SOCIAL SECURITY LE(SUPPLEMENT 20(

General Editor
David Bonner, LL.B., LL.M.

Commentary by
David Bonner, LL.B., LL.M.
Professor of Law, University of Leicester
Formerly Member, Social Security Appeal Tribunals

Ian Hooker, LL.B.
Lecturer in Law, University of Nottingham
Formerly Member, Social Security Appeal Tribunals

Richard Poynter B.C.L., M.A. (Oxon)
Solicitor, District Chairman,
Appeal Tribunals, Deputy Social Security Commissioner

Mark Rowland, LL.B.
Social Security Commissioner

Robin White, M.A., LL.M.
Professor of Law, University of Leicester,
Deputy Social Security Commissioner

Nick Wikeley, M.A.
Barrister, Professor of Law, University of Southampton,
Deputy Social Security Commissioner, Deputy District Chairman, Appeal Tribunals

David Williams, LL.M., Ph.D., C.T.A.
Solicitor, Social Security and Child Support Commissioner, Deputy Special Commissioner of Income Tax and part-time Chairman of VAT and Duties Tribunal

Penny Wood, LL.B., M.Sc.
Solicitor, District Chairman
Appeal Tribunals

Consultant to Vol. II
John Mesher, B.A., B.C.L., LL.M.
Barrister, Professor Associate of Law,
University of Sheffield,
Social Security and Child Support Commissioner

Consultant Editor
Child Poverty Action Group

LONDON
THOMSON
SWEET & MAXWELL
2008

Published in 2008 by
Sweet & Maxwell Limited of
100 Avenue Road, Swiss Cottage,
London NW3 3PF
(http://www.sweetandmaxwell.co.uk)
Typeset by Interactive Sciences Ltd, Gloucester
Printed in England by
Ashford Colour Press Ltd, Gosport, Hants

No natural forests were destroyed to make this product.
Only farmed timber was used and re-planted.

A catalogue record for this book is
available from the British Library

ISBN-9781847032577

All rights reserved. Crown Copyright Legislation is reproduced under
the terms of Crown Copyright Policy Guidance issued by HMSO.

No part of this publication may be reproduced or transmitted,
in any form or by any means, or stored in any retrieval system
of any nature without prior written permission, except for
permitted fair dealing under the Copyright, Designs and
Patents Act 1988, or in accordance with the terms of a licence
issued by the Copyright Licensing Agency in respect of
photocopying and/or reprographic reproduction.
Application for permission for other use of copyright material
including permission to reproduce extracts in other published
works shall be made to the publishers. Full acknowledgement
of author, publisher and source must be given.
Application for permission for other use of copyright material
controlled by the publisher shall be made to the publishers.
Material is contained in this publication for which publishing
permission has been sought, and for which copyright is
acknowledged. Permission to reproduce such material
cannot be granted by the publishers and application
must be made to the copyright holder.

Commentators have asserted their moral rights under
the Copyright, Designs and Patents Act 1988 to be identified
as the authors of the commentary in this Volume.

©

2008

PREFACE

This is the combined Supplement to the 2007 edition of the four volume work, *Social Security Legislation*, which was published in September 2007.

Part I of the Supplement contains new legislation (Acts and Regulations), presented in the same format as the main volumes. This will enable readers to note very quickly new sets of legislation.

Parts II, III, IV and V contain the updating material—a separate Part for each volume of the main work—which amends the legislative text and key aspects of the commentary so as to be up to date as at December 10, 2007. Part VI, the final section of the Supplement, gives some notice of changes forthcoming between that date and the date to which the main work (2008 edition) will be up to date (mid-April) and some indication of the April 2007 benefit rates, and takes account of changes known to us as at December 10, 2007.

As always we welcome comments from those who use this Supplement. Please address these to the General Editor, David Bonner, at the Faculty of Law, The University, Leicester LE1 7RH.

David Bonner
Ian Hooker
John Mesher
Richard Poynter
Mark Rowland
Robin White
Nick Wikeley
David Williams
Penny Wood
December 12, 2007

CONTENTS

	Page
Preface	*iii*
Using the Updated Material in this Supplement	*vii*
Pages of Main Volume Affected by Material in this Supplement	*ix*
Table of Abbreviations used in this Series	*xvii*
Table of Cases	*xxvii*
Table of Social Security Commissioner's Decisions	*xxix*
Table of European Materials	*xxxi*
Table of Statutes	*xxxiii*
Table of Statutory Instruments	*xxxvii*
Part I: New Legislation	1
Part II: Updating Material Volume I: Non-Means Tested Benefits	17
Part III: Updating Material Volume II: Income Support, Jobseeker's Allowance, State Pension Credit and the Social Fund	71
Part IV: Updating Material Volume III: Administration, Adjudication and the European Dimension	115
Part V: Updating Material Volume IV: Tax Credit and Employer Paid Social Security	147
Part VI: Forthcoming Changes and Up-Rating of Benefits	155

USING THE UPDATING MATERIAL IN THIS SUPPLEMENT

The amendments and updating contained in Pts II–V of this Supplement are keyed in to the page numbers of the relevant main volume of Social Security Legislation 2007. Where there have been a significant number of changes to a provision, the whole section, subsection, paragraph or regulation, as amended, will tend to be reproduced. Other changes may be noted by an instruction to insert or substitute new material or to delete part of the existing text. The date the change takes effect is also noted. Where explanation is needed of the change, or there is updating to do to existing annotations but no change to the legislation, you will also find commentary in this Supplement. The updating material explains new statutory material, takes on board Commissioners' or court decisions, or gives prominence to points which now seem to warrant more detailed attention.

This Supplement amends the text of the main volumes of Social Security Legislation 2007 to be up to date as at December 10, 2007.

David Bonner
General Editor

PAGES OF MAIN VOLUMES AFFECTED BY MATERIAL IN THIS SUPPLEMENT

Main volume page affected	Relevant paragraph in supplement
\multicolumn{2}{c}{**VOLUME I**}

Main volume page affected	Relevant paragraph in supplement
4	2.001
28	2.002
64	2.003
65	2.004
68	2.005
79	2.006
86	2.007
90	2.008–2.009
91	2.010
93	2.011
96	2.012
98	2.014
99	2.015
103	2.016
104	2.017
110	2.018
116	2.019
125–126	2.020
130	2.021
145	2.022
146	2.023
152	2.024
156–158	2.025
167	2.026
174	2.027
180–183	2.028
185	2.029–2.030
235	2.031
240	2.032
233	2.033
252	2.034
254	2.035–2.036
270	2.037
272	2.038
277	2.039
276–283	2.040
284	2.041
286	2.041A
289	2.042–2.043
293–294	2.044
295	2.045

Pages of Main Volumes Affected by Material in this Supplement

Main volume page affected	Relevant paragraph in supplement
337–338	2.046
353–354	2.047
354	2.048
368	2.049
370–371	2.050
381–382	2.051
382	2.052
383	2.053
384	2.054
396	2.055
397	2.056–2.057
399	2.058
400	2.059–2.060
406	2.061
421	2.062
422	2.063
425	2.064
486	2.064A
514	2.065–2.066
517	2.067
530	2.068–2.069
533	2.070
541	2.071
551	2.072
569	2.073
643	2.074
648	2.075
676	2.076
700	2.077
703	2.078
728	2.079
729–732	2.080
778	2.081
788	2.082
829	2.083
832	2.084
838	2.085
839	2.086
843	2.087–2.089
845	2.090
847	2.091–2.093
848	2.094
877–880	2.095
882	2.096
933	2.097
947	2.098
954–956	2.099

Pages of Main Volumes Affected by Material in this Supplement

Main volume page affected	Relevant paragraph in supplement
956–958	2.100
959–961	2.101
993	2.102
1003–1004	2.103

VOLUME II

Main volume page affected	Relevant paragraph in supplement
62	3.001
96–97	3.002
114	3.003
148	3.004
170–171	3.005
179	3.006
199	3.007–3.008
200	3.009–3.011
201	3.012–3.013
202	3.014
220	3.015–3.016
239	3.017
254	3.018
280	3.019
283	3.020
286	3.021
291–293	3.022
293–296	3.023
298	3.024–3.025
298–299	3.026
301	3.027
302	3.028
304	3.029
306	3.030
318–320	3.031
320	3.032
322	3.033
324–327	3.034
332	3.035
335	3.036
336	3.037
345–347	3.038
348–354	3.039
359–361	3.040
362–363	3.040A
362	3.041
363–364	3.042

Pages of Main Volumes Affected by Material in this Supplement

Main volume page affected	Relevant paragraph in supplement
364	3.043
367	3.044–3.045
369–372	3.046
375–380	3.047
384–385	3.048
389–390	3.049
391	3.050
393–399	3.051
394–397	3.052
404	3.053–3.054
407	3.055
413–414	3.056
416	3.057
414–419	3.058
420	3.059
465	3.060
473	3.061
482–485	3.062
501	3.063
516	3.064
521	3.065
527	3.066
567	3.067
578	3.068
603	3.069
604	3.070
608	3.071
608–609	3.071A
618	3.072–3.073
637	3.074
644	3.075–3.076
645	3.077
659	3.078
662	3.079
663–664	3.080
698–699	3.081
704	3.082
713–714	3.083
714	3.084
715	3.085–3.086
803	3.087–3.088
804	3.089
806	3.090
807	3.091
823	3.092
846	3.093
855	3.094

Pages of Main Volumes Affected by Material in this Supplement

Main volume page affected	Relevant paragraph in supplement
896	3.095
927	3.096
944	3.097
960	3.098
975	3.099
976	3.100
979–981	3.101
981–982	3.101A
986	3.102
987	3.103
990	3.104–3.105
994–998	3.106
1000	3.107
1003	3.108
1004	3.109
1025	3.110
1031	3.111
1071	3.112
1076	3.113
1084	3.114
1113	3.115–3.116
1117–1118	3.117
1128	3.118
1138	3.119
1150	3.120
1151	3.121
1155	3.122
1180	3.123
1182	3.124
1200	3.125
1236	3.126
1239	3.127

VOLUME III

Main volume page affected	Relevant paragraph in supplement
27	4.001
37	4.002–4.004
50	4.005–4.006
88	4.007
129	4.008
161	4.009
173	4.010
176	4.011
199	4.012
216–225	4.013

Pages of Main Volumes Affected by Material in this Supplement

Main volume page affected	Relevant paragraph in supplement
239–246	4.014
254–255	4.015
258	4.016
259–260	4.017
278	4.018
290	4.019
362	4.020
366	4.021
367	4.022
381	4.023
386	4.024
400	4.025
408	4.026–4.029
413	4.030
420	4.031
440	4.032
443	4.033
453	4.034
454	4.035
480	4.036
492	4.037
547	4.038
550–560	4.039–4.040
568	4.041
576	4.042
588	4.043
594	4.044
602	4.045–4.046
603	4.047
616	4.408
628–629	4.049
635	4.050
644	4.051
645	4.052
661–662	4.053
677	4.054
681	4.055
755	4.056
765	4.057
904	4.058
910	4.059
925	4.060
972	4.061
1183	4.062
1225	4.063
1226	4.064
1251	4.065

Pages of Main Volumes Affected by Material in this Supplement

VOLUME IV

Main volume page affected	Relevant paragraph in supplement
21	5.001
77	5.002
92	5.003
102	5.004
124	5.005–5.006
158	5.007
164	5.008
167	5.009
225	5.010
334	5.011
373	5.012–5.013
383–384	5.014
404	5.015
405	5.016
408	5.017
428	5.018
435	5.019
437	5.020
438	5.021
454	5.022
459	5.023
609–614	5.024
712	5.025
871	5.026

TABLE OF ABBREVIATIONS USED IN THIS SERIES

2002 Act	Tax Credits Act 2002
AA	Attendance Allowance
A.C.	Appeal Cases
A.C.D.	Administrative Court Digest
ADHD	Attention Deficit Hyperactivity Disorder
Adjudication Regulations	Social Security (Adjudication) Regulations 1986
Admin. L.R.	Administrative Law Reports
All E.R.	All England Law Reports (Butterworths)
All E.R. (EC)	All England Law Reports European Cases
AMA	Adjudicating Medical Authority
AO	Adjudication Officer
AOG	*Adjudication Officers' Guide*
Attendance Allowance Regulations	Social Security (Attendance Allowance) Regulations 1991
BAMS	Benefits Agency Medical Service
B.H.R.C.	Butterworths Human Rights Cases
B.L.G.R.	Butterworths Local Government Reports
Blue Books	*The Law Relating to Social Security*, Vols 1–11
B.M.L.R.	Butterworths Medico-Legal Reports
B.P.I.R.	Bankruptcy and Personal Insolvency Reports
B.T.C.	British Tax Cases
CAA 2001	Capital Allowance Act 2001
CAB	Citizens Advice Bureau
CAO	Chief Adjudication Officer
CBA	Child Benefit Act 1975
CBJSA	Contribution-based Jobseeker's Allowance
C.C.L. Rep.	Community Care Law Reports
CCM	Claimant Compliance Manual
CCN	New Tax Credits Claimant Compliance Manual
C.E.C.	European Community Cases
CERA	Cortical Evoked Response Audiogram
Ch.	Chancery Law Reports
Child Benefit Regulations	Child Benefit (General) Regulations 2006

Table of Abbreviations used in this Series

Claims and Payments Regulations 1979	Social Security (Claims and Payments) Regulations 1979
Claims and Payments Regulations 1987	Social Security (Claims and Payments) Regulations 1987
C.M.L.R.	Common Market Law Reports
C.O.D.	Crown Office Digest
Commissioners Procedure Regulations	Social Security Commissioners (Procedure) Regulations 1999
Computation of Earnings Regulations 1978	Social Security Benefit (Computation of Earnings) Regulations 1978
Computation of Earnings Regulations 1996	Social Security Benefit (Computation of Earnings) Regulations 1996
Const.L.J.	Construction Law Journal
Council Tax Benefit Regulations	Council Tax Benefit (General) Regulations 1992 (SI 1992/1814)
CP	Carer Premium
CPAG	Child Poverty Action Group
C.P.L.R.	Civil Practice Law Reports
CPR	Civil Procedure Rules
C.P.Rep.	Civil Procedure Reports
Cr.App.R.	Criminal Appeal Reports
Cr.App.R.(S)	Criminal Appeal Reports (Sentencing)
CRCA	Commissioners for Revenue and Customs Act 2005
Crim.L.R.	Criminal Law Review
Crim.L.R.	Criminal Law Review
CRU	Compensation Recovery Unit
CSA 1995	Child Support Act 1995
CS(NI)O	Child Support (Northern Ireland) Order 1995
CSO	Child Support Officer
CSPSSA	Child Support, Pensions and Social Security Act 2000
CTC	Child Tax Credit
DAT	Disability Appeal Tribunal
DCP	Disabled Child Premium
Decisions and Appeals Regulations 1999	Social Security and Child Support (Decisions and Appeals) Regulations 1999
Dependency Regulations	Social Security Benefit (Dependency) Regulations 1977
Disability Working Allowance Regulations	Disability Working Allowance (General) Regulations 1991
DLA	Disability Living Allowance

Table of Abbreviations used in this Series

DLADAA 1991	Disability Living Allowance and Disability Allowance Act 1991
DM	Decision Maker
DMA	Decision-making and Appeals
DMG	*Decision-Makers Guide*
DMP	Delegated Medical Practitioner
DPTC	Disabled Person's Tax Credit
DSDNI	Department for Social Development, Northern Ireland
DSS	Department of Social Security
DTI	Department of Trade and Industry
DWA	Disability Working Allowance
DWP	Department for Work and Pensions
EAA	Extrinsic Allergic Alveolitis
ECHR	European Court of Human Rights
E.C.R.	European Court Reports
ECSMA Agreement	European Convention on Social and Medical Assistance
EEA	European Economic Area
E.G.	Estates Gazette
E.H.R.R.	European Human Rights Reports
E.L.R.	Education Law Reports
EMA	Education Maintenance Allowance
EMO	Examining Medical Officer
EMP	Examining Medical Practitioner
ERA	Evoked Response Audiometry
ERA 1996	Employment Rights Act 1996
ER(NI)O	Employers Rights (Northern Ireland) Order 1996
Eur. L. Rev.	European Law Review
FA	Finance Act
Fam.Law	Family Law
Family Credit Regulations	Family Credit (General) Regulations 1987
FAS	Financial Assistance Scheme
FIS	Family Income Supplement
Fixing and Adjustment of Rates (Amendment) Regulations 1998	Child Benefit and Social Security (Fixing and Adjustment of Rates) (Amendment) Regulations 1998
Fixing and Adjustment of Rates Regulations 1976	Child Benefit and Social Security (Fixing and Adjustment of Rates) Regulations 1976
F.L.R.	Family Law Reports

Table of Abbreviations used in this Series

GA Regulations	Social Security (Guardian's Allowance) Regulations 1975
General Benefit Regulations	Social Security (General Benefit) Regulations 1982
General Regulations	Statutory Maternity Pay (General) Regulations 1986
G.P.	General Practitioner
Graduated Retirement Benefit Regulations 2005	Social Security (Graduated Retirement Benefit) Regulations 2005
GRP	Graduated Retirement Pension
G.W.D.	Green's Weekly Digest
HASSASSA	Health and Social Services and Social Security Adjudication Act 1983
HCD	House of Commons Debates
HCWA	House of Commons Written Answers
H.L.R.	Housing Law Reports
HMRC	Her Majesty's Revenue and Customs
HNCIP	(Housewives') Non-Contributory Invalidity Pension
Hospital In-Patients Regulations	Social Security (Hospital In-Patients) Regulations 1975
Housing Benefit Regulations	Housing Benefit (General) Regulations 1987 (SI 1987/1971)
HPP	Higher Pensioner Premium
HRA 1998	Human Rights Act 1998
H.R.L.R.	Human Rights Law Reports
HSE	Health and Safety Executive
IB	Incapacity Benefit
IB Regulations	Social Security (Incapacity Benefit) Regulations 1994
IBS	Irritable Bowel Syndrome
ICA	Invalid Care Allowance
I.C.R.	Industrial Cases Reports
ICTA	Income and Corporation Taxes Act 1988
IIAC	Industrial Injuries Advisory Council
I.L.J.	Industrial Law Journal
Imm.A.R.	Immigration Appeals Reports
Incapacity for Work Regulations	Social Security (Incapacity for Work) (General) Regulations 1995
Income Support Regulations	Income Support (General) Regulations 1987
Increases for Dependents Regulations	Social Security Benefit (Dependency) Regulations 1977

Table of Abbreviations used in this Series

IND	Immigration and Nationality Directorate of the Home Office
I.N.L.R.	Immigration and Nationality Law Reports
Invalid Care Allowance Regulations	Social Security (Invalid Care Allowance) Regulations 1976
IPPR	Institute of Public Policy Research
I.R.L.R.	Industrial Relations Law Reports
IS	Income Support
ISAs	Individual Savings Accounts
ITA	Income Tax Act 2007
ITEPA	Income Tax (Earnings and Pensions) Act 2003
ITTOIA	Income Tax (Trading and Other Income Act 2005)
ITS	Independent Tribunal Service
IWA	Social Security (Incapacity for Work) Act 1994
IW (Dependants) Regs	Social Security (Incapacity for Work) (Dependants) Regulations
IW (General) Regulations	Social Security (Incapacity for Work) (General) Regulations 1995
IW (Transitional) Regulations	Social Security (Incapacity for Work) (Transitional) Regulations 1995
IVB	Invalidity Benefit
J.P.	Justice of the Peace
JSA	Jobseeker's Allowance
JSA 1995	Jobseekers Act 1995
JSA Regulations	Jobseeker's Allowance Regulations 1996
JSA (Transitional) Regulations	Jobseeker's Allowance (Transitional) Regulations 1996
JS(NI)O	Jobseekers (Northern Ireland) Act 1995
J.S.W.F.L.	Journal of Social Welfare and Family Law
J.S.W.L.	Journal of Social Welfare Law
J.S.S.L.	Journal of Social Security Law
K.I.R.	Knights Industrial Reports
LEL	Lower Earnings Limit
Ll.L.Report	Lloyds' Law Report
Lloyd's Rep.	Lloyd's Law Reports
L.S.G.	Law Society Gazette
LTAHAW	Living Together As Husband And Wife
L.&T.R.	Landlord and Tenant Reports
MA	Maternity Allowance

Table of Abbreviations used in this Series

MAF	Medical Assessment Framework
MAT	Medical Appeal Tribunal
Maternity Benefit Regulations	Social Security (Maternity Benefit) Regulations 1975
Medical Evidence Regulations	Social Security (Medical Evidence) Regulations 1976
NCIP	Non-Contributory Invalidity Pension
NDPD	Notes on the Diagnosis of Prescribed Diseases
NI	National Insurance
N.I.	Northern Ireland Law Reports
NIC	National Insurance Contribution
N.L.J.	New Law Journal
N.P.C.	New Property Cases
Ogus, Barendt and Wikeley	A. Ogus, E. Barendt and N. Wikeley, *The Law of Social Security* (4th ed., Butterworths, 1995)
OPA	Overseas Pensions Act 1973
OPB	One Parent Benefit
OPPSSAT	Office of the President of the Social Security Appeals Tribunal
Overlapping Benefits Regulations	Social Security (Overlapping Benefits) Regulations 1979
Overpayments Regulations	Social Security (Payments on account, Overpayments and Recovery) Regulations
P.	Probate, Divorce and Admiralty
PAYE	Pay as You Earn
PCA	Personal Capability Assessment
P.&C.R.	Property, Planning & Compensation Reports
P.D.	Practice Direction
PD	Prescribed Disease
PPF	Pension Protection Fund
Pens.L.R.	Pensions Law Reports
Persons Abroad Regulations	Social Security Benefit (Persons Abroad) Regulations 1975
Persons Residing Together Regulations	Social Security Benefit (Persons Residing Together) Regulations 1977
PIE	Period of Interruption of Employment
PILON	Pay in Lieu of Notice
PIW	Period of Incapacity for Work
P.L.R.	Planning Law Reports

Table of Abbreviations used in this Series

Polygamous Marriage Regulations	Social Security and Family Allowances (Polygamous Marriages) Regulations 1975 (SI 1975/561)
PPF	Pension Protection Fund
Prescribed Diseases Regulations	Social Security (Industrial Injuries) (Prescribed Diseases) Regulations 1985
PTA	Pure Tone Audiometry
Q.B.	Queen's Bench
Recoupment Regulations	Social Security (Recoupment) Regulations 1990
REA	Reduced Earnings Allowance
RMO	Regional Medical Officer
RSI	Repetitive Strain Injury
R.T.R.	Road Traffic Reports
SAP	Statutory Adoption Pay
SAYE	Save As You Earn
S.C.	Session Cases
S.C.(H.L.)	Session Cases (House of Lords)
S.C.(P.C.)	Session Cases (Privy Council)
S.C.C.R.	Scottish Criminal Case Reports
S.C.L.R.	Scottish Civil Law Reports
SDA	Severe Disablement Allowance
SDP	Severe Disability Premium
SERPS	State Earnings-Related Pension Scheme
Severe Disablement Allowance	Social Security (Severe Disablement Regulations Allowance) Regulations 1984
S.J.	Solicitors' Journal
S.J.L.B.	Solicitors' Journal Law Brief
S.L.T.	Scots Law Times
SMP	Statutory Maternity Pay
SPC	State Pension Credit
SPCA	State Pension Credit Act 2002
SPCA(NI)	State Pension Credit Act (Northern Ireland) 2002
SPP	Statutory Paternity Pay
SPP and SAP (Administration) Regulations 2002	Statutory Paternity Pay and Statutory Adoption Pay (Administration) Regulations 2002
SPP and SAP (General) Regulations 2002	Statutory Paternity Pay and Statutory Adoption Pay (General) Regulations 2002
SPP and SAP (National Health Service Employees) Regulations 2002	Statutory Paternity Pay and Statutory Adoption Pay (National Health Service Employees) Regulations 2002

Table of Abbreviations used in this Series

SPP and SAP (Weekly Rates) Regulations 2002	Statutory Paternity Pay and Statutory Adoption Pay (Weekly Rates) Regulations 2002
SSA	Social Security Act
SSAA	Social Security Administration Act 1992*
SSAC	Social Security Advisory Committee
SSAT	Social Security Appeal Tribunal
SSCBA	Social Security Contributions and Benefits Act 1992*
SSCB(NI)	Social Security Contributions and Benefits (Northern Ireland) Act 1992
SS(CP)A	Social Security (Consequential Provisions) Act 1992
SSHBA	Social Security and Housing Benefits Act 1982
SS(MP)A	Social Security (Miscellaneous Provisions) Act 1977
SSP	Statutory Sick Pay
SSPA	Social Security Pensions Act 1975
S.T.C.	Simon's Tax Cases
S.T.C. (S.C.D.)	Simon's Tax Cases: Special Commissioners Decisions
STIB	Short-term Incapacity Benefit
S.T.I.	Simon's Tax Intelligence
TC	Tax Cases
TCA	Tax Credits Act
TC (Claims and Notifications) Regs	Tax Credit (Claims and Notifications) Regulations 2002
TCGA	Taxation of Chargeable Gains Act 1992
TCTM	Tax Credits Technical Manual
TMA	Taxes Management Act 1970
U.K.H.R.R.	United Kingdom Human Rights Reports
Unemployment, Sickness and Invalidity Benefit Regs	Social Security (Unemployment, Sickness and Invalidity Benefit) Regulations 1983
USI Regulations	Social Security (Unemployment, Sickness and Invalidity Benefit) Regulations 1983
VERA 1992	Vehicle Excise and Registration Act 1992
WFTC	Working Family Tax Credit
White Paper	Jobseeker's Allowance, Cm.2687 (October 1994)
Widow's Benefit and Retirement Pensions Regulations	Social Security (Widow's Benefit and Retirement Pensions) Regulations 1979
Wikeley, Annotations	N. Wikeley, "Annotations to Jobseekers Act 1995 (c. 18)" in *Current Law Statutes Annotated* (1995)

Table of Abbreviations used in this Series

Wikeley, Ogus and Barendt	Wikeley, Ogus and Barendt, *The Law of Social Security* (5th ed., Butterworths, 2002)
W.L.R.	Weekly Law Reports
Workmen's Compensation Acts	Workmen's Compensation Acts 1925 to 1945
WRPA	Welfare Reform and Pensions Act 1999
WRP(NI)O	Welfare Reform and Pensions (Northern Ireland) Order 1999
WTC	Working Tax Credit
WTC (Entitlement and Maximum Rate) Regulations 2002	Working Tax Credit (Entitlement and Maximum Rate) Regulations 2002
W.T.L.R.	Wills & Trusts Law Reports

* Where the context makes it seem more appropriate, these could also be referred to as Contributions and Benefits Act 1992, Administration Act 1992 (AA 1992).

TABLE OF CASES

AF Noonan (Architectural Practice) Ltd v Bournemouth & Boscombe Athletic Community Football Club Ltd; sub nom. Bournemouth & Boscombe Athletic Community Football Club Ltd, Re [2007] EWCA Civ 848; [2007] 1 W.L.R. 2614; (2007) 151 S.J.L.B. 923; [2007] C.P. Rep. 44, CA (Civ Div) 4.013

Ali v Secretary of State for the Home Department [2006] EWCA Civ 484; [2006] 3 C.M.L.R. 10; [2006] Eu. L.R. 1045; [2006] Imm. A.R. 532; [2006] I.N.L.R. 537; [2006] E.L.R. 423; (2006) 103(20) L.S.G. 25; (2006) 150 S.J.L.B. 606, CA (Civ Div) 3.028

Amjad v Steadman-Byrne. *See* Steadman-Byrne v Amjad; sub nom. Amjad v Steadman-Byrne

Baumbast v Secretary of State for the Home Department (C–413/99) [2002] E.C.R. I–7091; [2002] 3 C.M.L.R. 23; [2003] I.C.R. 1347; [2003] I.N.L.R. 1, ECJ 3.028

Chief Supplementary Benefit Officer v Leary [1985] 1 W.L.R. 84; [1985] 1 All E.R. 1061; (1984) 81 L.S.G. 3596; (1984) 128 S.J. 852, CA (Civ Div) 4.014

Couronne v Crawley BC and Secretary of State for Work and Pensions. *See* R. (on the application of Couronne) v Crawley BC; R. (on the application of Bontemps) v Secretary of State for Work and Pensions; sub nom. Couronne v Crawley BC

Department for Social Development v MacGeagh [2006] N.I. 125, CA (NI) 3.006

Hooper v Secretary of State for Work and Pensions [2007] EWCA Civ 495, CA (Civ Div) 4.043

Howard de Walden Estates Ltd v Aggio; Earl Cadogan v 26 Cadogan Square Ltd [2007] EWCA Civ 499; [2007] 3 W.L.R. 542; [2007] 3 All E.R. 910; [2007] L. & T.R. 29; [2007] 23 E.G. 165 (C.S.); (2007) 104(23) L.S.G. 29; (2007) 157 N.L.J. 815; [2007] N.P.C. 69, CA (Civ Div) 4.014

Kerr v Department for Social Development [2004] UKHL 23; [2004] 1 W.L.R. 1372; [2004] 4 All E.R. 385; [2004] N.I. 397, HL (NI) 4.013

Kola v Secretary of State for Work and Pensions; sub nom. R. (on the application of Kola) v Secretary of State for Work and Pensions [2007] UKHL 54, HL 3.062

Lees v Secretary of State for Social Services; sub nom. Lees v Department of Health & Social Security [1985] A.C. 930; [1985] 2 W.L.R. 805; [1985] 2 All E.R. 203; (1985) 82 L.S.G. 1944; (1985) 135 N.L.J. 437; (1985) 129 S.J. 316, HL 2.071

Leeves v Chief Adjudication Officer [1999] E.L.R. 90, CA (Civ Div) 3.034

R. v South Ribble BC Housing Benefit Review Board Ex p. Hamilton (2001) 33 H.L.R. 9, CA (Civ Div) 3.006

R. (on the application of Couronne) v Crawley BC; R. (on the application of Bontemps) v Secretary of State for Work and Pensions; sub nom. Couronne v Crawley BC [2007] EWCA Civ 1086, CA (Civ Div) 3.020

R. (on the application of Hook) v Social Security Commissioner [2007] EWHC 1705 (Admin), QBD (Admin) 3.056

R. (on the application of RJM) v Secretary of State for Work and Pensions [2006] EWCA Civ 1698, CA (Civ Div) 3.019

R. (on the application of Stennett) v Manchester City Council; R. (on the application of Armstrong) v Redcar and Cleveland BC; R. (on the application of Cobham) v Harrow LBC; sub nom. R. v Richmond LBC Ex p. Watson; R. v Manchester City Council Ex p. Stennett; R. v Harrow LBC Ex p. Cobham; R. v Redcar and Cleveland BC Ex p. Armstrong [2002] UKHL 34; [2002] 2 A.C. 1127; [2002] 3 W.L.R. 584; [2002] 4 All E.R. 124; [2002] B.L.G.R. 557; (2002) 5 C.C.L. Rep. 500; (2002) 68 B.M.L.R. 247; [2002] M.H.L.R. 377; (2002) 99(40) L.S.G. 33; (2002) 146 S.J.L.B. 202, HL 3.078

Table of Cases

Secretary of State for Social Security v Harmon; Secretary of State for Social Security v Carter; Secretary of State for Social Security v Cocks [1999] 1 W.L.R. 163; [1998] 2 F.L.R. 598; [1999] 1 F.C.R. 213; [1998] Fam. Law 519; (1999) 163 J.P.N. 192; (1998) 95(25) L.S.G. 32; (1998) 142 S.J.L.B. 183, CA (Civ Div) 3.006
Secretary of State for Work and Pensions v Morina [2007] EWCA Civ 749; (2007) 157 N.L.J. 1318, CA (Civ Div) 4.014, 4.015, 4.038, 4.048, 4.050
Shire v Secretary of State for Work and Pensions [2003] EWCA Civ 1465; [2004] C.P. Rep. 11; (2003) 100(42) L.S.G. 32, CA (Civ Div) 3.062
Steadman-Byrne v Amjad; sub nom. Amjad v Steadman-Byrne [2007] EWCA Civ 625; [2007] C.P. Rep. 38; (2007) 151 S.J.L.B. 890; [2007] 1 W.L.R. 2484, CA (Civ Div) 4.014
Tsiotras v Landeshauptstadt Stuttgart (C–171/91) [1993] E.C.R. I–2925, ECJ 3.023
Ullaslow v Secretary of State for Work and Pensions [2007] EWCA Civ 657, CA 3.122

TABLE OF SOCIAL SECURITY COMMISSIONERS DECISIONS

C8/06—07 (IB)	4.041	CIS/731/2007	3.023
CA/3943/2006	2.021	CIS/1121/2007	3.028
CAF/857/2006	4.038	CIS/1545/2007	3.026, 3.029
CAF/1569/2007	4.013	CIS/1685/2007	3.025, 3.028
CCR/2658/2006	4.009, 4.010, 4.011, 4.012	CIS/1775/2007	3.058
		CIS/1793/2007	3.022
CCS/4070/2006	3.006	CIS/1794/2007	4.014
CDLA/1678/1997	4.014	CIS/1915/2007	3.080
CDLA/792/2006	4.049, 4.051	CIS/1960/2007	4.006
CDLA/3461/2006	2.024	CIS/4010/2007	3.023
CDLA/3898/2006	2.071	CJSA/2663/2006	3.093
CDLA/4351/2006	2.022	CJSA/495/2007	3.002
CDLA/1256/2007	2.022	CJSA/505/2007	3.002
CDLA/2288/2007	4.014	CJSA/1814/2007	3.001, 3.094
CDLA/2466/2007	4.013, 4.016, 4.044	CJSA/3066/2007	3.022
CG/4060/2005	4.024	CP/3577/2006	2.046
CG/4139/2006	2.061	CPC/2920/2005	3.122
CH/3316/2005	3.022	CPC/4317/2006	3.021
CH/2995/2006	4.045, 4.047	CSDLA/202/2007	2.072
CH/1099/2007	3.041	CSIB/0223/2005	2.080
CI/3745/2006	2.095, 2.098, 2.101	CSIB/179/2006	2.080
CIB/5030/1998	4.013	CSIB/656/2006	2.080
CIB/26/2004	2.080	R (A) 2/06	4.040
CIB/3327/2004	2.039, 2.051	R (AF) 1/07	4.014
CIB/1695/2005	2.080	R (AF) 5/07	4.038
CIB/1602/2006	2.039, 2.050, 2.051	R (CR) 1/07	4.009, 4.010, 4.011
CIB/1620/2006	4.019	R (DLA) 1/00	2.072
CIB/2445/2006	2.053	R (DLA) 7/02	2.072
CIB/3339/2006	2.081	R (DLA) 1/04	2.071
CIB/16/2007	2.082	R (DLA) 3/07	4.012
CIB/143/2007	2.079, 2.080	R (FC) 1/93	3.041
CIB360/2007	2.080	R (H) 4/08	4.045, 4.047
CIS/213/2004	3.052, 4.013	R (I) 1/02	2.099
CIS/214/2004	3.052	R (I) 3/02	2.099
CIS/1363/2005	4.015	R (IB) 1/01	4.040
CIS/3315/2005	3.022	R (IB) 8/04	4.040
CIS/408/2006	3.028, 3.030	R (IB) 1/07	4.041
CIS/1757/2006	3.056	R (IB) 4/07	4.043
CIS/1833/2006	3.023	R (IS) 9/95	3.071
CIS/2448/2006	3.078	R (IS) 5/99	3.034
CIS/2538/2006	3.028, 3.030	R (IS) 14/99	3.062
CIS/3382/2006	3.067	R (IS) 15/99	4.014
CIS/3444/2006	3.028	R (IS) 6/07	4.014, 4.015, 4.038, 4.048, 4.050
CIS/3760/2006	3.078		
CIS/4156/2006	2.006	R (IS) 1/08	3.062
CIS/51/2007	4.025	R (M) 2/80	4.013
CIS/419/2007	3.024	R (PC) 2/07	3.021
CIS/623/2007	3.028	R (SF) 1/04	4.013
CIS/647/2007	3.034, 3.036, 3.046, 3.051, 3.057	R (SB) 52/83	4.014
		R (SB) 6/85	4.014

TABLE OF EUROPEAN MATERIALS

Treaties and Conventions
1950 European Convention on Human Rights
  Art.4 .... 3.002
  Art.8 .... 3.020
  Art.14 .... 3.020, 3.023, 3.093
  Protocol 1 Art.1 ...... 3.020, 3.023, 3.093
1957 Treaty establishing the European Community (post Treaty of Amsterdam) (as consolidated and further amended)
  Art.18(1) 3.030
1985 Hague Convention of the Law Applicable to Trusts and on their Recognition 3.052
  Art.7 .... 3.052

Regulations
1968 Reg.1612/68 on freedom of movement for workers within the Community [1968] O.J. L257/2 ...... 3.028

Directives
1993 Dir.93/96 on the right of residence for students [1993] O.J. L317/59 ..... 3.024, 3.026
  Art.16 .... 3.027
  Art.17 .... 3.027
2004 Dir.2004/38 on the right of citizens of the Union and their family members to move and reside freely within the territory of the Member States amending Reg.1612/68 and repealing several Directives [2004] O.J. L158/77 .... 3.030
  Art.12 .... 3.028
  Art.13 .... 3.028

xxxi

TABLE OF STATUTES

1960	Administration of Justice Act (8 & 9 Eliz.2 c.65)			(b)	2.005
	ss.12(1)(a)—(d)	4.013		s.44	2.007
	(e)	4.013		(1)	2.007
1970	Taxes Management Act			(b)	2.007
	(c.9)	5.007		(1A)	2.007
	s.20C	5.001		(5A)	2.007
	s.118	5.001		(6)	2.007
	(1)	5.001		(za)	2.007
1976	Race Relations Act (c.74)	3.020		(7)	2.007
1977	Social Security (Miscellaneous Provisions) Act			(c)	2.007
				s.44A	2.008, 2.009
	(c.5)	3.039		(A1)	2.008
1978	Employment Protection (Consolidation) Act			(1)	2.008
				(4)	2.008
	(c.44)	3.039, 3.101		(4A)	2.008
	s.12	3.071		s.44B	2.009
1979	Vaccine Damage Payments Act (c.17)			s.44C	2.009
				s.45	2.010
	s.1(1)(a)	2.001		(2)	2.010
1983	Mental Health Act (c.20)			(c)	2.010
	s.117	3.078		(d)	2.010
1984	Police and Criminal Evidence Act (c.60)	5.008		(3A)	2.010
				(b)	2.010
1987	Recognition of Trusts Act			s.46	2.011
	(c.14)	3.052		(3)	2.011
1988	Income and Corporation Taxes Act (c.1)	3.103, 3.105, 3.107		(4)	2.011
				s.48A	2.012
				(2)(a)	2.012
1991	Child Support Act (c.48)			(b)	2.012
	s.6	3.006		(2B)	2.012
1992	Social Security Contributions and Benefits Act (c.4)			(a)	2.012
				(b)	2.012
				(2ZA)	2.012
	s.22	2.002		(4)	2.012
	(2A)	2.002		(5)	2.012
	(2B)	2.002		s.48B	2.013
	(5)	2.002		(1)	2.013
	(5A)	2.002		(1A)	2.013
	s.38	2.003		(1ZA)	2.013
	(2)	2.003		(2)	2.013
	s.39	2.004		s.48BB	2.014
	(2)	2.004		(5)	2.014
	(2A)	2.004		s.48C	2.015
	(3)	2.004		(4)	2.015
	s.39C	2.005, 2.006		s.54	2.016
	(1)	2.005		(3)	2.016
	(1A)	2.005		s.55	2.017
	(2)	2.005		(3)(a)	2.017
	(3)	2.005		s.64	2.018
	(a)	2.005		(1)	2.018
				s.67	2.019

xxxiii

Table of Statutes

(2) 2.019	Social Security Administration Act (c.5)
s.72 .... 2.020, 2.021, 2.022, 2.023, 2.024	s.2AA 4.001
(1) 2.020	(2) 4.001
(1A) 2.020	(e) 4.001
(2) 2.020	s.7A 4.002
(2A) 2.020	s.7B 4.002
(5) 2.020	s.71 .... 4.006, 4.040
(6) 2.020, 2.072	(1) 4.005
(7) 2.020	(5) 4.006
(7A) 2.020	(5A) 4.006
(8) 2.020	s.71ZA(2) 4.007
s.73 .... 2.025	(a) 4.007
(1)(a) 2.072	(b) 4.007
(c) 2.072	s.122AA 5.002
(4) 2.025, 2.072	(1) 5.002
(4A) 2.025	(2)(d) 5.002
(5) 2.025	s.168 .... 4.008
(5A) 2.025	(3)(d) 4.008
(9) 2.025	(6) 4.008
(a) 2.025	1993 Pension Schemes Act (c.48)
s.75 .... 2.026	s.46 .... 2.046
(1) 2.026	1995 Jobseekers Act (c.18) 3.022
s.78 .... 2.027	s.1(2) 2.051
(4)(d) 2.027	s.7(1) 3.001
ss.83—85 .... 2.028	s.19(5) 3.002
s.88 .... 2.029	(9) 3.003
s.89 .... 2.030	Pensions Act (c.26)
(1) 2.030	s.126 .... 2.047
(1A) 2.030	Sch.4 .... 2.047
s.112(3) 3.039	Pt 1 para.1 .... 2.047
s.114 .... 2.031	Pt 2 .... 2.048
(4) 2.031	para.2 .... 2.048
s.122 .... 2.032	1996 Employment Rights Act (c.18) 3.039, 3.101
(6) 2.032	s.28 .... 3.039, 3.071
(7) 2.032	s.34 .... 3.039, 3.071, 3.117
(8) 2.032	s.64 .... 3.039, 3.071
s.149 .... 2.034	s.67 .... 3.039, 3.071
(3) 2.034	s.68 .... 3.039, 3.071
(4) 2.034	s.70 .... 3.039, 3.071, 3.117
s.150 .... 2.035	1997 Social Security (Recovery of Benefits) Act (c.27)
s.150A 2.035	s.1 .... 4.009
s.176 .... 2.037	s.11(1) 4.010
(1)(a) 2.037	s.12(3) 4.011
(c) 2.037	1998 Social Security Act (c.14)
(4) 2.037	s.6(3) 4.012
Sch.3 .... 2.038, 2.039, 2.040	s.9(3) 4.040
Pt 1 para.5 .... 2.038	s.12(2) 4.013
Sch.4 Pt 4 .... 2.041	s.13 .... 4.051
para.5 .... 2.041	s.14(1) 4.014
para.6 .... 2.041	ss.16(1)—(3) 4.015
Sch.4A 2.042	s.19 .... 4.016
Sch.4B 2.042	(1) 4.016
Sch.5 .... 2.044, 2.045	(2)(b) 4.016
para.2 .... 2.043	s.20 .... 4.017
(7) 2.043	(2) 4.017
para.5A(3) 2.044	(2A) 4.017
para.6(4) 2.044	s.39 .... 4.016, 4.017, 4.044, 4.046, 5.003
para.6A(2) 2.044	
para.8 .... 2.045	
(3) 2.045	

Table of Statutes

	(1) 4.018, 5.003	
	Sch.3 paras 10—19 .... 4.019	
1999	Social Security Contributions (Transfer of Functions, etc.) Act (c.2)	
	s.12(5) 5.004	
	Immigration and Asylum Act (c.33)	
	s.123 .... 3.005	
2001	Finance Act (c.9)	
	s.88(2) 5.004	
	Sch.29 para.39 .... 5.004	
2002	State Pension Credit Act (c.16)	
	s.3(1) 3.004	
	Tax Credits Act (c.21) 5.007	
	s.6 .... 5.005, 5.006	
	(3) 5.005	
	(3A) 5.005	
	(3B) 5.005	
	s.31 .... 5.007	
	s.36 .... 5.008	
	(2) 5.008	
	(3) 5.008	
	s.38 .... 5.009	
2003	Income Tax (Earnings and Pensions) Act (c.1)	
	s.219 .... 5.010	
	(5) 5.010	
	(6) 5.010	
2004	Finance Act (c.12)	
	Pt 4 ..... 3.015, 3.040, 3.048, 3.107	
	Asylum and Immigration (Treatment of Claimants, etc.) Act (c.19)	
	s.12(1) 3.005	
	(2)(a) 3.031, 3.063, 3.073	
	(3) 3.081	
	Pensions Act (c.35)	
	s.319 .... 5.002	
	Sch.12 para.7 .... 5.002	
2005	Commissioners for Revenue and Customs Act (c.11)	
	s.13 .... 5.011	
	(3)(b) 5.011	
	(c) 5.011	
	s.50(4) 5.002	
	Sch.4 para.46 .... 5.002	
2007	Income Tax Act (c.3) 3.043, 3.045, 3.050, 3.090, 3.103, 3.105, 3.107	
	s.6(2) 3.016	
	s.989 .... 3.016, 3.090	
	Welfare Reform Act (c.5)	
	s.41 .... 4.002	
	s.44 .... 4.006	
	s.52 .... 2.020	
	s.53(2) 2.025	
	s.60(1) 2.019	
	(2) 2.020	
	s.62(1) 4.016, 4.017, 4.018	

	(2) 4.016	
	(3) 4.017	
	(4) 4.017	
	(5) 4.018, 5.003	
	Sch.7 para.2(2) 2.025	
	para.3 .... 4.001, 4.008	
	Sch.8 .... 2.020, 2.025, 4.007, 4.008	
	Finance Act (c.11)	
	s.62 .... 5.010	
	s.84 .... 5.008, 5.011	
	s.97 .... 5.007	
	Sch.24 .... 5.007	
	Sch.27 Pt 5 .... 5.001, 5.008, 5.011	
	Pensions Act (c.22)	
	s.1 .... 2.038	
	s.5 .... 2.035	
	s.6(5) 2.004	
	(6) 2.005	
	s.9(1) 2.009	
	s.11 .... 2.010, 2.032	
	s.12 .... 2.002, 2.007, 2.032	
	s.13 .... 3.004	
	Sch.1 .... 2.013	
	para.1 .... 2.007	
	para.2 .... 2.012	
	para.6 .... 2.016	
	para.7 .... 2.017	
	para.8 .... 2.045	
	para.9 .... 2.002	
	para.10 .... 2.037	
	para.13 .... 2.027	
	para.14 .... 2.029	
	para.15 .... 2.030	
	para.16 .... 2.031	
	para.17 .... 2.034	
	para.18 .... 2.041	
	para.19 .... 2.043	
	para.33 .... 2.002	
	para.34 .... 2.008	
	para.35 .... 2.037	
	para.40 .... 2.003	
	para.41 .... 2.018	
	para.42 .... 2.026	
	para.43 .... 2.034	
	Sch.2 .... 2.042	
	Pt 3 para.3 .... 2.004	
	para.4 .... 2.005	
	para.5 .... 2.007	
	para.7 .... 2.012	
	para.8 .... 2.013	
	para.9 .... 2.014	
	para.10 .... 2.015	
	para.46 .... 2.011	
	Sch.3 para.3 .... 2.047	
	Sch.7 .... 2.012, 2.016, 2.027, 2.045	
	Pt.2 .... 2.028, 2.048	
	Pt 3 .... 2.044	
	Pt 5 .... 2.004	
	Sch.8 para.44 .... 3.004	

TABLE OF STATUTORY INSTRUMENTS

1975 Social Security (Credits) Regulations (SI 1975/556) 2.054
    reg.2 .... 2.049
    reg.3 .... 2.039, 2.050
    reg.8A 2.039, 2.050, 2.051
        (2)(b) 2.051
        (3)(a) 2.051
    reg.8B(2A)(a) 2.052
        (4) 2.053
        (b) 2.053
    reg.8C 2.054
    regs 8D—F 2.054
1976 Social Security (Invalid Care Allowance) Regulations (SI 1976/409)
    reg.8 .... 2.073
        (1) 2.073
1982 Social Security (General Benefit) Regulations (SI 1982/1408)
    reg.11 .... 2.095
    reg.16 .... 2.096
1985 Social Security (Industrial Injuries) (Prescribed Diseases) Regulations (SI 1985/967)
    Sch.1 PD A8 .... 2.098
        A10 .... 2.100
        A11 .... 2.097, 2.099, 2.100, 2.102
        A12 .... 2.101
1987 Income Support (General) Regulations (SI 1987/1967) 6.002
    reg.2(1) 3.007, 3.008, 3.009, 3.010, 3.011, 3.012, 3.013, 3.014, 3.015, 3.016, 3.040A, 3.043, 3.045, 3.048, 3.050
    reg.5 .... 3.017, 3.037
        (5) 3.017
        (5A) 3.017
    reg.12 .... 3.018
    reg.21 .... 3.019
    reg.21AA 3.020, 3.021, 3.022, 3.023, 3.024, 3.025, 3.026, 3.027, 3.028, 3.029, 3.030
    reg.21ZB 3.031
    reg.22A 3.032, 3.033
        (1)(a) 3.032

reg.23 .... 3.034, 3.036, 3.046, 3.051, 3.058
reg.29 .... 3.035
    (2B) 3.036
    (4B) 3.037
    (a) 3.035
reg.35 .... 3.038, 3.039
    (1)(g) 3.038, 3.071
    (gg) 3.038, 3.039
    (h) 3.038, 3.039, 3.071
    (2) 3.071
    (3) 3.071
    (a) 3.038
    (b) 3.038
reg.38 .... 3.040, 3.040A
    (1) 3.041
    (b) 3.040
    (3)(c) 3.040
    (9)(b) 3.040
    (11) 3.041
reg.39 .... 3.042
    (1) 3.042, 3.043
reg.39D 3.044, 3.045
    (1)(b) 3.044
    (c) 3.044
    (2) 3.044
reg.40 .... 3.046
reg.42 .... 3.047, 3.048
    (2)(g) 3.047, 3.048, 3.059, 3.079
    (2ZA)(a) 3.047
    (2ZA)—(2CA) 3.048, 3.059, 3.079
    (2A) 3.047
    (2B) 3.047
    (2C) 3.047
    (6) 3.049
    (6A) 3.049
    (c) 3.047
    (6AA) 3.049
    (8) 3.050
    (a) 3.047
reg.46 .... 3.051, 3.052
reg.49 .... 3.053, 3.054, 3.109
reg.51 .... 3.055
    (1) 3.056, 3.057, 3.058
    (2) 3.059
    (d) 3.055
reg.51A 3.058
reg.62(2A) 3.060
    (a) 3.060

xxxvii

Table of Statutory Instruments

(b)	3.060
reg.66A(5)	3.061
(a)	3.061
(b)	3.061
reg.70	3.062
Sch.1B para.18A	3.063
Sch.2 para.8A	3.064, 3.066
para.15(1A)	3.065
Sch.3 para.4	3.067
para.12	3.068
Sch.8 para.1	3.037, 3.068, 3.071, 3.117
(a)	3.071
(b)	3.071
para.1A	3.117
para.2	3.070, 3.071, 3.071A, 3.117
Sch.9 para.50	3.072
para.57	3.073, 3.074
Sch.10 para.7	3.078
para.23A	3.075, 3.079
para.26	3.080
para.29	3.076
para.40	3.077
Social Security (Claims and Payments) Regulations (SI 1987/1968)	6.002
reg.2	4.020
reg.3	4.021
(c)	4.021
(ca)	4.021
(d)	4.021
(da)	4.021
reg.4	4.022
(6A)	4.022
(c)	4.022
(d)	4.022
(6B)	4.022
(b)	4.022
(6C)	4.022
(c)	4.022
(cc)	4.022
reg.4D	4.023
(4)	4.023
(5)(c)	4.023
(cc)	4.023
reg.6	4.024
(1E)	4.024
(4AB)	4.024
(15)	4.024
(15A)	4.024
(19)	4.024
(b)	4.024
(20)	4.024
(a)	4.024
(b)	4.024
(c)	4.024
(21)	4.024
(a)	4.024
(b)	4.024
(21A)	4.024

	(30)(b)	4.024
	(33)	4.024
	(34)	4.024
	reg.7	4.025
	reg.13	4.026
	reg.13D	4.030
	(3)	4.030
	(4)	4.030
	reg.19	4.031
	(3B)	4.031
	(3C)	4.031
	reg.26	4.032
	reg.30	4.032
	(4)	4.032
	(4A)	4.032
	(4B)	4.032
	reg.32B	4.034
	reg.33	4.035
	reg.34B	4.037
	Sch.9	4.036
	para.1(1)	4.036
	para.7C	4.036
	para.7D	4.036
	Sch.9A	4.037
	para.2A(4)	4.037
1988	Social Security (Payments on account, Overpayments and Recovery) Regulations (SI 1988/664)	
	reg.14	4.005, 4.053
	Social Fund Cold Weather Payments (General) Regulations (SI 1988/1724)	
	Sch.1	3.126
	Sch.2	3.127
1991	Social Security (Attendance Allowance) Regulations (SI 1991/2740)	
	reg.7	2.065
	reg.8	2.067
	(6)	2.067
	Social Security (Disability Living Allowance) Regulations (SI 1991/2890)	
	reg.9	2.068
	reg.10	2.070
	(8)	2.070
	reg.12	2.071, 2.072
1992	Council Tax Benefit (General) Regulations (SI 1992/1814)	
	reg.22	3.041
	(1)	3.041
	(10)	3.041
1994	Social Security (Incapacity Benefit) Regulations (SI 1994/2946)	
	reg.4A	2.074
	reg.8	2.075

Table of Statutory Instruments

1995	Social Security (Incapacity for Work) (General) Regulations (SI 1995/311) 2.081		Sch.1 para.9A 3.112, 3.114	
	reg.2(1) 2.076		para.20(1A) 3.113	
	reg.17 .... 2.077, 2.078		Sch.6 para.1 .... 3.100, 3.115, 3.117	
	(3) 2.077		para.1A 3.117	
	(4) 2.077		para.2 .... 3.115, 3.117	
	reg.27 .... 2.079, 2.080		(1) 3.117	
	Sch. 2.082		para.3 .... 3.116	
1996	Jobseeker's Allowance Regulations (SI 1996/207) 6.002		(b) 3.116	
	reg.1(3) 3.087, 3.088, 3.089, 3.090, 3.091, 3.103, 3.105, 3.107		Sch.7 para.49 .... 3.118	
			Sch.8 para.38 .... 3.119	
			Social Security Benefit (Computation of Earnings) Regulations (SI 1996/2745)	
	reg.5(3) 3.092		reg.2 .... 2.061	
	reg.15 .... 3.093		reg.12 .... 2.062	
	(a) 3.093		(1) 2.062	
	reg.18(1) 3.001, 3.094		(2) 2.062	
	reg.19(1)(p) 2.051		reg.13 .... 2.063	
	reg.52 .... 3.095, 3.100		(6)(f) 2.063	
	(3) 3.095		(g) 2.063	
	(3A) 3.095		Sch.1 .... 2.064	
	reg.71 .... 3.096		para.11 .... 2.064	
	(1)(c) 3.096		para.12 .... 2.064	
	(2) 3.096	1999	Social Security and Child Support (Decisions and Appeals) Regulations (SI 1999/991)	
	reg.75(1)(a) 3.097			
	reg.85 .... 3.098			
	(1) 3.098		reg.1(3) 4.038	
	reg.94 .... 3.099		reg.3 .... 4.039	
	(6)—(9) 3.100		(5) 4.039	
	(8)(c) 3.099		(a) 4.040	
	reg.98 .... 3.101		(b) 4.040	
	(1)(f) 3.101		(c) 4.040	
	(ff) 3.101		(d) 4.040	
	(g) 3.101, 3.117		(5ZA)—(5ZC) 4.039, 4.040	
	(h) 3.117		(5ZB) 4.040	
	(2)(f) 3.101		(5B) 4.040	
	reg.102 .... 3.102, 3.103		reg.6 .... 4.040	
	(1) 3.102		(1) 4.041	
	reg.102D 3.104, 3.105		(2)(b) 4.040	
	(1)(c) 3.104		(c) 4.040	
	(2) 3.104		(3) 4.040	
	reg.105 .... 3.106, 3.107		reg.7 .... 4.040	
	(3) 3.106		(2) 4.042	
	(3A) 3.106		(bc) 4.042	
	(4) 3.106		(bd) 4.042	
	(5) 3.106		(5) 4.040	
	(13) 3.107		reg.7A(1) 4.043	
	(13A)(b) 3.106		reg.12 .... 4.044	
	(15) 3.106		(2) 4.044	
	(a) 3.106		(3)(b) 4.044	
	(16) 3.106		reg.18 .... 4.045	
	reg.111 .... 3.108, 3.109		reg.19 .... 4.047	
	reg.131 .... 3.110		(1) 4.046	
	(3)(a) 3.110		(3) 4.045, 4.047	
	(b) 3.110		reg.32(1) 4.048	
	reg.136 .... 3.111		reg.39 .... 4.049	
	(5)(a) 3.111		reg.46 .... 4.050	
	(b) 3.111		reg.57(1) 4.051	

Table of Statutory Instruments

	Sch.3B para.6 ...... 4.052
2000	Social Security (Immigration and Asylum) Consequential Amendments Regulations (SI 2000/636)
	reg.12(1) 3.081
	(2) 3.081
	Vaccine Damage Payments Act 1979 Statutory Sum Order (SI 2000/1983) 2.103
	Social Security Amendment (Bereavement Benefits) Regulations (SI 2000/2239)
	reg.6 ...... 3.066, 3.114
	Immigration (European Economic Area) Regulations (SI 2000/2326)
	reg.5(2) 3.023
	(a) 3.023
2001	Social Security (Crediting and Treatment of Contributions, and National Insurance Numbers) Regulations (SI 2001/769)
	reg.1 ...... 2.056
	(2) 2.055, 2.056
	(3) 2.056
	(4) 2.056
	reg.4 ...... 2.057, 2.058
	(1) 2.057
	(1A) 2.057
	(10) 2.058
	(11) 2.058
	reg.5 ...... 2.059
	reg.5A 2.059
	reg.6 ...... 2.060
	reg.6A 2.060
	reg.6B 2.060
2002	State Pension Credit Regulations (SI 2002/1792) 6.002
	reg.1 ...... 3.120, 3.121
	reg.2(4) 3.122
	reg.18 ...... 3.123
	(1A) 3.123
	(1C) 3.123
	(1CA) 3.123
	(1CB) 3.123
	reg.19 ...... 3.124
	Sch.II para 8 ...... 3.124
	(8) 3.124
	Working Tax Credit (Entitlement and Maximum Rate) Regulations (SI 2002/2005)
	reg.7D 5.012
	reg.14(2) 5.012
	(a) 5.012

	(f) 5.012
	Tax Credits (Definition and Calculation of Income) Regulations (SI 2002/2006)
	reg.2(2) 5.015, 5.016
	reg.3 ...... 5.017
	(7)(b) 5.017
	(8)(b) 5.017
	reg.8 ...... 5.018
	(d)(i) 5.018
	(ii) 5.018
	reg.11 ...... 5.019
	(3) 5.019
	reg.12 ...... 5.020
	(4) 5.020
	reg.14 ...... 5.021
	(2) 5.021
	(a) 5.021
	(b) 5.021
	(ba) 5.021
	Child Tax Credit Regulations (SI 2002/2007)
	reg.3 ...... 5.022
	reg.5 ...... 5.023
	(3)(ab) 5.023
	(3A) 5.023
	(5) 5.023
	Statutory Paternity Pay and Statutory Adoption Pay (Weekly Rates) Regulations (SI 2002/2818)
	reg.3 ...... 5.025
2004	Accession (Immigration and Worker Registration) Regulations (SI 2004/1219)
	reg.2 ...... 3.082
	(5) 3.082
	(5A) 3.082
	(6)(b) 3.082
	(7)(a) 3.082
	(c) 3.082
	Social Security (Crediting and Treatment of Contributions, and National Insurance Numbers) Amendment Regulations (SI 2004/1361)
	reg.2(b) 2.060
2005	Tax Credits (Approval of Child Care Providers) Scheme (SI 2005/93) 5.024
	Tax Credits Notification of Changes of Circumstances (Civil Partnership) (Transitional Provisions) Order (SI 2005/828) 5.005

xl

Table of Statutory Instruments

2006	Child Benefit (General) Regulations (SI 2006/223) 3.018	
	reg.1(3) 2.083	
	(a) 2.083	
	(d) 2.083	
	reg.3 .... 2.084	
	(2) 2.084	
	(b) 2.084	
	(c) 2.084	
	(d) 2.084	
	(4) 2.084	
	reg.14 .... 2.085	
	(1) 2.085	
	reg.15 .... 2.086	
	(1) 2.086	
	reg.21 .... 2.087	
	(1)(b) 2.087	
	reg.23 .... 2.088	
	(4) 2.088	
	reg.25 .... 2.089	
	(1)(b) 2.089	
	reg.27 .... 2.090	
	(4) 2.090	
	reg.30 .... 2.091	
	(1) 2.091	
	reg.31 .... 2.092	
	(1) 2.092	
	reg.32 .... 2.093	
	(1) 2.093	
	reg.34 .... 2.094	
	Accession (Immigration and Worker Authorisation) Regulations (SI 2006/3317)	
	reg.2 .... 3.083	
	(6A) 3.083	
	(8) 3.083	
	(12)(a) 3.083	
	reg.3 .... 3.084, 3.086	
	(1) 3.084, 3.086	
	reg.4 .... 3.085	
	(1)(b) 3.085	
2007	Social Security (Netherlands) Order (SI 2007/631) 2.033	
	Social Security Benefits Uprating Order (SI 2007/688) 5.025	
	Social Security, Occupational Pension Schemes and Statutory Payments (Consequential Provisions) Regulations (SI 2007/1154)	
	reg.2(2) 2.055, 2.058, 2.059	
	Tax Credits (Definition and Calculation of Income) (Amendment) Regulations (SI 2007/1305)	
	reg.3 .... 5.016	

reg.4 .... 5.017
reg.5 .... 5.018
reg.6 .... 5.019
reg.7 .... 5.020
reg.8 .... 5.021
Jobseeker's Allowance (Extension of the Intensive Activity Period) Amendment Regulations (SI 2007/1316)
reg.2 .... 3.097
Social Security, Housing Benefit and Council Tax Benefit (Miscellaneous Amendments) Regulations (SI 2007/1331) 4.026, 4.030
Asylum and Immigration (Treatment of Claimants, etc.) Act 2004 (Commencement No.7 and Transitional Provisions) Order (SI 2007/1602)
art.2(3) 3.005, 3.031, 3.063, 3.073, 3.081
(4) 3.005, 3.031, 3.063, 3.073, 3.081
Social Security (Miscellaneous Amendments) (No.2) Regulations (SI 2007/1626) 4.020, 4.032
reg.3(2) 2.076
reg.4(2) 4.044
(3) 4.046
Social Security (Students and Income-related Benefits) Amendment Regulations (SI 2007/1632)
reg.2(2)(a) 3.060
(b) 3.060
(3)(a) 3.061
(b) 3.061
reg.3(2)(a) 3.110
(b) 3.110
(3)(a) 3.111
(b) 3.111
Social Security (Miscellaneous Amendments) (No.3) Regulations (SI 2007/1749)
reg.2(2)(a) 3.009
(b) 3.010
(c) 3.011
(d) 3.014
(3) 3.040
(4)(a) 3.042
(b) 3.042
(5)(a) 3.044
(b) 3.044
(6)(a) 3.047

Table of Statutory Instruments

(b) 3.047
(c) 3.047
(d) 3.047
(e) 3.047
(f) 3.047
(7) 3.055
(8) 3.075
reg.3(2) 3.091
  (3)(a) 3.102, 3.104, 3.106
    (b) 3.102, 3.104, 3.106
  (4) 3.107
    (a) 3.106
    (b) 3.106
    (c) 3.106
    (d) 3.106
reg.8(2) 2.049
  (3) 2.052
Social Security (Industrial Injuries) (Prescribed Diseases) Amendment (No.2) Regulations (SI 2007/1753) 1.001, 2.099, 2.100, 2.102
reg.2(1) 2.097
  (2) 2.097
  (3) 2.097
Social Security (Claims and Payments) Amendment (No.2) Regulations (SI 2007/1866) 4.036
Vaccine Damage Payments Act 1979 Statutory Sum Order (SI 2007/1931) 1.006, 2.001
art.3 .... 2.103
Social Security (Ireland) Order (SI 2007/2122) 2.033
Secretary of State for Justice Order (SI 2007/2128) 1.011
Sch. para.13(2) 3.072
    (3) 3.077
para.16(2) 3.118
    (3) 3.119
Child Benefit (General) (Amendment) Regulations (SI 2007/2150) 2.083, 2.084, 2.085, 2.086, 2.087, 2.088, 2.089, 2.090, 2.091, 2.092, 2.093, 2.094, 3.018
Child Tax Credit (Amendments) Regulations (SI 2007/2151)
reg.3 .... 5.022
reg.4 .... 5.023

National Minimum Wage Regulations 1999 (Amendment) Regulations (SI 2007/2318) 3.003
Social Security (Miscellaneous Amendments) (No.4) Regulations (SI 2007/2470) 4.021, 4.031, 4.033, 4.035
reg.3(5) 4.040
  (6) 4.042
  (7) 4.042
  (8) 4.043
  (9) 4.052
Working Tax Credit (Entitlement and Maximum Rate) (Amendment No.2) Regulations (SI 2007/2479)
reg.2 .... 5.014
Tax Credits (Child Care Providers) (Miscellaneous Revocation and Transitional Provisions) (England) Scheme (SI 2007/2481) 1.022
art.4 .... 5.024
Independent Living Fund (2006) Order (SI 2007/2538)
art.2(2) 3.013
  (3) 3.076
art.4 .... 3.087
art.6(2) 3.120
  (3) 3.120
art.7 .... 5.015
Social Security (National Insurance Credits) Amendment Regulations (SI 2007/2582) 2.039
reg.2 .... 2.054
reg.3 .... 2.056
reg.4(3)(a) 2.057
    (b) 2.057
  (4) 2.060
Social Security Benefit (Computation of Earnings) (Amendment) Regulations (SI 2007/2613) 2.062, 2.063, 2.064
Social Security (Miscellaneous Amendments) (No.5) Regulations (SI 2007/2618)
reg.2 .... 3.008, 3.064, 3.065, 3.088, 3.112, 3.113
reg.3 .... 2.096
  (1) 2.073
reg.5(2) 3.007, 3.012
  (3) 3.017

xlii

Table of Statutory Instruments

(4)	3.032
(5)	3.035
(6)	3.039
(a)	3.038
(b)	3.038
(c)	3.038
(7)	3.042
(8)	3.044
(9)(a)	3.047
(b)	3.047
(10)	3.053
(11)(a)	3.069
(b)	3.070
reg.6	2.073
(4)	2.073
reg.7	2.077
reg.8(2)	3.089, 3.090
(3)	3.092
(4)	3.095
(5)	3.096
(6)	3.098
(7)	3.099
(8)(a)	3.101
(b)	3.101
(9)	3.102
(10)	3.104
(11)(a)	3.106, 3.107
(b)	3.106
(c)	3.106, 3.107
(12)	3.108
(14)(a)	3.115
(b)	3.116
reg.10(2)	3.121
(3)	3.123
(4)	3.124
(5)	3.125
Sch.	3.008, 3.064, 3.065, 3.088, 3.112, 3.113

Social Security (Attendance Allowance and Disability Living Allowance) (Amendment) Regulations (SI 2007/2875)

reg.2(2)	2.065
(3)	2.067
reg.3(2)	2.068
(3)	2.070

Social Security (Claims and Information) Regulations (SI 2007/2911) 1.028, 4.022, 4.023, 4.034

Social Fund Cold Weather Payments (General) Amendment Regulations (SI 2007/2912)

reg.3	3.126
reg.4	3.127
Sch.1	3.126
Sch.2	3.127

Accession (Worker Authorisation and Worker Registration) (Amendment) Regulations (SI 2007/3012)

reg.2	3.083, 3.084, 3.085
reg.3	3.082
reg.4	3.086

Social Security (Housing Costs and Miscellaneous Amendments) Regulations (SI 2007/3183) 4.037, 6.002

xliii

PART I

NEW LEGISLATION

NEW STATUTES

There are none for the period covered by this Supplement.

NEW REGULATIONS AND ORDERS

The Social Security (Industrial Injuries) (Prescribed Diseases) Amendment (No. 2) Regulations 2007

(2007 No. 1753)

ARRANGEMENT OF REGULATIONS

1. Citation, commencement and interpretation
2. Amendment of Schedule 1 to the principal Regulations
3. Transitional provision

1.001

In force October 1, 2007

The Secretary of State for Work and Pensions makes the following Regulations in exercise of the powers conferred by sections 108(2), 122(1) and 175(1), (3) and (4) of the Social Security Contributions and Benefits Act 1992 He is satisfied of the matters referred to in section 108(2)(a) and (b) of that Act.

In accordance with section 172(2) of the Social Security Administration Act 1992 he has referred proposals to make these Regulations to the Industrial Injuries Advisory Council.

1.002

Citation, commencement and interpretation

1.—(1) These Regulations may be cited as the Social Security (Industrial Injuries) (Prescribed Diseases) Amendment (No. 2) Regulations 2007 and shall come into force on 1st October 2007.

(2) In these Regulations "the principal Regulations" means the Social Security (Industrial Injuries) (Prescribed Diseases) Regulations 1985.

1.003

Amendment of Schedule 1 to the principal Regulations

2. [*Set out in the updates to the text of PD A11 in Sch. 1 to the Prescribed Diseases Regulations*].

1.004

Transitional provision

1.005 3.—(1) Regulation 2 shall not apply to a question relating to the blanching of a claimant's fingers where—
- (a) the question arises in connection with a period of assessment which relates to a claim which is made—
  - (i) before the commencement date, or
  - (ii) within 3 months after the commencement date in respect of a period which began before the commencement date, or
- (b) a person suffers from an attack of a disease and under regulation 7 of the principal Regulations (recrudescence) the attack is a recrudescence of a disease for which a claim was made before the commencement date or within 3 months after the commencement date in respect of a period which began before the commencement date.

(2) For the purposes of this regulation—
- (a) "commencement date" means the date on which these Regulations come into force; and
- (b) a period of assessment which begins on the day following the end of a preceding period of assessment, shall be treated as a continuation of the preceding period of assessment.

(2007 No. 1931)

The Vaccine Damage Payments Act 1979 Statutory Sum Order 2007

(2007 No. 1931)

ARRANGEMENT OF ORDER

1. Citation and commencement
2. Statutory sum for the purposes of the Vaccine Damage Payments Act 1979
3. Revocation

1.006

In force   **12th July 2007**

A draft of the following Order was laid before Parliament in accordance with section 1(4A) of the Vaccine Damage Payments Act 1979 and approved by resolution of each House of Parliament: **1.007**

The Secretary of State for Work and Pensions with the consent of the Treasury, in exercise of the powers conferred by section 1(1A) of the Vaccine Damage Payments Act 1979, makes the following Order:

Citation and commencement

1. This Order may be cited as the Vaccine Damage Payments Act 1979 Statutory Sum Order 2007 and shall come into force on 12th July 2007.   **1.008**

Statutory sum for the purposes of the Vaccine Damage Payments Act 1979

2. For the purposes of the Vaccine Damage Payments Act 1979 the statutory sum is £120,000.   **1.009**

Revocation

3. The Vaccine Damage Payments Act 1979 Statutory Sum Order 2000 is hereby revoked.   **1.010**

The Secretary of State for Justice Order 2007

The Secretary of State for Justice Order 2007

(2007 No. 2128)

ARRANGEMENT OF ORDER

1.011
1. Citation and commencement
2. Interpretation
3. Incorporation of the Secretary of State for Justice
4. Transfer of functions from Secretary of State etc.
5. Transfer of functions from Lord Chancellor
6. Transfer of property etc. to Secretary of State for Justice
7. Supplementary
8. Consequential amendments

In force   **August 22, 2007**

1.012   At the Court at Buckingham Palace, the 25th day of July 2007

Present,

The Queen's Most Excellent Majesty in Council

Her Majesty, in pursuance of sections 1 and 2 of the Ministers of the Crown Act 1975, is pleased, by and with the advice of Her Privy Council, to order, and it is ordered, as follows:

Citation and commencement

1.013   **1.**—(1) This Order may be cited as the Secretary of State for Justice Order 2007.
(2) This Order comes into force on 22nd August 2007.

Interpretation

1.014   2. In this Order—
(a) "instrument" includes, in particular, Royal Charters, Royal Warrants, Orders in Council, Letters Patent, judgments, decrees, orders, rules, regulations, schemes, bye-laws, awards, contracts and other agreements, memoranda and articles of association, certificates, deeds and other documents;
(b) a reference to the functions of a Minister under an enactment includes a reference to the functions of that Minister under an instrument having effect under that enactment.

Incorporation of the Secretary of State for Justice

3.—(1) The person who at the coming into force of this Order is the Secretary of State for Justice and any successor to that person is by that name a corporation sole. 1.015

(2) The corporate seal of the Secretary of State for Justice—
   (a) is to be authenticated by the signature of a Secretary of State or a person authorised by a Secretary of State to act in that behalf, and
   (b) is to be officially and judicially noticed.

(3) Every document purporting to be an instrument made or issued by the Secretary of State for Justice and to be—
   (a) sealed with the corporate seal of that Secretary of State authenticated in the manner provided for by paragraph (2), or
   (b) signed or executed by a person authorised by a Secretary of State to act in that behalf,

is to be received in evidence and to be deemed to be so made or issued without further proof, unless the contrary is shown.

(4) A certificate signed by the Secretary of State for Justice that an instrument purporting to be made or issued by—
   (a) the Secretary of State for Justice, or
   (b) the Secretary of State for Constitutional Affairs, or
   (c) the Secretary of State for the Home Department,

was so made or issued is conclusive evidence of that fact.

(5) The Documentary Evidence Act 1868 applies in relation to the Secretary of State for Justice—
   (a) as if references to regulations and orders included references to any document, and
   (b) as if the officers mentioned in column 2 of the Schedule included any officer authorised to act on behalf of the Secretary of State.

Transfer of functions from Secretary of State etc.

4.—(1) The functions of the Secretary of State under the following enactments are transferred to the Lord Chancellor— 1.016
   (a) in the Magistrates' Courts Act 1980, section 125A(3)(a);
   (b) in the Courts Act 2003, sections 70(2)(a), 72(3), 72A(4) and 73(1);
   (c) in the Criminal Justice Act 2003, sections 167(1)(b) and (c) and (9), 168(1)(c) and (5), 170(8)(b)(ii), 171(3)(a) and 173.

(2) The functions of the Secretary of State under the following enactments are transferred to the Secretary of State for Justice—
   (a) in the Domestic Violence, Crime and Victims Act 2004, sections 32, 33, 48, 49, 53, 54 and 55(1) to (6);
   (b) in Schedule 8 to that Act, paragraphs 1, 2, 8 and 9.

(3) The function of the Secretary of State for the Home Department under paragraph 1 of Schedule 1 to the Church Commissioners Measure 1947 is transferred to the Lord Chancellor.

The Secretary of State for Justice Order 2007

Transfer of functions from Lord Chancellor

1.017   5.—(1) The function of the Lord Chancellor under section 167(1)(c) of the Criminal Justice Act 2003 is transferred to the Secretary of State.

(2) The functions of the Lord Chancellor under the following enactments are transferred to the Secretary of State for the Home Department—

(a) in the Domestic Violence, Crime and Victims Act 2004, sections 33, 48, 49, 53, 54 and 55;

(b) in Schedule 8 to that Act, paragraphs 1, 2, 8 and 9.

Transfer of property etc. to Secretary of State for Justice

1.018   6.—(1) There are transferred to the Secretary of State for Justice—

(a) all property which, by virtue of section 35 of the Prison Act 1952, is vested in the Secretary of State at the coming into force of this Order, and

(b) all rights and liabilities to which the Secretary of State is entitled or subject at that time in connection with that property.

(2) There are transferred to the Secretary of State for Justice all property, rights and liabilities not falling within paragraph (1) to which the Secretary of State for the Home Department is entitled or subject at the coming into force of this Order in connection with—

(a) the functions transferred by article 4(2), or

(b) the functions that were immediately before 9th May 2007 entrusted to the Secretary of State for the Home Department and that have been entrusted to the Secretary of State for Justice before the making of this Order.

(3) There are transferred to the Secretary of State for Justice all property, rights and liabilities to which the Secretary of State for Constitutional Affairs is entitled or subject at the coming into force of this Order.

Supplementary

1.019   7.—(1) This article applies to—

(a) the functions transferred by article 4(1);
(b) the functions transferred by article 4(2);
(c) the function transferred by article 4(3);
(d) the function transferred by article 5(1);
(e) the functions transferred by article 5(2);
(f) anything transferred by article 6(1);
(g) anything transferred by article 6(2);
(h) the functions mentioned in article 6(2)(b);
(i) anything transferred by article 6(3);
(j) the functions that were immediately before 9th May 2007 entrusted to the Secretary of State for Constitutional Affairs and that have been entrusted to the Secretary of State for Justice before the making of this Order.

(2) In this article—

(a) "the transferor" means—
   (i) in relation to anything within paragraph (1)(a), (b) or (f), the Secretary of State;
   (ii) in relation to anything within paragraph (1)(c), (g) or (h), the Secretary of State for the Home Department;
   (iii) in relation to anything within paragraph (1)(d) or (e), the Lord Chancellor;
   (iv) in relation to anything within paragraph (1)(i) or (j), the Secretary of State for Constitutional Affairs;
(b) "the transferee" means—
   (i) in relation to anything within paragraph (1)(a) or (c), the Lord Chancellor;
   (ii) in relation to anything within paragraph (1)(b), (f), (g), (h), (i) or (j), the Secretary of State for Justice;
   (iii) in relation to anything within paragraph (1)(d), the Secretary of State;
   (iv) in relation to anything within paragraph (1)(e), the Secretary of State for the Home Department.

(3) This Order does not affect the validity of anything done (or having effect as if done) by or in relation to any of the transferors before the coming into force of this Order.

(4) Anything (including legal proceedings) which, at the coming into force of this Order, is in the process of being done by or in relation to the transferor may, so far as it relates to anything to which this article applies, be continued by or in relation to the transferee.

(5) Anything done (or having effect as if done) by or in relation to the transferor in connection with anything to which this article applies has effect, so far as necessary for continuing its effect after the coming into force of this Order, as if done by or in relation to the transferee.

(6) Documents or forms printed for use in connection with functions to which this article applies may be used in connection with those functions even though they contain, or are to be read as containing, references to the transferor, or to the department or an officer of the transferor; and for the purposes of the use of any such documents or forms after the coming into force of this Order, those references are to be read as references to the transferee, or to the department or an officer of the transferee (as appropriate).

(7) Any enactment or instrument passed or made before the coming into force of this Order has effect, so far as is necessary for the purposes of or in consequence of the transfer or entrusting to the transferee of anything to which this article applies, as if references to (and references which are to be read as references to) the transferor, or to the department or an officer of the transferor, were or included references to the transferee, or to the department or an officer of the transferee (as appropriate).

Consequential amendments

8. The Schedule (consequential amendments) has effect.

1.020

The Secretary of State for Justice Order 2007

SCHEDULE

ARTICLE 8

CONSEQUENTIAL AMENDMENTS

These have been incorporated into the updates to the text of relevant provisions.

GENERAL NOTE

1.021   This Order makes changes consequential on the establishment of the Ministry of Justice. It transfers to the Lord Chancellor certain functions and powers in connection with aspect of the criminal justice, sentencing and offender management systems previously vested in the Secretary of State, formerly the remit of the Home Secretary. It transfers to the Secretary of State for Justice Functions conferred on the Secretary of State at large and transfers to him some functions previously vested in the Lord Chancellor. Some of the changes impact on the social security area (income support, family credit, disability working allowance and jobseeker's allowance).

(2007 No. 2481)

The Tax Credits (Child Care Providers) (Miscellaneous Revocation and Transitional Provisions) (England) Scheme 2007

(2007 No. 2481)

ARRANGEMENT OF SCHEME

1. Citation, commencement and application
2. Interpretation
3. Partial revocation of the 1999 Regulations and transitional provision
4. Revocation of the 2005 Scheme and transitional provision

In force: October 1, 2007

The Secretary of State for Children, Schools and Families, being the appropriate national authority under section 12(6) of the Tax Credits Act 2002, and in exercise of the powers conferred by sections 12(5), (7) and (8) and 65(9) of that Act, makes the following Scheme:

Citation, commencement and application

1.—(1) This Scheme may be cited as the Tax Credits (Child Care Providers) (Miscellaneous Revocation and Transitional Provisions) (England) Scheme 2007.

(2) This Scheme comes into force—

(a) to the extent that it revokes the 2005 Scheme and the provisions of the 1999 Regulations other than regulations 11(a) and (b) and 12, on 1st October 2007; and

(b) to the extent that it revokes regulations 11(a) and (b) and 12 of the 1999 Regulations, on 1st October 2009.

(3) This Scheme applies in relation to England only.

Interpretation

2. In this Scheme—

"the 1999 Regulations" means the Tax Credit (New Category of Child Care Provider) Regulations 1999;

"the 2005 Scheme" means the Tax Credits (Approval of Child Care Providers) Scheme 2005;

"the inspection provisions" means regulations 11(a) and (b) and 12 of the 1999 Regulations (access to information and records by officers of the Secretary of State and Her Majesty's Revenue and Customs); and

"the transitional period" means the period beginning on 1st October 2007 and ending on 1st October 2009.

Partial revocation of the 1999 Regulations and transitional provision

1.025   **3.**—(1) The 1999 Regulations are revoked to the extent that they make a Scheme for determining the description of persons by whom child care is provided, and whose charges fall to be taken into account in computing the child care element of working tax credit, subject to paragraph (3) of this article.

(2) Any accreditation of an organisation by the Secretary of State pursuant to the Scheme provided for by the 1999 Regulations, and any approval granted by such an organisation, shall lapse on 1st October 2007, except for the purposes of the inspection provisions.

(3) During the transitional period the inspection provisions shall have effect as if—

(a) the reference in regulation 11 to the period for which an organisation is accredited were a reference to the transitional period; and

(b) the reference in regulation 12 to the period during which a child care provider is approved by an accredited organisation were a reference to the transitional period.

Revocation of the 2005 Scheme and transitional provision

1.026   **4.**—(1) The 2005 Scheme is revoked, subject to paragraph (2).

(2) The provisions of the 2005 Scheme continue to have effect in relation to—

(a) any approval granted to a child care provider under that Scheme which is valid immediately before 1st October 2007; and

(b) any application for approval under that Scheme which has not been granted before 1st October 2007.

GENERAL NOTE

1.027   This Scheme partially revokes the Tax Credit (New Category of Child Care Provider) Regulations 1999 (SI 1999/3110) and revokes the Tax Credits (Approval of Child Care Providers) Scheme 2005 (SI 2005/93), with transitional provisions. The Scheme applies in relation to England only. The revocations provided for by the Scheme mostly came into force on October 1, 2007.

Article 3(1) revokes the 1999 Regulations to the extent that they make a Scheme for determining the description of persons by whom child care is provided, and whose charges fall to be taken into account in computing the child care element of working tax credit. Article 3(2) makes various transitional provision concerning the access to information and records by HMRC officers and for allied matters.

Article 4(1) revokes the 2005 Scheme. Article 4(2) makes transitional provision to ensure that approvals granted under the 2005 Scheme that were valid immediately before October 1, 2007 continue to have effect until the end of their period of validity.

The 1999 Regulations and the 2005 Scheme have been revoked following the introduction of a system of voluntary registration for certain childcare providers under the Childcare Act 2006 (see the Childcare (Voluntary Registration) Regulations 2007 (SI 2007/730)).

(SI 2007/2911)

The Social Security (Claims and Information) Regulations 2007

(SI 2007/2911)

ARRANGEMENT OF REGULATIONS

1. Citation, commencement and interpretation
2. Use of social security information: local authorities
3. Use of social security information: Secretary of State
4. Social security information verified by local authorities.
5. Specified benefits for the purpose of section 7B(3) of the Administration Act.

6–10 *Omitted*

In force October 31, 2007

The Secretary of State for Work and Pensions makes the following Regulations in exercise of the powers conferred by sections 5(1)(a), 7A(1), (2) and (6)(d), 7B(2) and (5), 189(1) and (4) to (6) and 191 of the Social Security Administration Act 1992. In accordance with section 176(1)(a) of that Act, as regards provisions in the Regulations relating to housing benefit and council tax benefit, he has consulted organisations appearing to him to be representative of the authorities concerned. The Social Security Advisory Committee has agreed that proposals in respect of these Regulations should not be referred to it.

Citation, commencement and interpretation

1.—(1) These Regulations may be cited as the Social Security (Claims and Information) Regulations 2007 and shall come into force on 31st October 2007.

(2) In regulations 4 and 5 "the Administration Act" means the Social Security Administration Act 1992.

(3) In regulations 2 to 4—

"specified benefit" means one or more of the following benefits—
 (a) attendance allowance;
 (b) bereavement allowance;
 (c) bereavement payment;
 (d) carer's allowance;
 (e) disability living allowance;
 (f) incapacity benefit;
 (g) income support;
 (h) jobseeker's allowance;
 (i) retirement pension;

(j) state pension credit;
(k) widowed parent's allowance;
(l) winter fuel payment;

"the Secretary of State" includes persons providing services to the Secretary of State;

"local authority" includes persons providing services to a local authority and persons authorised to exercise any function of a local authority relating to housing benefit or council tax benefit.

Use of social security information: local authorities

2.—(1) This regulation applies where social security information held by a local authority was supplied by the Secretary of State to the local authority and this information—
   (a) was used by the Secretary of State in connection with a person's claim for, or award of, a specified benefit; and
   (b) is relevant to that person's claim for, or award of, council tax benefit or housing benefit.

(2) The local authority must, for the purposes of the person's claim for, or award of, council tax benefit or housing benefit, use that information without verifying its accuracy.

(3) Paragraph (2) does not apply where—
   (a) the information is supplied more than twelve months after it was used by the Secretary of State in connection with a claim for, or an award of, a specified benefit; or
   (b) the information is supplied within twelve months of its use by the Secretary of State but the local authority has reasonable grounds for believing the information has changed in the period between its use by the Secretary of State and its supply to the local authority; or
   (c) the date on which the information was used by the Secretary of State cannot be determined.

Use of social security information: Secretary of State

1.031   3.—(1) This regulation applies where social security information held by the Secretary of State was supplied by a local authority to the Secretary of State and this information—
   (a) was used by the local authority in connection with a person's claim for, or award of, council tax benefit or housing benefit; and
   (b) is relevant to that person's claim for, or award of, a specified benefit.

(2) The Secretary of State must, for the purposes of the person's claim for, or award of, a specified benefit, use that information without verifying its accuracy.

(3) Paragraph (2) does not apply where—
   (a) the information is supplied more than twelve months after it was used by a local authority in connection with a claim for, or an award of, council tax benefit or housing benefit; or
   (b) the information is supplied within twelve months of its use by the local authority but the Secretary of State has reasonable grounds

for believing the information has changed in the period between its use by the local authority and its supply to the Secretary of State; or
(c) the date on which the information was used by the local authority cannot be determined.

Social security information verified by local authorities

4.—(1) This regulation applies where social security information is verified by a local authority by virtue of regulations made under section 7A(2)(e) of the Administration Act and forwarded by that local authority to the Secretary of State.   1.032

(2) The Secretary of State must, for the purposes of a person's claim for, or award of, a specified benefit, use this information without verifying its accuracy.

(3) Paragraph (2) does not apply where—
(a) the Secretary of State has reasonable grounds for believing the social security information received from the local authority is inaccurate; or
(b) the Secretary of State receives the information more than four weeks after it was verified by the local authority.

Specified benefits for the purpose of section 7B(3) of the Administration Act

5. The benefits specified for the purpose of section 7B(3) of the Administration Act are—   1.033
(a) a "specified benefit" within the meaning given in regulation 1(3);
(b) housing benefit; and
(c) council tax benefit.

Regs 6–10 amend other legislation and the amendments are incorporated in the relevant regulations.

PART II

UPDATING MATERIAL
VOLUME I

NON-MEANS TESTED BENEFITS

Non-Means Tested Benefits

p.4, *annotation to the Vaccine Damage Payments Act 1979, s.1(1a) increase of the statutory sum)*

The statutory sum was increased to £120,000 by the Vaccine Damage Payments Act 1979 Statutory Sum Order 2007 (SI 2007/1931) with effect from July 12, 2007 (for text see the New Legislation section of this Supplement). 2.001

p.28, *amendment to Social Security Contributions and Benefits Act 1992, s.22*

With effect from September 26, 2007, s.22 was amended by s.12 of the Pensions Act 2007, as follows: 2.002
In subs.(2A) for "the upper earnings limit" substitute "the applicable limit";
And subs.(2A) was further amended by Sch.1 para.33 of the Pensions Act 2007 as follows:
At the end of that subs. insert—

"This subsection does not affect the operation of sections 44A and 44B (deemed earnings factors)."

After subs.(2A) insert—

"(2B) 'The applicable limit' means—
(a) in relation to a tax year before the flat rate introduction year, the upper earnings limit;
(b) in relation to the flat rate introduction year or any subsequent tax year, the upper accrual point."

With effect from the same date s.22 was also amended by Sch.1 para.9 of the Pensions Act 2007 as follows:
After subs.(5) insert—

"(5A) Section 23A makes provision for the crediting of Class 3 contributions for the purpose of determining entitlement to the benefits to which that section applies."

p.64, *amendment to Social Security Contributions and Benefits Act 1992, s.38*

With effect from July 26, 2007, s.38 was amended by Sch.1 para.40 of the Pensions Act 2007, as follows: 2.003
In subs.(2) for "the age of 65" substitute "pensionable age".

p.65, *amendment to Social Security Contributions and Benefits Act 1992, s.39*

With effect from July 26, 2007, s.39 was amended by s.6(5) of the Pensions Act 2007, as follows: 2.004
After subs.(2) insert—

"(2A) In its application by virtue of subsection (1) above, section 44(4) below is to be read as if for the first amount specified in that

Non-Means Tested Benefits

provision there were substituted a reference to the amount prescribed for the purposes of this subsection."

With effect from September 26, 2007, s.39 is amended by the Pensions Act 2007, Sch.7, Pt 5, by deleting the words "and Schedule 4A" wherever they occur.

From the same date s.39 is further amended by Sch.2, Pt 3, para.3 by omitting subs.(3).

p.68, *amendment to Social Security Contributions and Benefits Act 1992, s.39C*

2.005   With effect from July 26, 2007, s.39C was amended by s.6(6) of the Pensions Act 2007, as follows:
For subs.(2) substitute—

"(1A) In its application by virtue of subsection (1) above, section 44(4) below is to be read as if for the first amount specified in that provision there were substituted a reference to the amount prescribed for the purposes of this subsection.

(2) The weekly amount of a bereavement allowance is an amount equal to the amount prescribed for the purposes of subsection (1A) above."

In subs.(3), for the words "or (as the case may be) section 44 below by virtue of subsection (1) or (2) above" substitute "by virtue of subsection (1) above".

With effect from the same date, s.39C is further amended by Sch.2 Pt 3, para.4 of the Pensions Act 2007 as follows:
In subs.(1), after "section 46(2)" insert "and (4)"; and in subs.(3), in each of paras (a) and (b), for "sections" substitute "provisions".

p.79, *annotation to Social Security Contributions and Benefits Act 1992, s.39C (living together as man and wife)*

2.006   The importance of a sexual relationship, as well as the whole approach to be adopted in deciding whether a couple are living together as man and wife, has been examined again in *CIS/4156/2006*. This was a case where the couple had admittedly lived together in the past; but had resumed the shared occupation of a house (not the same home as they had shared previously) as "friends". The house they now shared was originally rented from the council by the claimant, but at some time in the course of their renewed relationship, she purchased it with the help of a loan from her (former) partner. The claimant was, throughout the period in question, in receipt of Income Support, and this was an appeal against a claim for recovery of overpaid benefit in the sum of £24.000. Deputy Commissioner Wikeley allowed the appeal on the grounds that the tribunal had failed to explain the reasons for their decision and in particular that they failed to explain why they were rejecting the argument advanced on behalf of the appellant that there was no sexual relationship involved in their renewed relationship. He makes reference specifically to some of the points made in the annotation in Vol.I.

Non-Means Tested Benefits

p.86, *amendment to Social Security Contributions and Benefits Act 1992, s.44*

With effect from September 26, 2007 s.44 was amended by Sch.1, para.1 of the Pensions Act 2007, as follows:
In subs.(1) for para.(b) substitute—

2.007

"(b) he satisfies the relevant conditions or condition";

and after subs.(1) insert—

"(1A) In subsection (1)(b) above 'the relevant conditions or condition' means—
(a) in a case where the person attains pensionable age before 6th April 2010, the conditions specified in Schedule 3, Part I, paragraph 5;
(b) in a case where the person attains pensionable age on or after that date, the condition specified in Schedule 3, Part I, paragraph 5A."

With effect from September 26, 2007 s.44 is further amended by Sch.2 Pt 3, para.5, as follows:
In subs.(5A), for "Schedule 4A" substitute "Schedules 4A and 4B"; and in subs.(6), for "Schedule 4A" substitute "Schedule 4A or 4B."
With effect from September 26, 2007, s.44 is amended by s.12 of the Pensions Act 2007, as follows:
In subs.(6) in para.(za) for "the upper earnings limit" substitute "the applicable limit";
In subs.(7), at the end, insert—

"(c) 'the applicable limit' means—
(i) in relation to a tax year before the flat rate introduction year, the upper earnings limit;
(ii) in relation to the flat rate introduction year or any subsequent tax year, the upper accrual point."

p.90, *amendment to Social Security Contributions and Benefits Act 1992, s.44A*

With effect from September 26, 2007 s.44A was amended by Sch.1 para.34 of the Pensions Act 2007 as follows:
Before subs.(1) insert—

2.008

"(A1) Subsections (1) to (4) below apply to the first appointed year or any subsequent tax year before 2010–11."

In subs.(1) after "a relevant year" insert "to which this subsection applies".
After subs.(4) insert—

"(4A) The following do not apply to a pensioner attaining pensionable age on or after 6th April 2010—
(a) the requirement referred to in subsection (2)(d) above, and
(b) subsections (3) and (4) above."

p.90, *amendment to Social Security Contributions and Benefits Act 1992, to follow s.44A*

2.009   With effect from September 26, 2007, the following sections were added after s.44A. by s.9(1) of the Pensions Act 2007.

"44B Deemed earnings factors: 2010–11 onwards

(1) This section applies to 2010–11 and subsequent tax years.

(2) For the purposes of section 44(6)(za) above, if any of Conditions A to C in subsections (3) to (5) below is satisfied for a relevant year to which this section applies, a pensioner is deemed to have an earnings factor for that year which—
   (a) is derived from so much of his earnings as did not exceed the applicable limit and on which primary Class 1 contributions were paid; and
   (b) is equal to the amount which, when added to any other earnings factors taken into account under that provision, produces an aggregate of earnings factors equal to the low earnings threshold.

(3) Condition A is that the pensioner would, apart from this section, have an earnings factor for the year—
   (a) equal to or greater than the qualifying earnings factor ('the QEF') for the year, but
   (b) less than the low earnings threshold for the year.

(4) Condition B is that the pensioner—
   (a) would, apart from this section and section 44C below, have an earnings factor for the year less than the QEF for the year, but
   (b) is entitled to an aggregate amount of earnings factor credits for that year under section 44C below equal to the difference between the QEF for the year and the earnings factor mentioned in paragraph (a) above.

(5) Condition C is that the pensioner is entitled to 52 earnings factor credits for that year under section 44C below.

(6) This section has effect in relation to the flat rate introduction year and any subsequent tax year as if—
   (a) subsection (2)(b) referred to an aggregate of earnings factors greater than the QEF, but less than the low earnings threshold, for the year (rather than to one equal to that threshold); and
   (b) Condition A in subsection (3) (and the reference to it in subsection (2)) were omitted.

(7) In this section—
   (a) 'the applicable limit' has the same meaning as in section 44 above;
   (b) 'the low earnings threshold' means the low earnings threshold for the year concerned as specified in section 44A above; and
   (c) in subsections (3) and (4), any reference to the pensioner's earnings factor for a relevant year is to be construed in accordance with section 44(6)(za) above.

Non-Means Tested Benefits

44C Earnings factor credits

(1) This section applies, for the purposes of Conditions B and C in section 44B(4) and (5) above, to 2010–11 and subsequent tax years.

(2) In respect of each week—
(a) which falls in a relevant year to which this section applies, and
(b) in respect of which a pensioner is eligible for earnings factor enhancement,

the pensioner is entitled to an earnings factor credit equal to 1/52 of the QEF for that year.

This is subject to subsection (5) below.

(3) A pensioner is eligible for earnings factor enhancement in respect of a week if one or more of the following apply—
(a) he was a relevant carer in respect of that week for the purposes of section 23A above (see section 23A(3));
(b) carer's allowance was payable to him for any part of that week, or would have been so payable but for the fact that under regulations the amount payable to him was reduced to nil because of his receipt of other benefits;
(c) severe disablement allowance was payable to him for any part of that week;
(d) long-term incapacity benefit was payable to him for any part of that week or would have been so payable but for the fact that—
  (i) he did not satisfy the contribution conditions in paragraph 2 of Schedule 3, or
  (ii) under regulations the amount payable to him was reduced to nil because of his receipt of other benefits or of payments from an occupational pension scheme or personal pension scheme;
(e) he satisfies such other conditions as may be prescribed.

(4) In subsection (3)(d)(ii) above 'occupational pension scheme' and 'personal pension scheme' have the meanings given by subsection (6) of section 30DD above for the purposes of subsection (5) of that section.

(5) For the purposes of Condition B in section 44B(4) above a person is not entitled to an aggregate amount of earnings factor credits in respect of a year that is greater than the difference referred to in that Condition.

(6) For the purposes of this section a week that falls partly in one tax year and partly in another is to be treated as falling in the year in which it begins and not in the following year.

(7) In section 44B above and this section—
(a) 'the QEF' means the qualifying earnings factor, and
(b) any reference to a person being entitled to an earnings factor credit of a particular amount (or to an aggregate amount of earnings factor credits) for a year is a reference to the person being treated as having for that year an earnings factor (within

23

Non-Means Tested Benefits

the meaning of section 44(6)(za) above) of the amount in question by virtue of subsection (2) above."

p.91, *amendment to Social Security Contributions and Benefits Act 1992, s.45*

2.010   With effect from September 26, 2007, s.45 was amended by s.11 of the Pensions Act 2007, as follows:
In subs.(2) after para.(c) insert—

"and
   (d) in relation to the flat rate introduction year and subsequent tax years, the weekly equivalent of the amount calculated in accordance with Schedule 4B to this Act."

In subs.(3A) at the end of para.(b) insert—

"before the flat rate introduction year".

p.93, *amendment to Social Security Contributions and Benefits Act 1992, s.46*

2.011   With effect from September 26, 2007, s.46 was amended by Sch.2, Pt 3, para.46 of the Pensions Act 2007, as follows:
After subs.(3) insert—

"(4) For the purpose of determining the additional pension falling to be calculated under section 45 above by virtue of section 39C(1) above in a case where the deceased spouse or civil partner died under pensionable age, section 45 has effect subject to the following additional modifications—
   (a) the omission of subsection (2)(d), and
   (b) the omission in subsection (3A)(b) of the words 'before the flat rate introduction year'."

p.96, *amendment to Social Security Contributions and Benefits Act 1992, s.48A*

2.012   With effect from September 26, 2007 s.48A was amended by s.2 and by Sch.7 of the Pensions Act, 2007 as follows:
In each of subss.(2)(a) and (2B)(a) omit "and become entitled to a Category A retirement pension".
Omit subs.(5)

With effect from September 26, 2007, s.48A is amended by Sch.1, para.2 of the Pensions Act 2007, as follows:
In subs.(2) for para.(b) substitute—

"(b) satisfies the relevant conditions or condition.";

and after subs.(2) insert—

"(2ZA) In subsection (2)(b) above 'the relevant conditions or condition' means—

(a) in a case where the spouse is a married man who attains pensionable age before 6th April 2010, the conditions specified in Schedule 3, Part I, paragraph 5;
(b) in a case where the spouse attains pensionable age on or after that date, the condition specified in Schedule 3, Part I, paragraph 5A."

In subs.(2B) for para.(b) substitute—

"(b) satisfies the condition specified in Schedule 3, Part I, paragraph 5A."

With effect from the same date s.48A is further amended by Sch.2, Pt 3, para.7 of the Pensions Act 2007, as follows:
In subs.(4) for "Schedule 4A" substitute "Schedules 4A and 4B".

p.97, *amendment to Social Security Contributions and Benefits Act 1992, s.48B*

With effect from September 26, 2007, s.48B was amended by Sch.1 of the Pensions Act 2007, as follows:
In subs.(1) for the words "the conditions specified in Schedule 3, Part I, paragraph 5" substitute "the relevant conditions or condition".
After subs.(1) insert—

2.013

"(1ZA) In subsection (1) above 'the relevant conditions or condition' means—
(a) in a case where the spouse—
(i) died before 6th April 2010, or
(ii) died on or after that date having attained pensionable age before that date, the conditions specified in Schedule 3, Part I, paragraph 5;
(b) in a case where the spouse died on or after that date without having attained pensionable age before that date, the condition specified in Schedule 3, Part I, paragraph 5A."

In subs.(1A) for the words "the conditions specified in Schedule 3, Part I, paragraph 5" substitute "the condition specified in Schedule 3, Part I, paragraph 5A".
With effect from the same date s.48B was further amended by Sch.2, Pt 3, para.8 as follows:
In subs.(2), for "Schedule 4A" substitute "Schedules 4A and 4B".

p.98, *amendment to Social Security Contributions and Benefits Act 1992, s.48BB*

With effect from September 26, 2007, s.48BB was amended by Sch.2, Pt 3, para.9 of the Pensions Act 2007, as follows:
In subs.(5)—
for "Schedule 4A" substitute "Schedules 4A and 4B"; and
for the words from "subject" to the end, substitute "subject to section 46(3) above and to the following provisions of this section and the modification in section 48C(4) below."

2.014

p.99, *amendment to Social Security Contributions and Benefits Act 1992, s.48C*

2.015 With effect from September 26, 2007, s.48C was amended by Sch.2, Pt 3, para.10 of the Pensions Act 2007, as follows:
In subs.(4), for "Schedule 4A" substitute "Schedules 4A and 4B".

p.103, *amendment to Social Security Contributions and Benefits Act 1992, s.54*

2.016 With effect from September 26, 2007, s.54 was amended by Sch.1, para.6 and by Sch.7 of the Pensions Act 2007, as follows:
Subs.(3) is omitted.

p.104, *amendment to Social Security Contributions and Benefits Act 1992, s.55*

2.017 With effect from September 26, 2007, s.55 was amended by Sch.1, para.7 of the Pensions Act 2007, as follows:
In subs.(3) for para.(a) substitute—

"(a) does not become entitled to that pension by reason only of not satisfying the conditions of section 1 of the Administration Act (entitlement to benefit dependent on claim), or".

p.110, *amendment to Social Security Contributions and Benefits Act 1992, s.64*

2.018 With effect from September 26, 2007, s.64 was amended by Sch.1, para.41 of the Pensions Act 2007, as follows:
In subs.(1) for "is aged 65 or over" substitute "has attained pensionable age".

p.116, *amendment to Social Security Contributions and Benefits Act 1992, s.67*

2.019 With effect from October 29, 2007, s.67(2) was amended by s.60 (1) of the Welfare Reform Act 2007, as follows:
For s.67(2) substitute the following:

"(2) Regulations may provide that an attendance allowance shall not be payable in respect of a person for a period when he is a resident of a care home in circumstances in which any of the costs of any qualifying services provided for him are borne out of public or local funds under a specified enactment.

(3) The reference in subsection (2) to a care home is to an establishment that provides accommodation together with nursing or personal care.

(4) The following are qualifying services for the purposes of subsection (2)—

(a) accommodation,

Non-Means Tested Benefits

(b) board, and
(c) personal care.

(5) The reference in subsection (2) to a specified enactment is to an enactment which is, or is of a description, specified for the purposes of that subsection by regulations.

(6) The power to specify an enactment for the purposes of subsection (2) includes power to specify it only in relation to its application for a particular purpose.

(7) In this section, 'enactment' includes an enactment comprised in, or in an instrument made under, an Act of the Scottish Parliament."

pp.125–126 *amendment of Social Security Contributions and Benefits Act 1992, s.72*

With effect from October 1, 2007, s.72 was amended by s.52 of the Welfare Reform Act, 2007, as follows:

After subs.(1) insert the following:

2.020

"(1A) In its application to a person in relation to so much of a period as falls before the day on which he reaches the age of 16, subsection (1) has effect subject to the following modifications—
  (a) the condition mentioned in subsection (1)(a)(ii) shall not apply, and
  (b) none of the other conditions mentioned in subsection (1) shall be taken to be satisfied unless—
    (i) he has requirements of a description mentioned in the condition substantially in excess of the normal requirements of persons of his age, or
    (ii) he has substantial requirements of such a description which younger persons in normal physical and mental health may also have but which persons of his age and in normal physical and mental health would not have."

After subs.(2) insert the following:

"(2A) The modifications mentioned in subsection (1A) shall have effect in relation to the application of subsection (1) for the purposes of subsection (2), but only—
  (a) in the case of a person who is under the age of 16 on the date on which the award of the care component would begin, and
  (b) in relation to so much of any period mentioned in subsection (2) as falls before the day on which he reaches the age of 16."

In subs.(5) after the words "person shall" insert "(notwithstanding subsection (1A)(b))".

Subs.(6) was repealed by Sch.8 of the Welfare Reform Act 2007.

In subs. (7) for the words "subsections (5) and (6)" substitute "subsection (5)".

After subs. (7) insert the following:

"(7A) Subsection (1A) has effect subject to regulations made under subsection (7) (except as otherwise prescribed)."

With effect from October 29, 2007 s.60(2) of the Welfare Reform Act 2007, amended s.72(8) by substituting the following:

"(8) Regulations may provide that no amount in respect of a disability living allowance which is attributable to entitlement to the care component shall be payable in respect of a person for a period when he is a resident of a care home in circumstances in which any of the costs of any qualifying services provided for him are borne out of public or local funds under a specified enactment.

(9) The reference in subsection (8) to a care home is to an establishment that provides accommodation together with nursing or personal care.

(10) The following are qualifying services for the purposes of subsection (8)—

(a) accommodation,

(b) board, and

(c) personal care.

(11) The reference in subsection (8) to a specified enactment is to an enactment which is, or is of a description, specified for the purposes of that subsection by regulations.

(12) The power to specify an enactment for the purposes of subsection (8) includes power to specify it only in relation to its application for a particular purpose.

(13) In this section, "enactment" includes an enactment comprised in, or in an instrument made under, an Act of the Scottish Parliament."

p.130, *annotation to Social Security Contributions and Benefits Act 1992, s.72 (attention reasonably required)*

2.021 In *CA/3943/2006*, the Deputy Commissioner held that it would be difficult ever to conclude that the use of a bucket in the kitchen, as a substitute for a lavatory, could be regarded as acceptable so as to render assistance that was needed to climb the stairs, no longer "reasonably required". The question of whether the use of a commode downstairs, if that were available, she decided, should be left to a subsequent tribunal.

p.145, *annotation to Social Security Contributions and Benefits Act 1992, s.72 (the cooking test)*

2.022 Where the claimant suffered from achondroplasia, a condition that restricted his height and meant that he had especially short arms and legs, it was held (in *CDLA/4351/2006*) that the availability of a "Baby Belling" cooker and a microwave, on which he could cook a main meal, meant the claim should fail.

p.146, *annotation to Social Security Contributions and Benefits Act 1992, s.72 (the cooking test—nausea)*

Whether nausea induced by the smells of cooking food could be regarded as a sufficient reason to regard the claimant as incapable of preparing a meal was considered again in *CDLA/1256/2007*. Commissioner Turnbull came down firmly in favour of the claimant.

2.023

p.152, *annotation to Social Security Contributions and Benefits Act 1992, s.72 (renewal claim and prospective period for entitlement)*

In *CDLA/3461/2006*, it was held that this requirement applies equally to a renewal claim as much as to a new claim. Thus where, on the medical evidence provided, it was reasonable to expect that the claimant would be recovered within the next 6months, even though he may not have recovered yet, the claim was properly refused.

2.024

pp.156–158, *amendment to Social Security Contributions and Benefits Act 1992, s.73*

With effect from October 1, 2007 s.73(4) was amended by s.53(2) of Welfare Reform Act 2007, as follows:
For subs.(4) substitute the following:

2.025

"(4A) In its application to a person in relation to so much of a period as falls before the day on which he reaches the age of 16, subsection (1) has effect subject to the modification that the condition mentioned in paragraph (d) shall not be taken to be satisfied unless—
(a) he requires substantially more guidance or supervision from another person than persons of his age in normal physical and mental health would require, or
(b) persons of his age in normal physical and mental health would not require such guidance or supervision"

GENERAL NOTE

The wording of this amendment appears to be designed to assist in the renewal of claims which bridge the date upon which the claimant may become entitled to benefit at a higher rate by virtue of achieving the age 16. The problem was highlighted in *CDLA 1190/06*, in the case of a child reaching the age of three, which was relevant in relation to s.73(1A), where the Commissioner was able to achieve the desired result by giving a more liberal interpretation to the Claims & Payments Regulations. It is odd that this amendment did not include that section also.

In subs.(5) the words "subject to subsection (4) above" were repealed by Sch.8 of the Welfare Reform Act, 2007.
After subs.(5) insert the following:

"(5A) Subsection (4A) has effect subject to regulations made under subsection (5) (except as otherwise prescribed)."

Non-Means Tested Benefits

After subs.(9) insert the following:

"(9A) The modifications mentioned in subsection (4A) shall have effect in relation to the application of subsection (1) for the purposes of subsection (9), but only—
- (a) in the case of a person who is under the age of 16 on the date on which the award of the mobility component would begin, and
- (b) in relation to so much of any period mentioned in subsection (9) as falls before the day on which he reaches the age of 16."

With effect from October 1, 2007, s.73(9) was amended by Sch.7 para.2(2) of the Welfare Reform Act 2007, as follows:
In subs.(9)(a) after "subsection (1)" insert "(a) to (d)".

p.167, *amendment to Social Security Contributions and Benefits Act 1992, s.75*

2.026   With effect from September 26, 2007, s.75 was amended by Sch.1, para.42 of the Pensions Act 2007, as follows:
In subs.(1) for "the age of 65" substitute "pensionable age"; and for the sidenote substitute "Persons who have attained pensionable age".

p.174, *amendment to Social Security Contributions and Benefits Act 1992, s.78*

2.027   With effect from September 26, 2007, s.78 was amended by Sch.1 para.13 and by Sch.7 of the Pensions Act 2007, as follows:
In subs.(4) para.(d) is omitted.

pp.180–183, *amendment to Social Security Contributions and Benefits Act 1992, ss.83–85*

2.028   With effect from September 26, 2007, ss.83, 84 and 85 were repealed by Sch.7, Pt 2, of the Pensions Act 2007.

p.185, *amendment to Social Security Contributions and Benefits Act 1992, s.88*

2.029   With effect from September 26, 2007, s.88 was amended by Sch.1 para.14 of the Pensions Act 2007, as follows:
For the words "under or by virtue of sections 83 to 86A" substitute "by virtue of section 86A".

p.185, *amendment to social Security Contributions and Benefits Act 1992, s.89*

2.030   With effect from September 26, 2007, s.89 was amended by Sch.1 para.15 of the Pensions Act 2007 as follows:
in each of subss.(1) and (1A), for "sections 82 to 86A" substitute "sections 82 and 86A".

Non-Means Tested Benefits

p.233, *Social Security Contributions and Benefits Act 1992, s.113, new reciprocal agreements*

A new agreement with the Netherlands has been concluded: see The Social Security (Netherlands) Order 2007 (SI 2007/631) coming into force on June 1, 2007.

A new agreement with Ireland has been concluded: see The Social Security (Ireland) order 2007 (SI 2007/2122) coming into force on October 1, 2007.

2.031

p.235, *amendment to Social Security Contributions and Benefits Act 1992, s.114*

With effect from September 26, 2007, s.114 was amended by Sch.1 para.16 of the Pensions Act 2007, as follows:
In subs.(4) the words "to 84" are omitted.

2.032

p.240, *amendment to Social Security Contributions and Benefits Act 1992, s.122*

With effect from September 26, 2007, s.122 was amended by s.11 of the Pensions Act as follows:
At the appropriate place insert the following new definition—

"'the flat rate introduction year' means such tax year as may be designated as such by order;".

From the same date s.122 was also amended by s.12 of the Pensions Act as follows:
At the appropriate place insert the following new definition—

"'the upper accrual point' is to be construed in accordance with subsections (7) and (8) below;";

After subs.(6) insert—

"(7) 'The upper accrual point' is the amount that is equal to the amount of the upper earnings limit for the flat rate introduction year multiplied by 52.
This is subject to subsection (8) below.
(8) The Secretary of State may, by order made before the beginning of that year, direct that the upper accrual point is to be such other amount (whether greater or lesser than that mentioned in subsection (7) above) as is specified in the order."

2.033

p.252, *amendment to Social Security Contributions and Benefits Act 1992, s.149*

With effect from September 26, 2007, s.149 was amended by Sch.1 para.17 of the Pensions Act 2007, as follows:
In subs.(3) the words "section 83(2) or (3) above or" are omitted.
From the same date s.149 was further amended by Sch.1 para.43 of the Pensions Act 2007, as follows:
In subs.(4) for "the age of 65" substitute "pensionable age".

2.034

31

p.254, *new s.150A to Contributions and Benefits Act 1992*

2.035   With effect from September 27, 2007, the Pensions Act 2007, s.5, inserted a new s.150A after s.150 as follows:

150A Annual up-rating of basic pension etc. and standard minimum guarantee

(1) The Secretary of State shall in each tax year review the following amounts in order to determine whether they have retained their value in relation to the general level of earnings obtaining in Great Britain—
   (a) the amount of the basic pension;
   (b) the specified amounts in the case of Category B, C or D retirement pensions;
   (c) the specified amounts in the case of industrial death benefit; and
   (d) the amounts of the standard minimum guarantee for the time being prescribed under s.2(4) and (5)(a) and (b) of the State Pension Credit Act 2002.

(2) Where it appears to the Secretary of State that the general level of earnings is greater at the end of the period under review than it was at the beginning of that period, he shall lay before Parliament the draft of an order which increases each of the amounts referred to in subs.(1) above by a percentage not less than the percentage by which the general level of earnings is greater at the end of the period than it was at the beginning.

(3) Subsection (2) above does not require the Secretary of State to provide for an increase in any case if it appears to him that the amount of the increase would be inconsiderable.

(4) The Secretary of State may, in providing for an increase in pursuance of subs.(2) above, adjust the amount of the increase so as to round the sum in question up or down to such extent as he thinks appropriate.

(5) The Secretary of State shall lay with a draft order under this section a copy of a report by the Government Actuary or the Deputy Government Actuary giving that Actuary's opinion on the likely effect on the National Insurance Fund of any parts of the order relating to sums payable out of that Fund.

(6) If a draft order laid before Parliament under this section is approved by a resolution of each House, the Secretary of State shall make the order in the form of the draft.

(7) An order under this section shall be framed so as to bring the increase in question into force in the week beginning with the first Monday in the tax year following that in which the order is made.

(8) For the purposes of any review under subs.(1) above the Secretary of State shall estimate the general level of earnings in such manner as he thinks fit.

(9) If a draft order under this section is combined with a draft up-rating order under s.150 above, the report required by virtue of

subs.(5) above may be combined with that required by virtue of s.150(8) above.

(10) In this section—

"the amount of the basic pension" means the first amount specified in s.44(4) of the Contributions and Benefits Act (weekly rate of Category A retirement pension);

"the specified amounts in the case of Category B, C or D retirement pensions" means—
  (a) the amount specified in para.5 of Pt 1 of Sch.4 to the Contributions and Benefits Act, and
  (b) the amounts specified in paras 6 and 7 of Pt 3 of that Schedule;

"the specified amounts in the case of industrial death benefit" means—
  (a) the amounts specified in para.10 of Pt 5 of that Schedule (apart from the amount of the initial rate), and
  (b) the amount specified in para.11 of that Part of that Schedule.

GENERAL NOTE

Section 5(3) to (7) of the Pensions Act 2007 provides as follows: 2.036

"(3) The section 150A inserted by subsection (1) and the amendments made by Part 5 of Schedule 1, so far as relating to the amounts referred to in section 150A(1)(a) to (c), have effect in relation to the designated tax year and subsequent tax years (with the result that the first review to be carried out under section 150A(1) in relation to those amounts is to be carried out in the designated tax year).

(4) 'The designated tax year' means such tax year as the Secretary of State may designate by an order made before 1st April 2011.

(5) The Secretary of State must exercise his power under subsection (4) in such a way as to secure that the tax year immediately following the designated tax year is one that begins before the relevant dissolution date.

(6) 'The relevant dissolution date' means the latest date on which, having regard to the maximum period for which a Parliament may exist, the Parliament in existence at the time of exercise of the power could be dissolved.

(7) The new section 150A inserted by subsection (1) and the amendments made by Part 5 of Schedule 1, so far as relating to the amounts mentioned in section 150A(1)(d), have effect in relation to the tax year in which this Act is passed and subsequent tax years."

p.270, *amendment to Social Security Contributions and Benefits Act 1992, s.176*

With effect from September 26, 2007, s.176 was amended by Sch.1 para.10 of the Pensions Act 2007, as follows: 2.037

In subs.1, after para.(a) insert—

"(aa) the first regulations made by virtue of section 23A(3)(c);".

And s.176 is also amended from the same date by Sch.1 para.35 of that act as follows:

In subs.(1)(c) at the appropriate place insert—

"section 122(8);";

In subs.(4) after "second appointed year" insert "or designating the flat rate introduction year".

p.272, *amendment to Social Security Contributions and Benefits Act 1992, Sch.3*

2.038   With effect from September 26, 2007, Sch.3 was amended by s.1 of the Pensions Act 2007, as follows:
In Pt 1, para.5, sub-para.(1) after "retirement pension" insert—

"(other than one in relation to which paragraph 5A applies)".

After para.5 insert—

"5A (1) This paragraph applies to—
(a) a Category A retirement pension in a case where the contributor concerned attains pensionable age on or after 6th April 2010;
(b) a Category B retirement pension payable by virtue of section 48A above in a case where the contributor concerned attains pensionable age on or after that date;
(c) a Category B retirement pension payable by virtue of section 48B above in a case where the contributor concerned dies on or after that date without having attained pensionable age before that date.

(2) The contribution condition for a Category A or Category B retirement pension in relation to which this paragraph applies is that—
(a) the contributor concerned must, in respect of each of not less than 30 years of his working life, have paid or been credited with contributions of a relevant class or been credited (in the case of 1987–88 or any subsequent year) with earnings; and
(b) in the case of each of those years, the earnings factor derived as mentioned in sub-paragraph (3) below must be not less than the qualifying earnings factor for that year.

(3) For the purposes of paragraph (b) of sub-paragraph (2) above, the earnings factor—
(a) in the case of 1987–88 or any subsequent year, is that which is derived from—
   (i) so much of the contributor's earnings as did not exceed the upper earnings limit and upon which such of the contributions mentioned in paragraph (a) of that sub-paragraph as are primary Class 1 contributions were paid or treated as paid or earnings credited; and
   (ii) any Class 2 or Class 3 contributions for the year; or
(b) in the case of any earlier year, is that which is derived from the contributions mentioned in paragraph (a) of that sub-paragraph.

Non-Means Tested Benefits

(4) Regulations may modify sub-paragraphs (2) and (3) above for the purposes of their application in a case where—
   (a) the contributor concerned has paid, or been credited with, contributions, or
   (b) contributions have been deemed to be, or treated as, paid by or credited to him, under the National Insurance Act 1946 or the National Insurance Act 1965."

p.277, *annotation to the Social Security Contributions and Benefits Act 1992, Sch.3 (referring to HM Revenue and Customs [formerly Board of Inland Revenue] questions on whether contributions have been paid)*

In *CIB/1602/2006*, Commissioner Williams, like Commissioner Rowland in interim decision *CIB/3327/2004*, criticised the administrative process on this, set out in the DMG guidance (Vol.3, Ch.3, paras 03230–03233). Reading it with the more accurate guidance in Vol.I, Ch.1, he thought the guidance to be:

2.039

> "internally inconsistent. Compare 01055 and 01056 with 56014. And it also guides administrators to make assumptions about contribution issues rather than decide them. See 01055 and 03231. And it does not tell the administrators to make it clear that their decisions depend on assumptions about a claimant's NI record rather than decisions about it. In my view the instruction to officials to make undisclosed assumptions about contribution issues combined with the failure to make it clear that there has been no decision on a contribution question have contributed to the systems failure to which Commissioner Rowland draws attention. In particular, there is a recurring failure to make a clear appealable decision on a question of credited earnings and a system in place that enables administrators to avoid the need to make the required decisions. This may explain why, even in this case where there was a decision, it has been assumed that there was no decision." (para.19)

He also considered DMG, paras 56014 and 56015 to "contain errors of law" (para.16).

In *CIB/1602/2006*, the matter in dispute was whether the claimant had sufficient credited earnings in tax/contribution year 2002–2003 to meet the second contribution condition. This turned on a much neglected area: in this case the complicated provisions of the Credits Regulations 1974, regs 3 and 8A. Commissioner Williams' decision on that is noted in the update to pp.370–371, below.

Commissioner Rowland's interim decision in *CIB/3327/2004* delineates the effect on a claimant's claim and appeals of the confusion generated by changes in jurisdiction on contributions matters (paras 2–4) and on the matter of awarding credits for spells of unemployment, a situation in which she was passed from pillar to post, a process during which Commissioner Rowland considered that there had been no actual decision on the award of credits for those spells, but only on non-

Non-Means Tested Benefits

entitlement to JSA (paras 19–21). This resulted in part from the changes on decision-making, appeals and jurisdictions wrought by the 1998 and 1999 legislation. But Commissioner Rowland rightly drew to attention for remedial action "some more fundamental flaws in the way on which the Department functions" in respect of these matters. Essentially, the key flaw was that no system had been put in place for informing the claimant that credits for unemployment had not been awarded. In the Commissioner's view, what was needed, "above all" was the establishment of

> "a system . . . to ensure that challenges to refusals of credits result in formal decisions that comply with regulation 28 of the [Decisions and Appeals Regulations] and inform the contributor of his or her right of appeal. That is so whether credits decisions are to be made during the relevant contribution year or after it has ended" (para.29).

Commissioner Williams considered in *CIB/1602/2006* that he had to reiterate that call for action:

> "That decision was made a year ago. It was an interim decision. I understand that as a result of later proceedings in the appeal the matter has now ceased to be an active appeal and that therefore the Commissioner will not be issuing a final decision. I have also seen no official response to that decision beyond the specific case. I therefore consider that I should adopt and repeat some of that analysis as it applies to this case in order to make clear why I entirely agree with him that the existing situation does not accord with the law. I depart from the approach of Commissioner Rowland in taking the view that in this case there is an appealable decision. But his criticisms of the lack of system are clearly part of the explanation for the confusion on the part of the secretary of state's representatives and the tribunal in this case" (para.14).

To that, this commentator can only add his support. This is a crucial area for contribution-based benefits and claimants and tribunals are entitled to expect at least as much decision-making clarity here as elsewhere in the benefits system. So far it is conspicuously lacking.

Some problems, of course, have arisen because of the mismatch in data on credits in the respective department's computer and recording systems: the DWP's Pension Service Computer System (PSCS) and the National Insurance Recording System (NIRS 2) system. Work is in hand to reconcile the latter with the former. It appears that up to 30,000 people may have been underpaid and about 90,000 may have been overpaid as a result of incorrect records. Overpayments are dealt with in amending regulations on the award of credits. These are noted in the updates to pp.368, 381–382, 382, 384 and 397, below. Underpayments are to be made good by administrative action. See further the Explanatory Memorandum to the amending regulations (SI 2007/2582) at *http://www.opsi.gov.uk/si/si200725.htm*. These changes, valuable as they are, do not as such, however, rectify the systemic problem identified by Commissioners Rowland and Williams.

Non-Means Tested Benefits

pp.276–283, *annotation to the Social Security Contributions and Benefits Act 1992, Sch.3 (Board of Inland Revenue)*

References to Board of Inland Revenue should now be read as ones to HM Revenue and Customs.   2.040

p.284, *amendment to Social Security Contributions and Benefits Act 1992, Sch.4, Pt 4*

With effect from September 26, 2007, Sch.4, Pt 4, was amended by Sch.1 para.18 of the Pensions Act 2007, as follows: 2.041
In para.5 for the figure in column (3) substitute "—";
and in para.6 for the figure in column (3) substitute "—".

p.286, *amendments to Social Security Contributions and Benefits Act 1992, sch.4A*

With effect from September 26, 2007, Sch.4A is amended by s.10, and Pt 5 of Sch.7, of the Pensions Act 2007, as follows: 2.041A
For the heading to this schedule substitute—

"ADDITIONAL PENSION: ACCRUAL RATES FOR PURPOSES OF SECTION 45(2)(c)".

In Pt 1, para.1, sub-para.(2) delete the number "39(1)"
In Pt 2, para.2, sub-para.(4), after "2009" insert "where the tax year concerned falls before 2010–11"
After sub-para.(4) insert—

"(4A) The appropriate table for persons attaining pensionable age on or after 6th April 2009 where the tax year is concerned is 2010–11 or a subsequent tax year is as follows—

TABLE 2A

	Amount of surplus Percentage
Band 1 Not exceeding LET	40
Band 2 Exceeding LET but not exceeding AUEL	10";

In Pt 2, para.2, sub-para.(6), after para.(c), insert—

"(d) 'AUEL' means the amount of equal to the upper earnings limit for the tax year concerned multiplied by 52"

In Pt 3, para.5, sup-para.(4), after "2009" insert—

"where the tax year concerned falls before 2010–11"

And after sub-para.(4) insert—

"4(A) The appropriate table for persons attaining pensionable age on or after 6th April 2009 where the tax year concerned is 2010–11 or a subsequent tax year is as follows—

Non-Means Tested Benefits

TABLE 4A

	Amount of surplus Percentage
Band 1 Not exceeding LET	40
Band 2 Exceeding LET but not exceeding AUEL	10";

In Pt 3, para.7, sub-para.(4), after "2009" insert—

"where the tax year concerned falls before 2010–11";

And after sub-para.(4) insert

"(4A) The appropriate table for persons attaining pensionable age on or after 6th April 2009 where the tax year concerned is 2010–11 or a subsequent tax year is as follows—

TABLE 6A

	Amount of surplus Percentage
Band 1 Not exceeding LET	40
Band 2 Exceeding LET but not exceeding AUEL	10";

In Pt 3, para.8, sub-para.(c) insert—

"(d) 'AUEL' means the amount of equal to the upper earnings limit for the tax year concerned multiplied by 52"

With effect from September 26, 2007 Sch.4A is further amended by Sch.2 Pt 3 para.11 as follows:
in para.1(2) omit "39(1)"

p.289, *amendment to Social Security Contributions and Benefits Act 1992, to follow Sch.4A*

2.042   With effect from September 26, 2007, Sch.4B was added by Sch.2 of the Pensions Act 2007 as follows:

"SCHEDULE 4B

Additional pension: accrual rates for purposes of section 45(2)(d)

Part 1

Amount for purposes of section 45(2)(d)

1(1) The amount referred to in section 45(2)(d) is to be calculated as follows—
(a) calculate the appropriate amount for each of the relevant years within section 45(2)(d) to which Part 2 of this Schedule applies;
(b) calculate the appropriate amount for each of the relevant years within section 45(2)(d) to which Part 3 of this Schedule applies; and
(c) add those amounts together.

(2) But if the resulting amount is a negative one, the amount referred to in section 45(2)(d) is nil.

Part 2

Normal rules: employment not contracted-out

Application

2 This Part applies to a relevant year if the contracted-out condition is not satisfied in respect of any tax week in the year.

Appropriate amount for year

3 The appropriate amount for the year for the purposes of paragraph 1 is either—
(a) the flat rate amount for the year (if there is a surplus in the pensioner's earnings factor for the year which does not exceed the LET), or
(b) the sum of the flat rate amount and the earnings-related amount for the year (if there is such a surplus which exceeds the LET).

4 The flat rate amount for the year is calculated by multiplying the FRAA in accordance with the last order under section 148AA of the Administration Act to come into force before the end of the final relevant year.

5 The earnings-related amount for the year is calculated as follows—
(a) take the part of the surplus for the year which exceeds the LET but which does not exceed the UAP;
(b) multiply that amount in accordance with the last order under section 148 of the Administration Act to come into force before the end of the final relevant year;
(c) multiply the amount found under paragraph (b) by 10%;
(d) divide the amount found under paragraph (c) by 44.

Part 3

Contracted-out employment

Application

6 This Part applies to a relevant year if the contracted-out condition is satisfied in respect of each tax week in the year.

Appropriate amount for year

7 The appropriate amount for the year for the purposes of paragraph 1 is calculated as follows—
(a) calculate amounts A and B in accordance with paragraphs 8 to 10;
(b) subtract amount B from amount A.

Amount A: assumed surplus not exceeding LET

8(1) Amount A is calculated in accordance with this paragraph if there is an assumed surplus in the pensioner's earnings factor for the year which does not exceed the LET.

(2) In such a case, amount A is the flat rate amount for the year.

(3) The flat rate amount for the year is calculated by multiplying the FRAA in accordance with the last order under section 148AA of the Administration Act to come into force before the end of the final relevant year.

Amount A: assumed surplus exceeding LET

9(1) Amount A is calculated in accordance with this paragraph if there is an assumed surplus in the pensioner's earnings factor for the year which exceeds the LET.

(2) In such a case, amount A is calculated as follows—
(a) take the part of the assumed surplus for the year which exceeds the LET but which does not exceed the UAP;

(b) multiply that amount in accordance with the last order under section 148 of the Administration Act to come into force before the end of the final relevant year;
(c) multiply the amount found under paragraph (b) by 10%;
(d) divide the amount found under paragraph (c) by 44;
(e) add the amount found under paragraph (d) to the flat rate amount for the year.

(3) The flat rate amount for the year is calculated by multiplying the FRAA in accordance with the last order under section 148AA of the Administration Act to come into force before the end of the final relevant year.

Amount B

10(1) Amount B is calculated as follows—
(a) take the part of the assumed surplus for the year which exceeds the QEF but which does not exceed the UAP;
(b) multiply that amount in accordance with the last order under section 148 of the Administration Act to come into force before the end of the final relevant year;
(c) multiply the amount found under paragraph (b) by 20%;
(d) divide the amount found under paragraph (c) by the number of relevant years in the pensioner's working life.

(2) Section 44B is to be ignored in applying section 44(6) for the purposes of this paragraph.

Part 4

Other cases

11 The Secretary of State may make regulations containing provision for finding for a tax year the amount referred to in section 45(2)(d)—
(a) in cases where the circumstances relating to the pensioner change in the course of the year, and
(b) in such other cases as the Secretary of State thinks fit.

Part 5

Interpretation

12 In this Schedule—
- 'assumed surplus', in relation to a pensioner's earnings factor for a year, means the surplus there would be in that factor for the year if section 48A(1) of the Pension Schemes Act 1993 (no primary Class 1 contributions deemed to be paid) did not apply in relation to any tax week falling in the year;
- 'the contracted-out condition', in relation to a tax week, means the condition that any earnings paid to or for the benefit of the pensioner in that week in respect of employment were in respect of employment qualifying him for a pension provided by a salary related contracted-out scheme (within the meaning of the Pension Schemes Act 1993);
- 'the FRAA' has the meaning given by paragraph 13;
- 'the LET', in relation to a tax year, means the low earnings threshold for the year as specified in section 44A above;
- 'the QEF', in relation to a tax year, means the qualifying earnings factor for the year;
- 'relevant year' and 'final relevant year' have the same meanings as in section 44 above;
- 'the UAP' means the upper accrual point.

13(1) 'The FRAA' means the flat rate accrual amount.

Non-Means Tested Benefits

(2) That amount is £72.80 for the flat rate introduction year and subsequent tax years (but subject to section 148AA of the Administration Act)."

p.289, *amendment to Social Security Contributions and Benefits Act 1992, Sch.5, para.2*

With effect from July 26, 2007, Sch.5, para.2 was amended by Sch.1 para.19 of the Pensions Act 2007, as follows:
In sub-para.(7) after "section 150" insert "or 150A".

2.043

pp.293–294, *amendment to Social Security Contributions and Benefits Act 1992, Sch.5*

With effect from September 26, 2007, Sch.5 is amended by Sch.7 Pt 3 of the Pensions Act 2007, as follows:
In each of paras 5A(3)(a), 6(4)(b) and 6A(2)(b), the words "after it has been reduced by the amount of any increases under section 109 of the Pensions Act" are repealed.

2.044

p.295, *amendment to Social Security Contributions and Benefits Act 1992, Sch.5*

With effect from September 26, 2007, Sch.5 para.8 was amended by Sch.1 para.8 and by Sch.7 of the Pensions Act 2007, as follows:
Sub-para.(3) of para.8 is omitted.

2.045

pp.337–338, *annotation to Pensions Schemes Act, 1993, s.46*

A further illustration of the sometimes surprising effect of this section is provided by *CP/3577/2006*. The appellant was a widow who had been claiming, prior to her husband's death, her own state retirement pension on the basis of her own contributions made during a long working life. As a married woman she was entitled to a weekly state benefit of £105.11. She was understandably upset to find that after her husband's death her entitlement, as his widow, was reduced to £94.18 per week. But her appeal was dismissed. Commissioner Williams demonstrates that this is the correct conclusion to be reached by the application of the principle in s.46. This is because the additional pension to which she was entitled as a widow (combining her own and her husband's additional pensions) was subject to a cap, while the maximum GMP to be deducted from it was the sum of the full amount of her own GMP and a GMP equal to half her husband's occupational pension. Although she gained small increases to her basic state pension and to the graduated retirement benefit, these were more than offset by the increased deduction to be made for the combined GMP. This is not to say that the claimant's overall income was reduced—it was not because it increased by a sum equal to half of her husband's occupational pension, but the "household" income was certainly reduced. It was reduced by half of his

2.046

Non-Means Tested Benefits

occupational pension, the whole of his state pension and a sum of almost £11 of her own pension!

pp.353–354, *amendment to Pensions Act, 1995, s.126, Sch.4*

2.047 With effect from September 26, 2007 s.126, Sch.4 was amended by Sch.3, para.3 of the Pensions Act 2007, as follows:

For the heading for Sch.4 substitute "Equalisation of and increase in pensionable age for men and women".

In Pt 1, para.1, sub-para.(1) after "man" insert "born before 6th April 1959"; and in sub-para.(3) for "the following table" substitute "table 1".

For sub-para.(4) substitute—

"(4) A woman born after 5th April 1955 but before 6th April 1959 attains pensionable age when she attains the age of 65."

For the heading for the table substitute "TABLE 1".
After the table insert—

"(5) A person born on any day in a period mentioned in column 1 of table 2 attains pensionable age at the commencement of the day shown against that period in column 2.

TABLE 2

(1)	(2)
Period within which birthday falls	*Day pensionable age attained*
6th April 1959 to 5th May 1959	6th May 2024
6th May 1959 to 5th June 1959	6th July 2024
6th June 1959 to 5th July 1959	6th September 2024
6th July 1959 to 5th August 1959	6th November 2024
6th August 1959 to 5th September 1959	6th January 2025
6th September 1959 to 5th October 1959	6th March 2025
6th October 1959 to 5th November 1959	6th May 2025
6th November 1959 to 5th December 1959	6th July 2025
6th December 1959 to 5th January 1960	6th September 2025
6th January 1960 to 5th February 1960	6th November 2025
6th February 1960 to 5th March 1960	6th January 2026
6th March 1960 to 5th April 1960	6th March 2026

(6) A person born after 5th April 1960 but before 6th April 1968 attains pensionable age when the person attains the age of 66.

(7) A person born on any day in a period mentioned in column 1 of table 3 attains pensionable age at the commencement of the day shown against that period in column 2.

Non-Means Tested Benefits

TABLE 3

(1)	(2)
Period within which birthday falls	Day pensionable age attained
6th April 1968 to 5th May 1968	6th May 2034
6th May 1968 to 5th June 1968	6th July 2034
6th June 1968 to 5th July 1968	6th September 2034
6th July 1968 to 5th August 1968	6th November 2034
6th August 1968 to 5th September 1968	6th January 2035
6th September 1968 to 5th October 1968	6th March 2035
6th October 1968 to 5th November 1968	6th May 2035
6th November 1968 to 5th December 1968	6th July 2035
6th December 1968 to 5th January 1969	6th September 2035
6th January 1969 to 5th February 1969	6th November 2035
6th February 1969 to 5th March 1969	6th January 2036
6th March 1969 to 5th April 1969	6th March 2036

(8) A person born after 5th April 1969 but before 6th April 1977 attains pensionable age when the person attains the age of 67.

(9) A person born on any day in a period mentioned in column 1 of table 4 attains pensionable age at the commencement of the day shown against that period in column 2.

TABLE 4

(1)	(2)
Period within which birthday falls	Day pensionable age attained
6th April 1977 to 5th May 1977	6th May 2044
6th May 1977 to 5th June 1977	6th July 2044
6th June 1977 to 5th July 1977	6th September 2044
6th July 1977 to 5th August 1977	6th November 2044
6th August 1977 to 5th September 1977	6th January 2045
6th September 1977 to 5th October 1977	6th March 2045
6th October 1977 to 5th November 1977	6th May 2045
6th November 1977 to 5th December 1977	6th July 2045
6th December 1977 to 5th January 1978	6th September 2045
6th January 1978 to 5th February 1978	6th November 2045
6th February 1978 to 5th March 1978	6th January 2046
6th March 1978 to 5th April 1978	6th March 2046

Non-Means Tested Benefits

(10) A person born after 5th April 1978 attains pensionable age when the person attains the age of 68."

p.354, *amendment to Pensions Act, 1995, Sch.4 Pt 2*

2.048   With effect from September 26, 2007 Sch.4, Pt 2, para.2 was repealed by Sch.7, Pt 2 of the Pensions Act 2007.

p.368, *amendment to the Credits Regulations 1975, reg.2 (definition of "reckonable year")*

2.049   With effect from July 16, 2007, reg.8(2) of the Social Security (Miscellaneous Amendments) (No.3) Regulations 2007 (SI 2007/1749) amended the definition of "reckonable year" to read:
"reckonable year" means a year for which the relevant earnings factor of the contributor concerned was sufficient to satisfy—
(a) in relation to short-term incapacity benefit, widowed mother's allowance, [widowed parent's allowance, bereavement benefits,] widow's pension or Category A or Category B retirement pension, para.(b) of the second contribution condition specified in relation to that benefit in Sch.3 to the Contributions and Benefits Act; or
(b) in relation to contribution-based jobseeker's allowance, the additional condition specified in s.2(3) of the Jobseekers Act 1995;

pp.370–371, *annotation to the Credits Regulations 1975, reg.3.*

2.050   The role and importance of reg.3 is generally overlooked. It is, however, crucial in determining whether "credits" (crediting earnings and earnings factors to a claimant's contribution account) for which the claimant is eligible under other provisions of these regulations can actually be awarded in respect of the specified benefits. It is, moreover, a provision that causes problems in respect of its interaction with the provision on credits for unemployment in reg.8A. Commissioner Williams sets out the law on crediting contributions in *CIB/1602/2006*:

"Provision is made to allow credited earnings under section 22(5) of the 1992 Act. This provides, as relevant to this appeal:
'Regulations may provide for crediting—
(a) for 1987–88 or any subsequent year, earnings . . .
for the purpose of bringing a person's earnings factor for that tax year to a figure which will enable him to satisfy contribution conditions of entitlement to . . . any prescribed description of benefit . . . '
This applies to D's claim for incapacity benefit. It makes clear that credited earnings can only apply when the individual has not paid enough actual contributions for the year. This, equally clearly, can only be decided after the end of the tax year, which occurs in April each calendar year. (For employed earners this will be in practice after the time limit in the following May or June when all employers are required to make a return of total contributions collected for their

Non-Means Tested Benefits

employees during the year ending in April. See Schedule 4, paragraph 22 to the Social Security (Contributions) Regulations 2001 (SI 2001 No 1004)).

The regulations allowing credited earnings for periods of unemployment are regulations 3 (general provisions relating to the crediting of contributions and earnings) and 8A (credits for unemployment) of the Social Security (Credits) Regulations 1975 ('the Credits Regulations') (SI 1975 No 556). These are complicated and much amended regulations. Little attention has been paid for years past to the structure of the Credits Regulations and the way that they are empowered by, and link to, section 22(5) of the 1992 Act and its predecessors back to section 13 of the Social Security Act 1975. The Regulations follow the usual pattern of stating the commencement provisions in regulation 1 and definitions in regulation 2. Regulation 3 then lays down general provisions relating to the crediting of contributions and earnings. Regulations 4 to 9D follow with provisions for specific forms of credit or credited earnings in specific situations. It is abundantly clear from this that, reflecting the authority granted in section 22(5), regulation 3 is to be applied in each case along with the specific regulation. That has not happened here. As Commissioner Rowland commented in CIB 3327 2004, regulation 3 is rarely mentioned in connection with the award of credited earnings. It is not the subject, so far as I can see, of any comment in the *DMG*. Nor has it been mentioned in this appeal.

The Credits Regulations have been amended many times since first being written. The most important of the amendments—only partially executed—take account of the abolition of contribution credits on 6 04 1987. From that date (the start of the tax year 1987–88) the previous system of awarding weekly credits was abolished. It was replaced by a system of crediting earnings and earnings factors to a claimant only when necessary at the end of a tax year. Commissioner Rowland explores these concepts in CIB 3327 2004, and I do not repeat that. The difficulties in cases such as this are because the fundamental change in the nature of contribution 'credits' does not appear yet to have been absorbed into the relevant administrative processes for identifying and awarding credited earnings. That failure is in part hidden because of a failure fully to amend the Credits Regulations themselves to reflect the changes made in 1987" (paras 24–26).

The problem this generates with claims for credits for unemployment were then considered by Commissioner Williams (and a solution found). The matter is considered in the update to the annotation to reg.8A (update to pp.381–382), below.

pp.381–382, *annotation to the Credits Regulations 1975, reg.8A (credits for unemployment)*

As with all of the Regulations making claimants eligible for the award of credits, this must be read with reg.3 (*CIB/1602/2006; CIB/3327/2004*): and see further updates to p.277 and pp.370–371, above. One can only

2.051

have them insofar as they are necessary to bring one's record up to the level required for satisfying the second contribution condition for the relevant benefit. The position is that it thus cannot be known whether a claimant is entitled to claim credits (credited with earnings) until some time after the end of the tax year for which the claim for them is made. The difficulties that can be caused by this complex interaction of Credits Regulations with those applicable to Jobseeker's Allowance, in a context in which there appear to be decision-making problems as a result of responsibilities divided between the DWP and HMRC, are explored in *CIB/1602/2006*.

Regulation 8A(3)(a)(i) stipulates that to be eligible for unemployment credits, in respect of a period of non-payment of JSA, a person must give notice in writing of the grounds on which he claims to be entitled to be credited with earnings "(i) on the first day of the period for which he claims to be entitled in which the week in question fell; or (ii) within such further time as may be reasonable in the circumstances of the case". In reality it is the second (fallback) option which will have to apply. This means that in a case such as that in *CIB/1602/2006*, where the claimant on a claim for incapacity benefit was arguing that he should have been awarded credits for a period of unemployment several years earlier in which she was not entitled to payment of JSA, that:

> "the Secretary of State can do no more than require that a claimant makes a claim in writing, setting out the grounds for it, within a reasonable time of becoming entitled. That is a question of fact. It will take into account the guidance given to a claimant (all of which is set out above, unless something is added orally).
>
> Noting the guidance and correspondence put in evidence to the tribunal in this appeal, I have little difficulty in finding on the facts that D's correspondence with the Jobcentre and with the Member of Parliament and the Minister did raise the matter adequately in writing and within a reasonable time" (paras 33, 34).

The decision on whether earnings should be credited is not a HMRC decision, but one for the Secretary of State and appealable to the appeals tribunal, the Commissioner and the courts. In *CI/1602/2006*, it was whether reg.8A(2)(b) applied in the claimant's case. The claimant needed two weeks credited earnings to bring his record to the requisite level (50 times the lower earnings limit), having already been credited with 48 times that limit. Here, the Commissioner found from the correspondence that a decision had been made to refuse to credit the claimant with earnings for the period at issue because during the time at issue he was out of the United Kingdom. The Commissioner found that, although on holiday, he had satisfied the availability condition because he had informed the Jobcentre of his holiday with his children (and could thus have returned on request with the 48-hour notice period allowed). In terms of actively seeking work he could also take advantage of the "deemed actively seeking work" for two weeks of properly notified holiday (Jobseeker's Regulations 1996, reg.19(1)(p)). Absence from Great Britain precludes entitlement to JSA. But it does not as such preclude entitlement to unemployment credits for the period of absence, since

Non-Means Tested Benefits

reg.8A(2)(b) while linking back to specifically enumerated conditions in Jobseekers Act 1995, s.1(2), does not include the "present in Great Britain" condition. Accordingly, Commissioner Williams concluded that the claimant met the second contribution condition for entitlement to incapacity benefit.

p.382, *amendment to the Credits Regulations 1975, reg.8B (2A)(a)(i) (credits for incapacity for work)*

With effect from July 16, 2007, reg.8(3) of the Social Security (Miscellaneous Amendments) (No.3) Regulations 2007 (SI 2007/1749) amended subpara.(a)(i) by deleting the words in square brackets.

2.052

p.383, *annotation to the Credits Regulations 1975, reg.8B(4)(b) ("such further time as may be reasonable in the circumstances")*

Commissioner Mesher considered this phrase in *CIB/2445/2006* when concluding that the appeal tribunal was within its permitted area of judgment when concluding that what would have been a reasonable time for claiming credits for any of the years 1989/90 to 2000/01 had expired by the time the claimant claimed them on May 13, 2005 (para.27). As the Commissioner pointed out, the test in reg.8B(4) is not one of "good cause" for a late claim but

2.053

> "the more general test of what is a reasonable time in the circumstances for a claim to be made. Therefore . . . the length of the time after the period for which credits are claimed is a factor, along with all the other circumstances. When entitlement to credits rests on proof of incapacity for work, the assessment of the evidence and the making of a proper decision becomes more difficult the further away from the period in question one gets. As a general proposition it can be accepted that the longer the gap from the tax year in question the more compelling the other circumstances must be for it to be concluded that the time for claiming, outside the following benefit year, is reasonable" (para.29).

Even with respect to the most recent tax years in respect of which credits were claimed (2000/01), the range of communications indicating a shortfall in his contributions record were such that the tribunal was entitled to conclude that the time for claiming credits was, by May 2005, no longer reasonable.

p.384, *amendment to the Credits Regulations 1975: insertion of new regulations 8D–F*

With effect from October 1, 2007, reg.2 of the Social Security (National Insurance Credits) Amendment Regulations 2007 (SI 2007/2582) inserted after reg.8C new regs numbered 8D–F as follows:

2.054

Credits for the purposes of entitlement to incapacity benefit following official error

8D.—(1) This regulation applies for the purpose only of enabling a person who was previously entitled to incapacity benefit to satisfy the condition referred to in para.2(3)(a) of Sch.3 to the Contributions and Benefits Act in respect of a subsequent claim for incapacity benefit where his period of incapacity for work is, together with a previous period of incapacity for work, to be treated as one period of incapacity for work under s.30C of that Act.

(2) Where—
(a) a person was previously entitled to incapacity benefit;
(b) the award of incapacity benefit was as a result of satisfying the condition referred to in para.(1) by virtue of being credited with earnings for incapacity for work or approved training in the tax years from 1993–94 to 2007–08;
(c) some or all of those credits were credited by virtue of official error derived from the failure to transpose correctly information relating to those credits from the Department for Work and Pensions' Pension Strategy Computer System to Her Majesty's Revenue and Customs' computer system (NIRS2) or from related clerical procedures;
(d) that person makes a further claim for incapacity benefit; and
(e) his period of incapacity for work is, together with the period of incapacity for work to which his previous entitlement referred to in sub-para.(a) related, to be treated as one period of incapacity for work under s.30C of the Contributions and Benefits Act,

that person shall be credited with such earnings as may be required to enable the condition referred to in para.(1) to be satisfied.

(3) In this regulation and in regs 8E and 8F, "official error" means an error made by—
(a) an officer of the Department for Work and Pensions or an officer of Revenue and Customs acting as such which no person outside the Department or Her Majesty's Revenue and Customs caused or to which no person outside the Department for Work and Pensions or Her Majesty's Revenue and Customs materially contributed; or
(b) a person employed by a service provider and to which no person who was not so employed materially contributed,

but excludes any error of law which is shown to have been an error by virtue of a subsequent decision of a Commissioner or the court.

(4) In para.(3)—
"Commissioner" means the Chief Social Security Commissioner or any other Social Security Commissioner and includes a tribunal of three or more Commissioners constituted under s.16(7) of the Social Security Act 1998;
"service provider" means a person providing services to the Secretary of State for Work and Pensions or to Her Majesty's Revenue and Customs.

Credits for the purposes of entitlement to retirement pension following official error

8E.—(1) This regulation applies for the purpose only of enabling the condition referred to in para.5(3)(a) of Sch.3 to the Contributions and Benefits Act to be satisfied in respect of a claim for retirement pension made by a person ("the claimant")—
(a) who would attain pensionable age no later than May 31, 2008;
(b) not falling within sub-para.(a) but based on the satisfaction of that condition by another person—
   (i) who would attain, or would have attained, pensionable age no later than May 31, 2008; or
   (ii) in respect of whose death the claimant received a bereavement benefit.
(2) Where—
(a) a person claims retirement pension;
(b) the satisfaction of the condition referred to in para.(1) would be based on earnings credited for incapacity for work or approved training in the tax years from 1993–94 to 2007–08; and
(c) some or all of those credits were credited by virtue of official error derived from the failure to transpose correctly information relating to those credits from the Department for Work and Pensions' Pension Strategy Computer System to Her Majesty's Revenue and Customs' computer system (NIRS2) or from related clerical procedures,
those earnings shall be credited.

(3) In this regulation, "bereavement benefit" means a bereavement allowance, a widowed mother's allowance, a widowed parent's allowance or a widow's pension.

Credits for the purposes of entitlement to contribution-based jobseeker's allowance following official error

8F.—(1) This regulation applies for the purpose only of enabling a person to satisfy the condition referred to in s.2(1)(b) of the Jobseekers Act 1995.
(2) Where—
(a) a person claims a jobseeker's allowance;
(b) the satisfaction of the condition referred to in para.(1) would be based on earnings credited for incapacity for work or approved training in the tax years from 1993–94 to 2007–08; and
(c) some or all of those credits were credited by virtue of official error derived from the failure to transpose correctly information relating to those credits from the Department for Work and Pensions' Pension Strategy Computer System to Her Majesty's Revenue and Customs' computer system (NIRS2) or from related clerical procedures,
that person shall be credited with those earnings.

Non-Means Tested Benefits

p.396, *amendment to the Crediting and Treatment of Contributions, and National Insurance Numbers Regulations 2001, reg.1(2) (definition of "due date")*

2.055   With effect from April 6, 2007, reg.2(2) of the Social Security, Occupational Pension Schemes and Statutory Payments (Consequential Provisions) Regulations 2007 (SI 2007/1154) amended the definition of "due date" to read as follows:
"due date" [(subject to reg.4(11))] means, in relation to any contribution which a person is—
  (a) liable to pay, the date by which payment falls to be made in accordance with Pt IV of the Contributions Regulations;
  (b) entitled, but not liable, to pay, the date 42 days after the end of the year in respect of which it is paid;

p.397, *amendment to the Crediting and Treatment of Contributions, and National Insurance Numbers Regulations 2001, reg.1: insertion of new paras (3) and (4)*

2.056   With effect from October 1, 2007, reg.3 of the Social Security (National Insurance Credits) Amendment Regulations 2007 (SI 2007/2582) inserted after para.(2) new paras (3) and (4) as follows:

(3) In these Regulations, "official error" means an error made by—
  (a) an officer of the Department for Work and Pensions or an officer of Revenue and Customs acting as such which no person outside the Department or Her Majesty's Revenue and Customs caused or to which no person outside the Department or Her Majesty's Revenue and Customs materially contributed; or
  (b) a person employed by a service provider and to which no person who was not so employed materially contributed,
but excludes any error of law which is shown to have been an error by virtue of a subsequent decision of a Commissioner or the court.
(4) In para.(3)—
"Commissioner" means the Chief Social Security Commissioner or any other Social Security Commissioner and includes a tribunal of three or more Commissioners constituted under s.16(7) of the Social Security Act 1998;
"service provider" means a person providing services to the Secretary of State for Work and Pensions or to Her Majesty's Revenue and Customs.

p.397, *amendments to the Crediting and Treatment of Contributions, and National Insurance Numbers Regulations 2001, reg.4*

2.057   With effect from October 1, 2007, reg.4(3)(a) of the Social Security (National Insurance Credits) Amendment Regulations 2007 (SI 2007/2582) amended para.(1) to read as follows:

(1) Subject to the provisions of regs 5 [to 6B] below and reg.40 of the Contributions Regulations (voluntary Class 2 contributions not paid within permitted period), for the purpose of entitlement to any contributory benefit, paras (2) to (9) below shall apply to contributions ("relevant contributions")—
  (a) paid after the due date; or
  (b) treated as paid after the due date under reg.7(2) below.

From the same date, reg.4(3)(b) of those amending regulations inserted after para.(1) a new para.(1A) to read as follows:

(1A) Any relevant contribution which is paid—
(a) by virtue of an official error; and
(b) more than six years after the end of the year in which the contributor was first advised of that error,
shall be treated as not paid.

p.399, *amendment to the Crediting and Treatment of Contributions, and National Insurance Numbers) Regulations 2001, reg.4 (insertion of para.(11))*

With effect from April 6, 2007, reg.2(2) of the Social Security, Occupational Pension Schemes and Statutory Payments (Consequential Provisions) Regulations 2007 (SI 2007/1154) inserted para.(11) after para.(10) to read as follows:

2.058

(11) Where an amount is retrospectively treated as earnings ("retrospective earnings") by regulations made by virtue of s.4B(2) of the Act, the "due date" for earnings-related contributions in respect of those earnings is the date given by para.11A of Sch.4 to the Social Security (Contributions) Regulations 2001, for the purposes of this regulation and regs 5 and 5A.

p.400, *amendment to the Crediting and Treatment of Contributions, and National Insurance Numbers Regulations 2001 (insertion of new reg.5A)*

With effect from April 6, 2007, reg.2(2) of the Social Security, Occupational Pension Schemes and Statutory Payments (Consequential Provisions) Regulations 2007 (SI 2007/1154) inserted new reg.5A after reg.5 to read as follows:

2.059

Treatment for the purpose of any contributory benefit of duly paid primary Class 1 contributions in respect of retrospective earnings

5A. Where a primary Class 1 contribution payable in respect of retrospective earnings is paid by the due date, it shall be treated—
  (a) for the purposes of the first contribution condition of entitlement to a contribution-based jobseeker's allowance or short-term incapacity benefit, as paid on the day on which payment is made of the retrospective earnings in respect of which the contribution is payable; and

Non-Means Tested Benefits

(b) for any other purpose relating to entitlement to any contributory benefit, as paid on the due date.

p.400, *amendment to the Crediting and Treatment of Contributions, and National Insurance Numbers Regulations 2001 (insertion of new regs 6A and 6B)*

2.060   With effect from May 17, 2004, reg.2(b) of the Social Security (Crediting and Treatment of Contributions, and National Insurance Numbers) Amendment Regulations 2004 (SI 2004/1361) inserted after reg.6 a new reg.6A to read as follows:

Treatment for the purposes of any contributory benefit of certain Class 3 contributions

6A.—(1) For the purposes of entitlement to any contributory benefit, this regulation applies in the case of a Class 3 contribution paid after the due date—
(a) which would otherwise under reg.4—
    (i) have been treated as paid on a day other than on the day on which it was actually paid; or
    (ii) have been treated as not paid; and
(b) which is paid in respect of a year after April 5, 1996 but before April 6, 2002.

(2) A contribution referred to in para.(1), where it is paid on or before April 5, 2009 by or in respect of a person who attains pensionable age on or after April 6, 2008, shall be treated as paid on the day on which it is paid.

(3) A contribution referred to in para.(1), where it is paid on or before April 5, 2009 by or in respect of a person who attains pensionable age on or after October 24, 2004 but before April 6, 2008, shall be treated as paid on—
(a) the day on which it is paid; or
(b) the date on which the person attained pensionable age, whichever is the earlier.

(4) A contribution referred to in para.(1), where it is paid on or before April 5, 2010 by or in respect of a person who attains pensionable age on or after April 6, 1998 but before October 24, 2004, shall be treated as paid on—
(a) October 1, 1998; or
(b) the date on which the person attained pensionable age, whichever is the later.

With effect from October 1, 2007, reg.4(4) of the Social Security (National Insurance Credits) Amendment Regulations 2007 (SI 2007/2582) inserted after reg.6A, a new reg.6B to read as follows

Treatment for the purpose of any contributory benefit of certain Class 2 or Class 3 contributions

6B. For the purpose of entitlement to any contributory benefit, a Class 2 or a Class 3 contribution paid after the due date—

Non-Means Tested Benefits

    (a) which would otherwise under reg.4 (apart from para.(1A) of that regulation)—
        (i) have been treated as paid on a day other than the day on which it was actually paid; or
        (ii) have been treated as not paid; and
    (b) which was paid after the due date by virtue of an official error,
shall be treated as paid on the day on which it is paid.

p.406, *annotations to Computation of Earnings Regs 1996, reg.2*

For a decision which is of significance in drawing the dividing line between employee earners and self-employed earners, which arose in the context of computing the earnings of a GCSE examiner, see *CG/4139/2006*. The Commissioner concludes his decision with the words: 2.061

"12. . . . I also hope that the Secretary of State takes steps to ensure that the guidance given to officers dealing with carer's allowance and other benefits to which the Computation of Earnings Regulations are relevant takes account of the deeming in regulation 2(3) of an paragraph 6 of Schedule 1 to the Categorisation of Earners Regulations."

p.421, *amendment to Computation of Earnings Regs 1996, reg.12*

With effect from October 1, 2007, The Social Security Benefit (Computation of Earnings) (Amendment) Regulations 2007 (SI 2007/2613) amend reg.12 as follows: 2.062
In para.(1), omit "Subject to paragraph (2),";
Omit para.(2).

p.422, *amendment to Computation of Earnings Regs 1996, reg.13*

With effect from October 1, 2007, The Social Security Benefit (Computation of Earnings) (Amendment) Regulations 2007 (SI 2007/2613) amend reg.13 as follows: 2.063
After para.(6)(f) add—

"(g) where the claimant provides accommodation to another person in the dwelling the claimant occupies as his home, any expenses defrayed by the claimant in providing the accommodation to that person (including any defrayed in providing board as well as lodging)."

p.425, *amendment to Computation of Earnings Regs 1996, Sch.1*

With effect from October 1, 2007, The Social Security Benefit (Computation of Earnings) (Amendment) Regulations 2007 (SI 2007/2613) amend Sch.1 as follows: 2.064
After para.11 add—

"12.—(1) Any earnings, other than items to which sub-paragraph (2) applies, paid or due to be paid from the claimant's employment as an employed earner which ended before the day in respect of which the claimant first satisfies the conditions for entitlement to the benefit, pension or allowance to which the claim relates.

(2) This sub-paragraph applies to—
(a) any payment by way of occupational or personal pension; and
(b) except in a case where the claimant's employment terminated by reason of retirement at a time when he had attained pensionable age (within the meaning given by rules in paragraph 1 of Schedule 4 to the Pensions Act 1995)—
   (i) any payment or remuneration of the nature described in regulation 9(1)(e) or (j), and
   (ii) any award or sum of the nature described in regulation 9(1)(g) or (h) (including any payment made following the settlement of a complaint to an employment tribunal or of court proceedings).

(3) Sub-paragraph (1) is subject to the following provisions.

(4) Sub-paragraph (1) does not apply in relation to a claim for, or an award of, incapacity benefit (within the meaning given by paragraph 11 of Schedule 4 to the Welfare Reform Act 2007) or severe disablement allowance (also within the meaning given by that paragraph).

(5) Sub-paragraph (1) applies in relation to a claim for an increase in benefit under Part IV of the Contributions and Benefits Act (increases in respect of dependants) only in a case where—
(a) the spouse or partner or other adult in respect of whom that claim is made was in employment as an employed earner, but
(b) that employment ended before the day referred to in sub-paragraph (1)."

p.486, *reg.5 of the Persons Abroad Regulations*

2.064A Regulation 5(1) and (2) should read as follows and not as printed in the main volume:

5.—(1) Where regulations made in consequence of an order under [¹ s.63 of the Social Security Act 1986 (up-rating of benefits and increments in guaranteed minimum pensions)] provide for the application of this regulation to any additional benefit becoming payable by virtue of that order, the following provisions of this regulation shall, subject to reg.12 below and the provisions of those regulations, have effect in relation to the entitlement to that benefit of persons absent from Great Britain.

(2) In this regulation [² and in reg.5A]—
(a) references to additional benefit of any description are to be construed as referring to additional benefit of that description which is, or but for this regulation would be, payable by virtue (either directly or indirectly) of the said order; and
(b) "the appointed date" means the date appointed for the coming into force of the said order.

Non-Means Tested Benefits

p.514, *amendment of Social Security (Attendance Allowance) Regulations 1991, reg.7.*

With effect from October 29, 2007, reg.7 is amended by reg.2(2) of the Social Security (Attendance Allowance and Disability Living Allowance) (Amendment) Regulations 2007, (SI 2007/2875) as follows: 2.065
For reg.7 substitute

"Persons in care homes

7.—(1) Subject to regulation 8, a person shall not be paid any amount in respect of an attendance allowance for any period where throughout that period he is a resident in a care home in circumstances where any of the costs of any qualifying services provided for him are borne out of public or local funds under a specified enactment.

(2) The specified enactments for the purposes of paragraph (1) are—
 (a) (i) Part III of the National Assistance Act 1948
   (ii) Part IV of the Social Work (Scotland) Act 1968),
   (iii) the Mental Health (Care and Treatment) (Scotland) Act 2003,
   (iv) the Community Care and Health (Scotland) Act 2002,
   (v) the Mental Health Act 1983, or
 (b) any other enactment relating to persons under disability.

(3) In this regulation, and in regulation 8, references to the costs of any qualifying services shall not include the cost of—
 (a) domiciliary services, including personal care, provided in respect of a person in a private dwelling; or
 (b) improvements made to, or furniture or equipment provided for, a private dwelling on account of the needs of a person under disability; or
 (c) improvements made to, or furniture or equipment provided for, a care home in respect of which a grant or payment has been made out of public or local funds except where the grant or payment is of a regular or repeated nature; or
 (d) social and recreational activities provided outside the care home in respect of which grants or payments are made out of public or local funds; or
 (e) the purchase or running of a motor vehicle to be used in connection with any qualifying service provided in a care home in respect of which grants or payments are made out of public or local funds; or
 (f) services provided pursuant to the National Health Service Act 2006, the National Health Service (Wales) Act 2006, or the National Health Service (Scotland) Act 1978.

(4) For the purposes of paragraph (1), a period during which a person is a resident in a care home in the circumstances set out in that paragraph shall, subject to paragraphs (5) and (6), be deemed—
 (a) to begin on the day after the day on which he enters a care home, and

Non-Means Tested Benefits

(b) to end on the day before the day on which he leaves a care home.

(5) Where a person enters a care home from a hospital or similar institution in circumstances in which paragraph (1) of regulation 6 applies, the period during which he is a resident in the care home shall be deemed to begin on the day he enters that care home.

(6) Where a person leaves a care home and enters a hospital or similar institution in circumstances in which paragraph (1) of regulation 6 applies, the period during which he is a resident in the care home shall be deemed to end on the day he leaves that care home."

GENERAL NOTE

2.066 There is a transitional and saving provision in reg.4 of the Amendment regulations to the effect that this amendment shall not prevent any day before the coming into force of the amended regulations from counting towards the first 28 day period specified in reg.8.

p.517, *amendment of Social Security (Attendance Allowance) Regulations 1991, reg.8.*

2.067 With effect from October 29, 2007, reg.8 was amended by reg.2(3) of the Social Security (Attendance Allowance and Disability Living Allowance) (Amendment) Regulations 2007, (SI 2007/2875) as follows:
For para.(6) of the regulation substitute—

"(6) Regulation 7 shall not apply in any particular case for any period during which the whole costs of all of the qualifying services are met—
  (a) out of the resources of the person for whom the qualifying services are provided, or partly out of his own resources and partly with assistance from another person or a charity, or
  (b) on his behalf by another person or a charity."

p.530, *amendment to Social Security (Disability Living Allowance) Regulations 1991, reg.9.*

2.068 With effect from October 29, 2007, reg.9 is amended by reg.3(2) of the Social Security (Attendance Allowance and Disability Living Allowance) (Amendment) Regulations 2007, (SI 2007/2875) as follows:
For reg.9 substitute

"Persons in care homes

9.—(1) Except in the cases specified in paragraphs (3) to (5), and subject to regulation 10, a person shall not be paid any amount in respect of a disability living allowance which is attributable to entitlement to the care component for any period where throughout that period he is a resident in a care home in circumstances where any of the costs of any qualifying services provided for him are borne out of public or local funds under a specified enactment.

Non-Means Tested Benefits

(2) The specified enactments for the purposes of paragraph (1) are—
- (a) (i) Part III of the National Assistance Act 1948,
    - (ii) Part IV of the Social Work (Scotland) Act 1968,
    - (iii) the Mental Health (Care and Treatment) (Scotland) Act 2003,
    - (iv) the Community Care and Health (Scotland) Act 2002,
    - (v) the Mental Health Act 1983; or
- (b) any other enactment relating to persons under disability or to young persons or to education or training.

(3) Paragraph (2)(b) shall not apply in circumstances where any of the costs of the qualifying services provided for him are borne wholly or partly out of public or local funds by virtue of—
- (a) section 485 of the Education Act 1996), section 14 of the Education Act 2002) or section 73 of the Education (Scotland) Act 1980) (which relate to grants in aid of educational services);
- (b) sections 1, 2 or 3 of the Education Act 1962 (which relate respectively to awards by local education authorities in respect of degree courses and further education and awards by the Secretary of State to persons undergoing teacher training or postgraduate courses) or sections 49 or 73 of the Education (Scotland) Act 1980 (which relate respectively to the power of education authorities to assist persons to take advantage of educational facilities and the powers of the Secretary of State to make grants to education authorities and others);
- (c) section 65 of the Further and Higher Education Act 1992 or sections 4 or 11 of the Further and Higher Education (Scotland) Act 2005) (which relate respectively to the funding of further education and the administration of funds);
- (d) section 1 of the Education (Student Loans) Act 1990 (which relates to student loans); or
- (e) section 22 of the Teaching and Higher Education Act 1998

(4) Subject to paragraph (5), paragraphs (1) and (2) shall not apply in the case of a child who—
- (a) has not attained the age of 16 and is being looked after by a local authority; or
- (b) has not attained the age of 18 and to whom—
    - (i) section 17(10)(b) of the Children Act 1989 or section 93(4)(a)(ii) of the Children (Scotland) Act 1995 (impairment of health and development) applies because his health is likely to be significantly impaired, or further impaired, without the provision of services for him, or
    - (ii) section 17(10)(c) of the Children Act 1989 (disability) or section 93(4)(a)(iii) of the Children (Scotland) Act 1995 (disability) applies; or
- (c) who is accommodated outside the United Kingdom and the costs of any qualifying services are borne wholly or partly by a local authority pursuant to their powers under section 320 of

Non-Means Tested Benefits

the Education Act 1996 or section 25 of the Education (Additional Support for Learning) (Scotland) Act 2004.

(5) Sub-paragraphs (a) and (b) of paragraph (4) shall only apply during any period which the local authority looking after the child place him in a private dwelling with a family, or a relative of his, or some other suitable person.

(6) In this regulation and in regulation 10, references to the costs of any qualifying services shall not include the cost of—
   (a) domiciliary services, including personal care, provided in respect of a person in a private dwelling; or
   (b) improvements made to, or furniture or equipment provided for, a private dwelling on account of the needs of a person under disability; or
   (c) improvements made to, or furniture or equipment provided for, a care home in respect of which a grant or payment has been made out of public or local funds except where the grant or payment is of a regular or repeated nature; or
   (d) social and recreational activities provided outside the care home in respect of which grants or payments are made out of public or local funds; or
   (e) the purchase or running of a motor vehicle to be used in connection with any qualifying service provided in a care home in respect of which grants or payments are made out of public or local funds; or
   (f) services provided pursuant to the National Health Service Act 2006, the National Health Service (Wales) Act 2006, or the National Health Service (Scotland) Act 1978.

(7) For the purposes of paragraph (1), a period during which a person is a resident in a care home in the circumstances set out in that paragraph shall, subject to paragraphs (8) and (9), be deemed—
   (a) to begin on the day after the day on which he enters a care home, and
   (b) to end on the day before the day on which he leaves a care home.

(8) Where a person enters a care home from a hospital or similar institution in circumstances in which paragraph (1) of regulation 6 applies, the period during which he is a resident in the care home shall be deemed to begin on the day he enters that care home.

(9) Where a person leaves a care home and enters a hospital or similar institution in circumstances in which paragraph (1) of regulation 6 applies, the period during which he is a resident in the care home shall be deemed to end on the day he leaves that care home".

GENERAL NOTE

2.069 There is a transitional and saving provision in reg.4 of the Amendment regulations to the effect that this amendment shall not prevent any day before the coming into force of the amended regulation from counting towards the 28-day and 84-day periods specified in reg.10

Non-Means Tested Benefits

p.533, *amendment to Social Security (Disability Living Allowance) Regulations 1991, reg.10*

With effect from October 29, 2007, reg.10 was amended by reg.3(3) of the Social Security (Attendance Allowance and Disability Living Allowance) (Amendment) Regulations 2007, (SI 2007/2875) as follows:

For para.(8) of the regulation substitute—

"(8) Regulation 9 shall not apply in any particular case for any period during which the whole costs of all of the qualifying services are met—
  (a) out of the resources of the person for whom the qualifying services are provided, or partly out of his own resources and partly with the assistance from another person or a charity, or
  (b) on his behalf by another person or a charity."

2.070

p.541, *annotation to Disability Living Allowance Regulations 1991, reg.12 (physical condition as a whole)*

An attempt to extend the reasoning of *R (DLA) 1/04* to the case of a blind man suffering from depression was made in *CDLA/3898/2006*. The claimant's depression was said to derive from his blindness and that it caused the claimant to suffer anxiety to the point of severe discomfort so that he was virtually unable to walk outside. He would thus qualify for the higher rate of benefit. This claim was refused and his appeal was rejected by Commissioner Mesher. The Commissioner held that the appeal must fail because the appeal tribunal had found, as a fact, that the claimant did not suffer discomfort from anxiety so long as he had guidance and support from someone to accompany him. The claimant argued that this finding was unjustified because his anxiety would continue unless the particular person he had for company was someone with whom he had a particular relationship of trust, and in whom he could then be confident. But no evidence of this was before the appeal tribunal, and the commissioner held, therefore, that there could be no error of law in the conclusion they had reached. But the Commissioner comments more generally upon the argument that had been put to him. It is important, he says, in a field such as this, which is so complex as to be sometimes almost unjusticiable, (in the sense that it may appear difficult to distinguish clearly and consistently between those cases which succeed and those which fail) that one should return to the basics as explained in *Lees*, and having done so he says:

2.071

"I doubt in the light of *Lees*, and of the decision of the Tribunal of Commissioners in *R (M) 3/86*, whether 'mere' mental distress, turmoil or anxiety (as opposed to physical manifestations like breathlessness, palpitations, dizziness, chest pain or nausea) can amount to severe discomfort even where a physical disorder contributes to the effect to more than a minimal extent. There would also, if such things could count, be difficulty in distinguishing a perfectly rational heightening of

Non-Means Tested Benefits

caution, vigilance and concentration which presumably could not be regarded as severe discomfort on any basis."

p.551, *annotation to Disability Living Allowance Regulations 1991, reg.12*

2.072 In *CSDLA/202/2007*, a claim for higher rate mobility component made on behalf of a child of three, who was autistic, was returned for consideration by a new tribunal because the first appeal tribunal had failed to consider both of the possible routes by which such a claim might succeed; *viz.* either under s.73(1)(a) (temporary paralysis as to walking resulting from the autism), or, by s.73(1)(c) (severely mentally impaired and severe behavioural problems, etc). In doing so, Commissioner Parker adopts both *R(DLA)1/00* and *R(DLA)7/02*. She observes, as well, that neither of these routes to entitlement involves specific reference to the age of the child (*cf.* s.73(4) and s.72(6)). But, she suggests, the factor of age is inherent in each of these routes because, in the case of s.73(1)(a), the ability to walk must be the result of some physical disablement and that test would not be satisfied by any inability, such as lack of stamina, that resulted only from the claimant's immaturity; while a claim under s.73(1)(c) (in addition to needing to satisfy s.72(6) for the highest rate of the care component) will also need to show that the claimant's severe behavioural problems result from severe mental impairment, rather than just the tantrums of a normal child.

p.569, *amendments to Invalid Care Allowance Regulations 1976, reg.8.*

2.073 With effect from October 1, 2007, reg.8 is amended by reg.3(1) of the Social Security (Miscellaneous Amendments) (No.5) Regulations 2007, (SI 2007/2618) as follows:

In para.(1) for the words "an amount equal to the lower earnings limit in force by virtue of regulations under section 5 of the Contributions and Benefit Act on the last day of that week" in each place that those words occur, substitute "£95".

p.643, *amendment to the Incapacity Benefit Regulations 1994, reg.4A (days to be treated as days of incapacity for work)*

2.074 With effect from October 1, 2007, reg.6 of the Social Security (Miscellaneous Amendments) (No.5) Regulations 2007 (SI 2007/2618) amended reg.4A to read:

4A.—[(1)] For the purposes of incapacity benefit for persons incapacitated in youth under s.30A(2A) of the Contributions and Benefits Act, any day in respect of which a person is entitled to statutory sick pay immediately before the relevant day shall be treated as a day of incapacity for work.

[(2) Where—
(a) any day was, as a result of official error, a day of incapacity for work in a period of incapacity for work for the purposes of the previous entitlement to incapacity benefit referred to in reg.8D(2)(a) of the Social Security (Credits) Regulations 1975

Non-Means Tested Benefits

(credits for the purposes of entitlement to incapacity benefit following official error); and

(b) that official error derived from the failure to transpose correctly information relating to credits for incapacity for work or approved training in the tax years from 1993–94 to 2007–08 from the Department of Work and Pensions' Pension Strategy Computer System to Her Majesty's Revenue and Customs' Computer System (NIRS2) or from related clerical procedures,

that day shall be treated as a day of incapacity for work for the purposes of the later claim referred to in para.(2)(d) of that regulation.

(3) In this regulation—

"Commissioner" means the Chief Social Security Commissioner or any other Social Security Commissioner and includes a tribunal of three or more Commissioners constituted under s.16(7) of the Social Security Act 1998;

"credits for incapacity for work or approved training" means earnings credited pursuant to the Social Security (Credits) Regulations 1975 for incapacity for work or approved training;

"official error" means an error made by—

(a) an officer of the Department for Work and Pensions or an officer of Revenue and Customs acting as such which no person outside the Department or Her Majesty's Revenue and Customs caused or to which no person outside the Department for Work and Pensions or Her Majesty's Revenue and Customs materially contributed, or

(b) a person employed by a service provider and to which no person who was not so employed materially contributed,

but excludes any error of law which is shown to have been an error by virtue of a subsequent decision of a Commissioner or the court;

"service provider" means a person providing services to the Secretary of State for Work and Pensions or to Her Majesty's Revenue and Customs.]

p.648, *amendment to the Incapacity Benefit Regulations 1994, reg.8 (amount of councillor's allowance)*

With effect from October 1, 2007, reg.6(4) of the Social Security (Miscellaneous Amendments) (No.5) Regulations 2007 (SI 2007/2618) amended reg.8 so as to increase the prescribed amount of councillor's allowance from £86.00 to £88.50.

2.075

p.676, *insertion of a new definition into the Incapacity for Work (General) regulations 1995, reg.2(1) ("health care professional")*

With effect from July 3, 2007, reg.3(2) of the Social Security (Miscellaneous Amendments) (No.2) Regulations 2007 (SI 2007/1626)

2.076

inserted, between the definition of "doctor" and that of "medical evidence", a new definition to read as follows:

"health care professional" means—
- (a) a registered medical practitioner,
- (b) a registered nurse,
- (c) an occupational therapist or physiotherapist registered with a regulatory body established by an Order in Council under s.60 of the Health Care Act 1999, or
- (d) a member of such other profession, regulated by a body mentioned in s.25(3) of the National Health Service Reform and Health Care Professions Act 2002, prescribed by the Secretary of State in accordance with powers under s.39(1) of the Social Security Act 1998.

p.700, *amendment to the Incapacity for Work (General) Regulations 1995, reg.17 (permitted earnings limits)*

2.077 With effect from October 1, 2007, reg.7 of the Social Security (Miscellaneous Amendments) (No.5) Regulations 2007 (SI 2007/2618) amended reg.17(3) and (4) so as to increase the permitted earnings limit from £86.00 to £88.50. Amounts in the annotation to reg.17 (pp.702–704) should be read accordingly from that date.

p.703, *annotation to Incapacity for Work (General) Regulations 1995, reg.17 (exempt work—category 7)*

2.078 The permitted earnings limit should have read "£86.00" not "£81.00", and, in any event, was increased to £88.50 from October 1, 2007 (see update to p.700, above).

p.728, *annotation to Incapacity for Work (General) Regulations 1995, reg.27*

2.079 Commissioner Williams in *CIB/143/2007* thought the disagreement between Commissioners May and Levenson referred to in the commentary

"more apparent than real as it depends on the level of decision making being considered. The opening words of regulation 27 have changed between the wording in issue in CIB 248 1997 and the current wording. The current wording is in my view unambiguous. An official must decide that the assessment is not satisfied before moving on to consider regulation 27.

CSIB 146 2004 was an unusual case because the tribunal rejected the official evidence about the claimant's personal capability assessment before deciding that regulation 27 applied to the claimant. As Commissioner May commented at paragraph 11, that removed the evidential basis for the official decision that the claimant failed the personal capability assessment. On the facts the tribunal therefore left the assessment undecided. But I disagree with his generalisation from those unusual facts to the proposition that all tribunals must look at the personal capability assessment before examining regulation 27. An official must do that. A tribunal need not. It has the benefit of section 12(8)(a) of the Social Security Act 1998. It need not consider any issue that is not raised in the appeal. If there is no dispute about the application of the assessment in a particular appeal, then it need not be in issue" (paras 20–21).

pp.729–732, *annotation to Incapacity for Work (General) Regulations 1995, reg.27 (pre-1997 head (b) as preserved by* Howker*): the need to look at the work the claimant might have to do if found not incapable of work*

More decisions seem to be supporting the general approach to this provision of Commissioners Jacobs/Parker than that of Commissioner May, albeit that the latter has reiterated in two further decisions of his own (*CSIB/179/2006* and *CSIB/656/2006*) the approach he propounded in *CSIB/0223/2005*.

2.080

In *CIB/360/2007*, deputy Commissioner Paines thought it clear that the provision is not confined to cases in which merely learning of the finding of capacity for work would cause damage to health but also the health consequences of the claimant returning to the workplace. This perforce involves some consideration of the work the claimant would be required to do, something on which a tribunal with its knowledge of work and of the claimant's background and condition, can readily form a view to enable it to decide whether, within that range of work, there is work he could do without the risk to health contemplated by the provision. So, in the case of a claimant with a depressive condition, determining any effect on his mental health in response to the demands of a return to work, a tribunal would need to decide whether, as his consultant had suggested, "the demands of any form of work that the claimant would have the physical or intellectual ability to perform would be too much for him given his susceptibility to stress" (para.19). In an earlier decision, *CIB/1695/2005*, the deputy Commissioner had considered the case of a claimant with epilepsy. There he thought the requirements of the provision were not met

> "because—while one could readily imagine types of work that the claimant could not safely perform, such as work involving driving or the operation of heavy machinery—there was an adequate range of work that the claimant could do in which there would not be a substantial risk to health from his suffering a seizure in the workplace."

In that case, the deputy Commissioner endorsed Commissioner Jacobs' approach in *CIB/26/2004*, so that where someone suffers from a specific disease or disablement (in that case, epilepsy), the issue of whether there would be a substantial risk to his own or someone else's health ensuing from the finding that he was not incapable of work falls to be decided by reference, among other things, to the type of work that he would be likely to be required to be available for. Endorsing what he called the Jacobs/Parker/Paines approach, Commissioner Williams in *CIB/143/2007* built on the epilepsy example to suggest that identifying the two risks reduced the practical effect of the differences in approach between that approach and the one taken by Commissioner May:

> "regulation 27(b) can be seen to be asking officials and tribunals to make two separate assessments of risk: that to the claimant and that to other people in a work situation with the claimant. Those risks may or may not be parallel. For example, on the facts in CIB 1695 2005, an epileptic may put both herself and work colleagues at risk if she collapses without warning, perhaps dropping hot food or liquid or falling downstairs.
>
> By contrast, risks caused by some systemic disabilities may pose a major risk to the individual with the weakness but little risk to others.
>
> . . . Take the example of heart disease . . . Approved doctors are asked to consider the position of someone found capable of work with uncontrolled heart disease, particularly if also suffering from other problems such as lung disease. In such cases there may be a substantial risk to the individual whatever he or she is asked to do, notwithstanding that he or she does not score 15 points in the personal capability assessment on the day of examination. Any work may occasion that risk, and the nature of the work may be irrelevant. It is not evident that there will also be a high risk to others arising from the heart disease of a workmate or colleague.
>
> Another example is the risk of violence or psychological harm by the claimant to others . . . This may pose little risk to the claimant. The nature of the risk to others will depend to some extent on the kind of work that the claimant may be asked to do. That requires going beyond the non-specific idea that the risk is to be assessed without any focus on the kind of work the claimant may do. Consider this example further. If it were known that a person whose presence in the workplace might, because of a specific mental disablement, lead to a risk of violence that may on occasion be severe, it could be relevant to know the context of that individual's work before the risk could be assessed. Commissioner May's approach appears to assume that this could be dealt with by assumptions about the jobseeker's agreement that the individual would be asked to agree. But that is a question of evidence not of assumption. What has the claimant done in the past? What was the claimant doing at the time of the decision? What are the claimant's qualifications? Take the case of a qualified person who now suffers from unpredictable violent behaviour following an accident or illness. Different views might be taken of someone whose background suggested that the person might work with children or old or defenceless adults—in other words, in one of the millions of jobs in health, education, welfare, caring and similar activities, as compared with someone whose background suggested that the sort of work to be expected is manual work in a disciplined context" (paras 41–43).

Here, however, the evidence about the effect of the claimant's specific disease or disablement (alcohol dependency disorder aggravated by drug misuse) did not suggest a risk to the claimant's health; that came from his lifestyle, and work might in fact assist his situation.

p.778, *annotation to Incapacity for Work (General) Regulations 1995: new entry: Activity 13: descriptor (e): "loses control of bowels occasionally"*

In *CIB/3339/2006*, Commissioner Rowland stated: 2.081

"if a claimant merely feels an urgent desire to go to the toilet and is able to control his bowels for long enough to get there, he is not entitled to any points under activity 13 in the Schedule. . . . Applying a purposive construction to this legislation, as one must, it is clear that an occasional partial loss of control is sufficient to meet the terms of descriptor 13(e) unless the extent of the loss of control can be said to be *de minimis* in its effects" (para.5).

p.788, *annotation to Incapacity for Work (General) Regulations 1995, Sch.: new entry: Activity 17: coping with pressure; descriptor (d): "is unable to cope with changes in daily routine"*

In *CIB/16/2007*, deputy Commissioner Ovey was of the opinion that 2.082

"a daily routine may have some variable elements if there is overall a broadly settled and regular pattern. In particular, it does not seem to me that a regular trip, such as the claimant's trip to Newcastle, which is not made every day necessarily amounts to a change in daily routine for this purpose if it is nevertheless something done regularly. The descriptor is not, in my view, directed to day-to-day variations determined by the claimant in a pattern which she has herself established" (para.31).

p.829, *amendment to the Child Benefit (General) Regulations 2006, reg.1(3)*

With effect from August 16, 2007, reg.1(3) was amended by the Child 2.083 Benefit (General) (Amendment) Regulations 2007, (SI 2007/2150), as follows:
In the definition of "approved training" in subpara.(a) for "Programme Led Pathways" substitute "Programme Led Apprenticeships" and in subpara.(d) for "Jobskills Traineeships" substitute "Training for Success: Professional and Technical Training".

p.832, *amendment to the Child Benefit (General) Regulations 2006, reg.3*

With effect from August 16, 2007, reg.3 was amended by the Child 2.084 Benefit (General) (Amendment) Regulations 2007, (SI 2007/2150), as follows:
In reg.3(2)(b) for the words following "paragraph (a)" substitute the words "has been accepted or is enrolled to undertake a further such course."

Non-Means Tested Benefits

In reg.3(2) after sub-para.(c) insert:

"or

(d) having undertaken a course mentioned in paragraph (a) or approved training mentioned in paragraph (c), has been accepted or is enrolled to undertake such approved training"

In reg.3(4) after the word "sub-paragraph" insert the words "or was accepted or enrolled to undertake that education or training"

p.839, *amendment to the Child Benefit (General) Regulations 2006, reg.14*

2.085   With effect from August 16, 2007, reg.14 was amended by the Child Benefit (General) (Amendment) Regulations 2007, (SI 2007/2150), as follows:

In para.(1) after the words "approved by the Commissioners" insert the words "or by telephone to an officer of Revenue and Customs at an appropriate office"

p.838, *amendment to the Child Benefit (General) Regulations 2006, reg.15*

2.086   With effect from August 16, 2007, reg.15 was amended by the Child Benefit (General) (Amendment) Regulations 2007, (SI 2007/2150), as follows:

In para.(1) after the words "an appropriate office" insert the words "or gives an officer of the Inland Revenue and Customs notice by telephone at such an office"

p.843, *amendment to the Child Benefit (General) Regulations 2006, reg.21*

2.087   With effect from August 16, 2007, reg.21 was amended by the Child Benefit (General) (Amendment) Regulations 2007, (SI 2007/2150), as follows:

In para.(1)(b) for the words "recognised educational establishment" in both places where those words occur, substitute the words "school or college".

p.843, *amendment to the Child Benefit (General) Regulations 2006, reg.23*

2.088   With effect from August 16, 2007, reg.23 was amended by the Child Benefit (General) (Amendment) Regulations 2007, (SI 2007/2150), as follows:

In para.(4) after the word "he" insert the words "makes a claim for child benefit on or after 1st May 2004 and".

p.843, *amendment to the Child Benefit (General) Regulations 2006, reg.25*

With effect from August 16, 2007, reg.25 was amended by the Child Benefit (General) (Amendment) Regulations 2007, (SI 2007/2150), as follows:
In para.(1)(b) for the words "recognised educational establishment" in both places where those words occur, substitute the words "school or college".

2.089

p.845, *amendment to the Child Benefit (General) Regulations 2006, reg.27*

With effect from August 16, 2007, reg.27 was amended by the Child Benefit (General) (Amendment) Regulations 2007, (SI 2007/2150), as follows:
In para.(4) after the word "he" insert the words "makes a claim for child benefit on or after 1st May 2004 and".

2.090

p.847, *amendment to the Child Benefit (General) Regulations 2006, reg.30*

With effect from August 16, 2007, reg.30 was amended by the Child Benefit (General) (Amendment) Regulations 2007, (SI 2007/2150), as follows:
In para.(1) for the number "146 (1)" substitute "146 (2)".

2.091

p.847, *amendment to the Child Benefit (General) Regulations 2006, reg.31*

With effect from August 16, 2007, reg.31 was amended by the Child Benefit (General) (Amendment) Regulations 2007, (SI 2007/2150), as follows:
In para.(1) for the number "146 (1)" substitute "146 (2)".

2.092

p.847, *amendment to the Child Benefit (General) Regulations 2006, reg.32*

With effect from August 16, 2007, reg.32 was amended by the Child Benefit (General) (Amendment) Regulations 2007, (SI 2007/2150), as follows:
In para.(1) for the number "146 (2)" substitute "146 (1)".

2.093

p.848, *amendment to the Child Benefit (General) Regulations 2006, reg.34*

With effect from August 16, 2007, reg.34 was amended by the Child Benefit (General) (Amendment) Regulations 2007, (SI 2007/2150), as follows:
After the words "parent of a child" insert "or, qualifying young person".

2.094

Non-Means Tested Benefits

pp.877–880, *annotation to the General Benefit Regulations 1982, reg.11*

2.095   For an illustration of the complexities of applying the "multiple effective cause" provisions of reg.11, see *CI/3745/2006*. The Schedule to the decision also contains useful evidence from the medical adviser to the DWP (Dr Reed) on PD A8 (tenosynovitis) and PD A12 (carpal tunnel syndrome).

p.882, *amendment to the General Benefit Regulations 1982, reg.16 (increase of earnings level)*

2.096   With effect from October 1, 2007, reg.3 of the Social Security (Miscellaneous Amendments) (No.5) Regulations 2007 (SI 2007/2618) increased the earnings level from £4,472.00 to £4,602.

p.933, *amendment to the Prescribed Diseases Regulations 1985, Sch.1 PD A11 (vibration white finger)*

2.097   With effect from October 1, 2007, reg.2(1), (2) of the Social Security (Industrial Injuries) (Prescribed Diseases) Amendment (No.2) Regulations 2007 (SI 2007/1753) substituted a new "column 1 entry" (prescribed disease or injury) for A11 to read as follows:

"**A11.**
(a) Intense blanching of the skin, with a sharp demarcation line between affected and non-affected skin, where the blanching is cold-induced, episodic, occurs throughout the year and affects the skin of the distal with the middle and proximal phalanges, or distal with the middle phalanx (or in the case of a thumb the distal with the proximal phalanx), of—
  (i) in the case of a person with five fingers (including thumb) on one hand, any three of those fingers; or
  (ii) in the case of a person with only four such fingers, any two of those fingers; or
  (iii) in the case of a person with less than four such fingers, any one of them or, as the case may be, the one remaining finger;
where none of the person's fingers was subject to any degree of cold-induced, episodic blanching of the skin prior to the person's employment in an occupation described in the second column in relation to this paragraph, or
(b) significant, demonstrable reduction in both sensory perception and manipulative dexterity with continuous numbness or continuous tingling all present at the same time in the distal phalanx of any finger (including thumb) where none of the person's fingers was subject to any degree of reduction in sensory perception, manipulative dexterity, numbness or tingling prior to the person's employment in an occupation described in the second column in relation to this paragraph, where the symptoms in para.(a) or para.(b) were caused by vibration."

The change is subject to a transitional provision in reg.3 of those 2007 regulations (for text see the *New Legislation* section of this Supplement).

From the same date and subject to the same transitional provisions, reg.2(1), (3) of those 2007 regulations amended prescribed occupation PD A11(a) to read as follows:

"(a) the use of hand-held chain saws [on wood];".

p.947, *annotation to Prescribed Diseases Regulations 1985, Sch.1: new annotation on PD A8 (tenosynovitis)*

For useful evidence from the medical adviser to the DWP (Dr Reed) on PD A8 (tenosynovitis), see the Schedule to *CI/3745/2006*. 2.098

pp.954–956, *annotation to Prescribed Diseases Regulations 1985, Sch.1, PD A11 (vibration white finger)*

The terms of prescription of the prescribed disease or injury PD A11 were altered, subject to a transitional provision, with effect from October 1, 2007 so as to add sensorineural symptoms to the description of the disease and a proviso that both sets of symptoms are caused by vibration. It also provides that the prescription shall not cover blanching of the skin or sensorineural symptoms prior to employment in a prescribed occupation. For text of the changes, see update to p.933, above, and for the text of the transitional provision see the Social Security (Industrial Injuries) (Prescribed Diseases) Amendment (No.2) Regulations 2007 (SI 2007/1753) in the *New Legislation* section of this Supplement. Without renaming PD A11 as "hand-arm vibration syndrome" as there recommended, the changes in some degree reflect ones put forward by the Industrial Injuries Advisory Council in reports in Cm. 2844 (May 1995) and Cm. 6098 (July 2004), and reiterated in its review of the list of prescribed diseases in Cm. 7003 (January 2007) (see paras 38, 39), although the Explanatory Note to the amending regulations makes no mention of any of these reports. The change may also reflect the impact of *R(I)3/02* as regards taking on board sensory effects in ascertaining loss of faculty, and *R(I)1/02* in seeing them as relevant to compensation as well as the vascular effects. 2.099

pp.956–958, *annotation to Prescribed Diseases Regulations 1985, Sch.1, PD A11 (vibration white finger) (prescribed occupation (a))*

The words "in forestry" were replaced with the broader term "on wood" with effect (subject to a transitional provision) from October 1, 2007, thus giving effect to recommendations of the Industrial Injuries Advisory Council on the confusion generated by "in forestry" (see Cm. 6098 (July 2004), paras 67, 78 and Cm. 7003 (January 2007), para.38). Happily, the case law on the meaning and scope of "in forestry", which had itself effected a broadening of the term, is thus now only relevant to claims in respect of a period of assessment which relates to a claim made, or having effect, before the date these 2007 Regulations came into force 2.100

Non-Means Tested Benefits

or to a renewed break-out of a condition for which a claim was made before their entry into force. The change brings PD A11 into line with PD A10 where the broader term "on wood" has been applied since September 22, 2003. For the meaning of "wood", see the annotation to PD A10(e) in para.10.131 of Vol.I. For the text of the transitional provision see the Social Security (Industrial Injuries) (Prescribed Diseases) Amendment (No.2) Regulations 2007 (SI 2007/1753) in the *New Legislation* section of this Supplement.

pp.959–961, *annotation to the Prescribed Diseases Regulations 1985, Sch.1: PD A12 (carpal tunnel syndrome)*

2.101 For useful evidence from the medical adviser to the DWP (Dr Reed) on PD A12 (carpal tunnel syndrome), see the Schedule to *CI/3745/2006*.

p.993, *insertion of a new transitional provision*

2.102 For text of the Social Security (Industrial Injuries) (Prescribed Diseases) Amendment (No.2) Regulations 2007 (SI 2007/1753), see the New Legislation section of this Supplement. Effective from October 1, 2007, subject to a transitional provision, the regulations insert a new formulation of the prescribed disease or injury for PD A11. See further updates to pp.933 and 954–956, above.

pp.1003–1004, *Vaccine Damage Payments Act 1979 Statutory Sum Order 2000 (revocation of the Order)*

2.103 The Order was revoked from July 12, 2007 by Art.3 of the Vaccine Damage Payments Act 1979 Statutory Sum Order 2007 (SI 2007/1931), which increased the sum to £120,000. For the text of the revoking Order see the *New Legislation* section of this Supplement.

PART III

UPDATING MATERIAL
VOLUME II

INCOME SUPPORT, JOBSEEKER'S ALLOWANCE, STATE PENSION CREDIT AND THE SOCIAL FUND

Income Support, Jobseekers' Allowance, etc.

p.62, *annotation to Jobseekers Act 1995, s.7(1) (actively seeking work)*

As Commissioner Williams rightly points out in *CJSA/1814/2007* (paras 9–15), this requires the application of a positive rather than a negative test. It asks what the claimant did in the week in question, rather than what he did not do. It is not a matter of whether each of the steps in the claimant's Jobseeker's Agreement were met, but rather whether the tests in s.7(1) and JSA Regs, reg.18(1) are met by what the claimant actually did in the week at issue. The questions to be answered were thus

3.001

> "(a) Should the claimant be expected to take at least three jobsearch steps that week, or is it reasonable that only one or two be taken?
> (b) What steps were taken?
> (c) In the light of that reasonable expectation and those findings, were the steps taken by the claimant "such steps as he can reasonably be expected to have to take in order to have the best prospects of securing employment" (section 7(1))?
> If the steps by the claimant taken meet that test, it is irrelevant that the claimant did not also take some other step, whether or not it is in the jobseeker's agreement." (para.15)

pp.96–97, *annotation to Jobseekers Act 1995, s.19(5) (preclusion in respect of training schemes or employment programmes)*

In *CSJSA/495/2007* and *CSJSA/505/2007*, Commissioner May rejected as unarguable the claimant's arguments that the application to him of sanctions for failing to take up a place on an intensive activity period employment programme infringed Art.4 ECHR (freedom from slavery or forced labour). Nor was there an arguable case of discrimination.

3.002

p.114, *annotation to the Jobseekers Act 1995, s.19(9) (national minimum wage rates)*

With effect from October 1, 2007, the hourly rates become £5.52 for those 22 and over; £4.60 for those aged 18–21; and £3.40 for those workers under 18 who have ceased to be of compulsory school age. The change in rates was effected by the National Minimum Wage Regulations 1999 (Amendment) Regulations 2007 (SI 2007/2318).

3.003

p.148, *annotation to the State Pension Credit Act 2002, s.3(1) (savings credit)*

Note that the words "the age of 65" will be replaced by the expression "pensionable age" but only with effect from April 6, 2024 (Pensions Act 2007, s.13 and Sch.8, para.44).

3.004

Income Support, Jobseekers' Allowance, etc.

pp.170–171, *Immigration and Asylum Act 1999, s.123 (Back-dating of benefits where person recorded as a refugee)*

3.005 With effect from June 14, 2007, s.12(1) of the Asylum and Immigration (Treatment of Claimants, etc.) Act 2004 (c.19), repealed s.123.

By Art.2(3) of the Asylum and Immigration (Treatment of Claimants, etc.) Act 2004 (Commencement No.7 and Transitional Provisions) Order 2007 (SI 2007/1602), the repeal of s.123 "shall not apply to a person who is recorded as a refugee on or before June 14, 2007". For those purposes a person is recorded as a refugee on the day on which the Home Secretary notifies him that he has been recognised as a refugee and granted asylum in the UK (see Art.2(4)).

p.179, *annotation to the Child Support Act 1991, s.6*

3.006 In *CCS/4070/2006* the Commissioner holds that where the parent with care's claim for benefit is fraudulently made, s.6 cannot apply and the Secretary of State has no jurisdiction to make a maintenance calculation (applying *R. v South Ribble Borough Council ex p. Hamilton* [2001] 33 H.L.R. 9 and distinguishing *Harman* (see the main volume) on the ground that there was no known fraud in *Harman* (nor in *MacGeagh*, also referred to in the main volume)).

p.199, *Income Support (General) Regulations 1987, reg.2(1) (Definition of "maternity leave")*

3.007 With effect from October 1, 2007, reg.5(2) of the Social Security (Miscellaneous Amendments) (No.5) Regulations 2007 (S.I. 2007/2618), amended the definition of "maternity leave" in reg.2(1) to read as follows:

> "'maternity leave' means a period during which a woman is absent from work because she is pregnant or has given birth to a child, and at the end of which she has a right to return to work either under the terms of her contract of employment or under [Part VIII of the Employment Rights Act 1996];"

p.199, *Income Support Regulations, reg.2(1) (Definition of "lower rate")*

3.008 With effect from October 1, 2007, reg.2 of, and the Schedule to, the Social Security (Miscellaneous Amendments) (No.5) Regulations 2007 (SI 2007/2618), revoked the definition of "lower rate" in reg.2(1).

p.200, *Income Support (General) Regulations 1987, reg.2(1) (Definition of "pension fund holder")*

3.009 With effect from July 17, 2007, reg.2(2)(a) of the Social Security (Miscellaneous Amendments) (No.3) Regulations 2007 (S.I. 2007/1749) amended the definition of "pension fund holder" in reg.2(1) to read as follows:

Income Support, Jobseekers' Allowance, etc.

"'pension fund holder' means with respect to a personal pension scheme or [an occupational pension scheme], the trustees, managers or scheme administrators, as the case may be, of the scheme [. . .] concerned;"

p.200, *Income Support (General) Regulations 1987, reg.2(1) (Definition of "personal pension scheme")*

With effect from July 17, 2007, reg.2(2)(b) of the Social Security (Miscellaneous Amendments) (No.3) Regulations 2007 (SI 2007/1749) substituted a new definition of "personal pension scheme" in reg.2(1) as follows:

3.010

"'personal pension scheme' means—
(a) a personal pension scheme as defined by section 1 of the Pension Schemes Act 1993;
(b) an annuity contract or trust scheme approved under section 620 or 621 of the Income and Corporation Taxes Act 1988 or a substituted contract within the meaning of section 622(3) of that Act which is treated as having become a registered pension scheme by virtue of paragraph 1(1)(f) of Schedule 36 to the Finance Act 2004;
(c) a personal pension scheme approved under Chapter 4 of Part 14 of the Income and Corporation Taxes Act 1988 which is treated as having become a registered pension scheme by virtue of paragraph 1(1)(g) of Schedule 36 to the Finance Act 2004;"

p.200, *Income Support (General) Regulations 1987, reg.2(1) (Definition of "retirement annuity contract")*

With effect from July 17, 2007, reg.2(2)(c) of the Social Security (Miscellaneous Amendments) (No.3) Regulations 2007 (SI 2007/1749) revoked the definition of "retirement annuity contract" in reg.2(1).

3.011

p.201, *Income Support (General) Regulations 1987, reg.2(1) (Definition of "starting rate")*

With effect from October 1, 2007, reg.5(2) of the Social Security (Miscellaneous Amendments) (No.5) Regulations 2007 (SI 2007/2618), inserted a new definition of "starting rate" immediately after the definition of "sports award" in reg.2(1) as follows:

3.012

"'starting rate', where it relates to the rate of tax, has the same meaning as in the Income Tax Act 2007 (see section 989 of that Act);"

p.201, *Income Support (General) Regulations 1987, reg.2(1) (Definition of "the Independent Living Fund (2006)" and "the Independent Living Funds")*

With effect from October 1, 2007, reg.2(2) of the Independent Living Fund (2006) Order 2007 (SI 2007/2538), inserted a new definition of "the Independent Living Fund (2006)" as follows:

3.013

Income Support, Jobseekers' Allowance, etc.

" 'the Independent Living Fund (2006)' means the Trust of that name established by a deed dated 10th April 2006 and made between the Secretary of State for Work and Pensions of the one part and Margaret Rosemary Cooper, Michael Beresford Boyall and Marie Theresa Martin of the other part;"

and amended the definition of "the Independent Living Funds" to read as follows:

" 'the Independent Living Funds' means the Independent Living Fund, [the Independent Living (Extension) Fund, the Independent Living (1993) Fund and the Independent Living Fund (2006)];"

p.202, *Income Support (General) Regulations 1987, reg.2(1) (Definition of "war widower's pension")*

3.014   With effect from July 17, 2007, reg.2(2)(d) of the Social Security (Miscellaneous Amendments) (No.3) Regulations 2007 (SI 2007/1749) amended the definition of "war widower's pension" in reg.2(1) to read as follows:

" 'war widower's pension' means any widower's or surviving civil partner's pension or allowance granted in respect of a death due to service or war injury and payable by virtue of the Air Force (Constitution) Act 1917, the Personal Injuries (Emergency Provisions) Act 1939, the Pensions (Navy, Army, Air Force and Mercantile Marine) Act 1939, the Polish Resettlement Act 1947 or Part VII or section 151 of the Reserve Forces Act 1980 or a pension or allowance for a widower granted under any scheme mentioned in [section 641(1)(e) or (f) of the Income Tax (Earnings and Pensions) Act 2003];"

p.220, *annotation to the Income Support (General) Regulations 1987, reg.2(1), definition of "personal pension scheme"*

3.015   The definition of "personal pension scheme" has been amended with effect from July 16, 2007 to reflect the fact that following the changes made by Pt 4 of the Finance Act 2004 there is no longer any distinction between personal pension schemes for employed and self-employed earners—they are simply referred to as "personal pension schemes". In addition the definition of "retirement annuity contract" has been omitted as these contracts now come within the definition of "personal pension scheme".

p.220, *annotation to the Income Support (General) Regulations 1987, reg.2(1), definition of "starting rate"*

3.016   "*starting rate*": The meaning in s.989 of the Income Tax Act 2007 is "the rate of income tax determined in pursuance of section 6(2)". Section 6(2) provides that "The starting rate, basic rate and higher rate for a tax year are the rates determined as such by Parliament for the tax year".

Income Support, Jobseekers' Allowance, etc.

p.239, *Income Support (General) Regulations 1987, reg.5 (Persons treated as engaged in remunerative work)*

With effect from October 1, 2007, reg.5(3) of the Social Security (Miscellaneous Amendments) (No.5) Regulations 2007 (SI 2007/2618), amended reg.5(5) to read as follows:

3.017

"(5) [Subject to paragraph (5A), a person] who was, or was treated as being, engaged in remunerative work and in respect of that work earnings to which regulation 35(1)(b) to (d) and (i) (earnings of employed earners) applies are paid shall be treated as engaged in remunerative work for the period for which those earnings are taken into account in accordance with Part V."

and inserted a new paragraph immediately after para.5 as follows:

"(5A) Paragraph (5) shall not apply to earnings disregarded under paragraph 1 of Schedule 8 to these regulations."

p.254, *annotation to the Income Support (General) Regulations 1987, reg.12*

The Child Benefit (General) Regulations 2006 have been amended by the Child Benefit (General) (Amendment) Regulations 2007 (SI 2007/2150). The principal effect of these regulations is to extend the definition of "qualifying young person" so that it includes a person who is enrolled on or has been accepted to undertake approved training or a course of full-time education even though it begins after he is 19, provided that he was enrolled or accepted on the training/course before he became 19. In addition, in the definition of "approved training", "Programme Led Pathways" have now become "Programme Led Apprenticeships".

3.018

p.280, *commentary to Income Support (General) Regulations 1987, reg.21 (Special cases)*

The claimant in *RJM v Secretary of State for Work and Pensions* has been granted permission to appeal to the House of Lords.

3.019

p.283, *commentary to Income Support (General) Regulations 1987, reg.21AA (Special cases: supplemental—persons from abroad)—Introduction and Historical Background*

A further challenge to the habitual residence test has been unsuccessful. In *Couronne v Crawley BC and Secretary of State for Work and Pensions* [2007] EWCA Civ 1086, the Court of Appeal held that the test did not discriminate unlawfully against British Citizens from the Chagos Islands in comparison with British Citizens of Irish ethnic or national origin either under the Race Relations Act 1976 or Art.14 and Art.8 and or Art.1 First Protocol ECHR. The application of the test to the appellants

3.020

Income Support, Jobseekers' Allowance, etc.

(who had been unlawfully prevented by the British government from returning to their homeland) was not irrational.

p.286, commentary to Income Support (General) Regulations 1987, reg.21AA (Special cases: supplemental—persons from abroad)—British nationals

3.021   CPC/4317/2006 has been reported as *R(PC) 2/07*.

pp.291–293, commentary to Income Support (General) Regulations 1987, reg.21AA (Special cases: supplemental—persons from abroad)—Workers

3.022   In *CJSA/3066/2007*, the Commissioner holds that, in JSA cases, the right to reside test does not usually impose a greater hurdle for EU citizens than is imposed by the Jobseekers Act. It is not appropriate to treat the right to reside test as a preliminary issue in JSA cases.

In *CIS/1793/2007*, the Commissioner stated that he did "not wholly agree" with the analysis in *CH/3316/2005* and *CIS/3315/2005*. However, he found on the facts that where the claimant had worked for only 10 weeks over a period of three or four years (the longest continuous period being three weeks) that work was marginal and ancillary rather than genuine and effective.

pp.293–296, commentary to Income Support (General) Regulations 1987, reg.21AA (Special cases: supplemental—persons from abroad)—Persons who retain the status of worker

3.023   In *CIS/1833/2006*, the Commissioner held, applying the decision of the ECJ in Case C-171/91, *Tsiotras v Landeshauptstadt Stuttgart*, that work undertaken by a Maltese national in the UK before Malta acceded to the EU on 1.5.04 does not count for the purposes of the temporary illness or involuntary unemployment provisions of reg.5(2) of the Immigration (European Economic Area) Regulations 2000.

In *CIS/4010/2007*, the Commissioner held that pregnancy, *per se*, is not an "illness or accident" within reg.5(2)(a) of the Immigration (European Economic Area) Regulations 2000. and that the different treatment of illness and pregnancy does not amount to unlawful discrimination contrary to Art.14 and Art.1, First Protocol ECHR. However, the same Commissioner decided in *CIS/731/2007* that in an individual case a pregnant woman may nevertheless be suffering from an illness within reg.5(2)(a) by reason of her pregnancy.

p.298, commentary to Income Support (General) Regulations 1987, reg.21AA (Special cases: supplemental—persons from abroad)—Students

3.024   In *CIS/419/2007*, the Commissioner holds that a Polish single parent intercalating student who is not looking for work does not have a right of residence under the former Directive 93/96/EEC.

Income Support, Jobseekers' Allowance, etc.

p.298, *commentary to Income Support (General) Regulations 1987, reg.21AA (Special cases: supplemental—persons from abroad)—Family members and extended family members*

In *CIS/1685/2007*, the Commissioner held that, in an appropriate case, a tribunal must consider whether the claimant has a right of residence as a family member of a qualified person as well as considering his/her rights as a qualified person.

3.025

pp.298–299, *commentary to Income Support (General) Regulations 1987, reg.21AA (Special cases: supplemental—persons from abroad)—Family member*

In *CIS/1545/2007*, the Commissioner held that the dependent child of a *student* (and the primary carer of that child) only have a right to reside under the former Directive 93/96 where there are sufficient resources to avoid becoming a burden on the social assistance system.

3.026

p.301, *commentary to Income Support (General) Regulations 1987, reg.21AA (Special cases: supplemental—persons from abroad)—Permanent right of residence*

The commentary at para.2.169 is technically incorrect to state that: "[e]veryone with a permanent right to reside is exempt from the habitual residence test". Under the provisions cited, the exemption only extends to those who have a permanent right to reside under Art.17 of the Directive, not those whose right derives from Art.16. The practical point, however, is correct. Anyone with a permanent right to reside under Art.16 will inevitably be actually habitually resident.

3.027

p.302, *commentary to Income Support (General) Regulations 1987, reg.21AA (Special cases: supplemental—persons from abroad)—Right to reside where children are in education: Baumbast*

There have been a number of decisions in which Commissioners have considered the scope of the *Baumbast* case. In *CIS/1685/2007*, the Commissioner held that the *Baumbast* decision (as it relates to the children of workers) derives from the children's rights under Regulation (EEC) 1612/68 and does not depend upon the qualifying worker no longer being in the United Kingdom. However, another Commissioner has sought to limit the scope of the decision by reference to the reasoning in *CIS/2538/2006* and *CIS/408/2006*. In *CIS/3444/2006* and *CIS/623/2007*, he held that the issues raised in *Baumbast* are now addressed by Arts 12 and 13 of Directive 2004/38/EC and the ruling in that case must be taken as having been qualified by the Directive. Moreover, a move from one Member State to another is not necessarily inconsistent with a child's right to a proper education. In *CIS/1121/2007*, he held that although *Baumbast* could be distinguished from the decision of the Court of Appeal in *Ali v Home Secretary* [2006] EWCA Civ 484, *Baumbast* did not apply to confer a right of residence on the facts of the appeal

3.028

Income Support, Jobseekers' Allowance, etc.

p.304, *commentary to Income Support (General) Regulations 1987, reg.21AA (Special cases: supplemental—persons from abroad)—A8 and A2 nationals*

3.029   In *CIS/1545/2007*, the Commissioner held that work undertaken by an A8 worker requiring registration for which s/he does not have a registration certificate is disregarded for when calculating the 12 months' qualifying period.

p.306, *commentary to Income Support (General) Regulations 1987, reg.21AA (Special cases: supplemental—persons from abroad)— Compatibility of the right to reside test with EC law*

3.030   In *CIS/2538/2006*, the Commissioner holds that the "limitations and conditions" mentioned in Art.18(1) EC are to be implied from the Directives conferring rights of residence, it being implicit that where a right of residence is not conferred, there is no right of residence under Community law unless the denial of such a right would offend the general principles of Community law and, in particular, the principle of proportionality, in which case there may be a freestanding right of residence under Art.18(1). Directive 2004/38/EC provides the benchmark for proportionality even in cases arising before that Directive came into force. Article 18(1) cannot confer rights that go beyond what would have been conferred by the Directive except where it can be shown that there is a lacuna in the Directive. For an example of circumstances in which the same Commissioner held that such a lacuna existed, see *CIS/408/2006*.

pp.318–320, *Income Support (General) Regulations 1987, reg.21ZB (Treatment of refugees)*

3.031   With effect from June 14, 2007, s.12(2)(a)(i) of the Asylum and Immigration (Treatment of Claimants, etc.) Act 2004 (c.19), revoked reg.21ZB.

By Art.2(3) of the Asylum and Immigration (Treatment of Claimants, etc.) Act 2004 (Commencement No.7 and Transitional Provisions) Order 2007 (SI 2007/1602), the revocation of reg.21ZB "shall not apply to a person who is recorded as a refugee on or before June 14, 2007". For those purposes a person is recorded as a refugee on the day on which the Home Secretary notifies him that he has been recognised as a refugee and granted asylum in the UK (see Art.2(4)).

p.320, *amendment to the Income Support (General) Regulations 1987, reg.22A (Reduction in applicable amount where the claimant is appealing against a decision which embodies a determination that he is not incapable of work)*

3.032   With effect from October 1, 2007, the words "16, 17(c)(i) or (d)(i)" in reg.22A(1)(a) were omitted by reg.5(4) of the Social Security (Miscellaneous Amendments) (No.5) Regulations 2007 (SI 2007/2618).

Income Support, Jobseekers' Allowance, etc.

p.322, *annotation to the Income Support (General) Regulations 1987, reg.22A*

The amendment made with effect from October 1, 2007 simply removes outdated references to paragraphs that no longer exist.

3.033

pp.324–327, *annotation to the Income Support (General) Regulations 1987, reg.23*

In *CIS/647/2007* the claimant had been working and receiving working tax credit. She then stopped work and claimed income support in August 2005. At this point she was still receiving working tax credit. However in October 2005 the Revenue decided that she had to repay her working tax credit. In November 2005 an income support decision-maker decided that she was not entitled to income support up to October 2005 because her tax credit exceeded her applicable amount but she was entitled from October 2005. A tribunal allowed her appeal on the ground that the Revenue had decided that she was required to repay the working tax credit before the income support claim was decided.

3.034

The Commissioner, however, allowed the Secretary of State's appeal. The Court of Appeal in *Leeves* (reported as *R(IS) 5/99*) had decided that money which the claimant was under a certain and immediate obligation to repay did not amount to income. But the Court had made it clear that the effect of a demand for repayment was only effective as regards income to be attributed to the future. The demand did not have retrospective effect to remove the quality of income from payments that had already been made and attributed. The key date was the date of the demand for repayment. It was irrelevant whether that date was before or after the date of the income support decision under appeal.

p.332, *amendment to the Income Support (General) Regulations 1987, reg.29 (Calculation of earnings derived from employed earner's employment and income other than earnings)*

With effect from October 1, 2007, reg.5(5) of the Social Security (Miscellaneous Amendments) (No.5) Regulations 2007 (SI 2007/2618) substituted the words "section 227(1) of the Employment Rights Act 1996" for the words "paragraph 8(1)(c) of Schedule 14 to the Employment Protection (Consolidation) Act 1978" in reg.29(4B)(a).

3.035

p.335, *annotation to the Income Support (General) Regulations 1987, reg.29(2B)*

See *CIS/647/2007* in the note to reg.23 above.

3.036

p.336, *annotation to the Income Support (General) Regulations 1987, reg.29(4B)*

Note the amendment to reg.5 (see above) and the extended disregard of payments made on the termination of full-time employment under the new form of para.1 of Sch.8 (see below).

3.037

Income Support, Jobseekers' Allowance, etc.

pp.345–347, *amendment to the Income Support (General) Regulations 1987, reg.35 (Earnings of employed earners)*

3.038   With effect from October 1, 2007, reg.5(6)(a)(i) of the Social Security (Miscellaneous Amendments) (No.5) Regulations 2007 (SI 2007/2618) substituted the words "112(4) or 117(3)(a) of the Employment Rights Act 1996 (the remedies: orders and compensation, enforcement of order and compensation)" for the words "68(2) or 71(2)(a) of the Employment Protection (Consolidation) Act 1978 (remedies for unfair dismissal and compensation)" in reg.35(1)(g).

From the same date, reg.5(6)(a)(ii) of the same amending regulations inserted the following new sub-para.(gg) after sub-para.(g) in reg.35(1):

"(gg) any payment or remuneration made under section 28, 34, 64, 68 or 70 of the Employment Rights Act 1996 (right to guarantee payments, remuneration on suspension on medical or maternity grounds, complaints to employment tribunals);".

From the same date, reg.5(6)(a)(iii) of the same amending regulations substituted the words "112(3) of the Contributions and Benefits Act" for the words "18(2) of the Social Security (Miscellaneous Provisions) Act 1977" in reg.35(1)(h).

From the same date, reg.5(6)(b) of the same amending regulations substituted the words "135(1) of the Employment Rights Act 1996" for the words "81(1) of the Employment Protection (Consolidation) Act 1978" in reg.35(3)(a)(iii).

From the same date, reg.5(6)(c) of the same amending regulations substituted the words "section 227(1) of the Employment Rights Act 1996" for the words "paragraph 8(1)(c) of Schedule 14 to the Employment Protection (Consolidation) Act 1978" in reg.35(3)(b).

pp.348–354, *annotation to the Income Support (General) Regulations 1987, reg.35*

3.039   The amendments made by reg.5(6) of the Social Security (Miscellaneous Amendments) (No.5) Regulations 2007 primarily replace references to revoked provisions in the Employment Protection (Consolidation) Act 1978 with references to the relevant provisions in the Employment Rights Act 1996. The payments referred to in the new reg.35(1)(gg) are guarantee payments under s.28, remuneration while suspended on medical grounds under s.64 and remuneration while suspended on maternity grounds under s.68 of the Employment Rights Act 1996 (s.34 of that Act provides for a complaint to an employment tribunal if an employer fails to pay under s.28, and s.70 for a complaint to an employment tribunal if an employer fails to pay under s.64 or s.68 or under s.67 fails to offer alternative suitable work where this is available before suspending on maternity grounds). The reference in reg.35(1)(h) to the Social Security (Miscellaneous Provisions) Act 1977 has also been updated so that the reference is now to s.112(3) of the Contributions and Benefits Act. The sums referred to in s.112(3) are arrears of pay under an order for reinstatement or re-engagement; a sum payable under an

Income Support, Jobseekers' Allowance, etc.

award for the continuation of a contract of employment; and remuneration under a protective award.

pp.359–361, *amendment to the Income Support (General) Regulations 1987, reg.38 (Calculation of net profit of self-employed earners)*

With effect from July 16, 2007, the words "a retirement annuity contract or" in paras (1)(b)(ii), (3)(c) and (9)(b) of reg.38 were omitted by reg.2(3) of the Social Security (Miscellaneous Amendments) (No.3) Regulations 2007 (SI 2007/1749). 　3.040

pp.362–363, *annotation to the Income Support (General) Regulations 1987, reg.38*

Before the changes made by Pt 4 of the Finance Act 2004 retirement annuity contracts were treated separately for tax purposes but they are now subsumed under the general classification of "personal pension scheme" (see the amended definition of "personal pension scheme" in reg.2(1) above which reflects this change). As a consequence there is no longer any need to distinguish between retirement annuity contracts and personal pension schemes in the Income Support Regulations and so references to retirement annuity contracts have been removed from reg.38 and the other regulations in which they appear. 　3.040A

p.362, *annotation to the Income Support (General) Regulations 1987, reg.38(1)*

In *CH/1099/2007* (which concerned reg.22 of the Council Tax Benefit Regulations 1992, the then equivalent council tax benefit regulation) the claimant argued that the loss in his business should be deducted from his wife's earnings from her part-time employment (not in his business). The Commissioner accepted that reg.22(10) (the equivalent of reg.38(11)) did not apply because this only applied where the *claimant* was engaged in two or more employments. However, reg.22(1) (the equivalent of reg.38(1)) spoke of "net *profit*". A "net *profit*" of a business could not be less than nil (see also para.10 of *R(FC) 1/93* in which the Commissioner took the same approach). There was thus nothing to deduct. 　3.041

pp.363–364, *amendment to the Income Support (General) Regulations 1987, reg.39 (Deduction of tax and contributions for self-employed earners)*

With effect from July 16, 2007, reg.2(4)(a) of the Social Security (Miscellaneous Amendments) (No.3) Regulations 2007 (SI 2007/1749) substituted the words "personal allowance" for the words "personal relief", in each place in which they occur, in reg.39(1). 　3.042

From the same date, reg.2(4)(b) of the same amending regulations substituted the words "section 257(1) of the Income and Corporation Taxes Act 1988" for the words "sections 8(1) and (2) and 14(1)(a) and (2) of the Income and Corporation Taxes Act 1970" in reg.39(1).

Income Support, Jobseekers' Allowance, etc.

With effect from October 1, 2007, reg.5(7) of the Social Security (Miscellaneous Amendments) (No.5) Regulations 2007 (SI 2007/2618) substituted the words "starting rate" for the words "lower rate", in each place in which they occur, in reg.39(1).

p.364, *annotation to the Income Support (General) Regulations 1987, reg.39(1)*

3.043 The outdated references to "personal relief", "the Income and Corporation Taxes Act 1970" and "lower rate" have been updated. "Lower rate" was replaced by "starting rate" in relation to the rates at which income tax is charged by the Income Tax Act 2007 with effect from April 6, 2007 (see the new definition of "starting rate" inserted into reg.2(1) above).

p.367, *amendment to the Income Support (General) Regulations 1987, reg.39D (Deduction in respect of tax for participants in the self-employment route)*

3.044 With effect from July 16, 2007, reg.2(5)(a) of the Social Security (Miscellaneous Amendments) (No.3) Regulations 2007 (SI 2007/1749) substituted the following sub-paragraph for sub-para.(b) of reg.39D(1):

"(b) the personal allowance applicable to a person receiving assistance under the self-employment route by virtue of section 257(1) of the Income and Corporation Taxes Act 1988 (personal allowance) is allowable against that income;".

From the same date, reg.2(5)(b) of the same amending regulations substituted the words "personal allowance" for the words "personal relief" in reg.39D(2).

With effect from October 1, 2007, reg.5(8) of the Social Security (Miscellaneous Amendments) (No.5) Regulations 2007 (SI 2007/2618) substituted the words "starting rate" for the words "lower rate", in each place in which they occur, in reg.39D(1)(c) and (2).

p.367, *annotation to the Income Support (General) Regulations 1987, reg.39D*

3.045 The outdated references to "personal relief" and "lower rate" have been updated. "Lower rate" was replaced by "starting rate" in relation to the rates at which income tax is charged by the Income Tax Act 2007 with effect from April 6, 2007 (see the new definition of "starting rate" inserted into reg.2(1) above).

pp.369–372, *annotation to the Income Support (General) Regulations 1987, reg.40*

3.046 See *CIS/647/2007* in the note to reg.23 above.

Income Support, Jobseekers' Allowance, etc.

pp.375–380, *amendment to the Income Support (General) Regulations 1987, reg.42 (Notional income)*

With effect from July 16, 2007, the words ", retirement annuity contract" in para.(2)(g) of reg.42 were omitted by reg.2(6)(a) of the Social Security (Miscellaneous Amendments) (No.3) Regulations 2007 (SI 2007/1749).

3.047

From the same date, the words ", a retirement annuity contract" in para.(2ZA)(a) of reg.42 were omitted by reg.2(6)(b) of the same amending regulations.

From the same date, reg.2(6)(c) of the same amending regulations substituted the following paragraphs for para.(2A) of reg.42:

"(2A) This paragraph applies where a person aged not less than 60—
(a) is entitled to money purchase benefits under an occupational pension scheme or a personal pension scheme;
(b) fails to purchase an annuity with the funds available in that scheme; and
(c) either—
  (i) defers in whole or in part the payment of any income which would have been payable to him by his pension fund holder, or
  (ii) fails to take any necessary action to secure that the whole of any income which would be payable to him by his pension fund holder upon his applying for it, is so paid, or
  (iii) income withdrawal is not available to him under that scheme.

(2AA) Where paragraph (2A) applies, the amount of any income foregone shall be treated as possessed by that person, but only from the date on which it could be expected to be acquired were an application for it to be made."

From the same date, reg.2(6)(d) of the same amending regulations substituted the words "where paragraph (2A)(c)(i) or (ii)" for the words "to which either head (2A)(a)(i) or (ii)" in para.(2B) of reg.42.

From the same date, reg.2(6)(e)(i) of the same amending regulations substituted the words " where paragraph (2A)(c)(iii)" for the words "to which either head (2A)(a)(iii) or sub-paragraph (2A)(b)" in para.(2C) of reg.42.

From the same date, the words "or retirement annuity contract" in para.(2C) of reg.42 were omitted by reg.2(6)(e)(ii) of the same amending regulations.

From the same date, reg.2(6)(f)(i) of the same amending regulations substituted the words "personal allowance" for the words "personal relief", in each place in which they occur, in para.(8)(a) of reg.42.

From the same date, reg.2(6)(f)(ii) of the same amending regulations substituted the words "section 257(1) of the Income and Corporation Taxes Act 1988" for the words "sections 8(1) and (2) and 14(1)(a) and

Income Support, Jobseekers' Allowance, etc.

(2) of the Income and Corporation Taxes Act 1970" in para.(8)(a) of reg.42.

With effect from October 1, 2007, reg.5(9)(a) of the Social Security (Miscellaneous Amendments) (No.5) Regulations 2007 (SI 2007/2618) added the following new sub-paragraph and new paragraph at the end of para.(6A)(c)(ii) of reg.42:

" ; or

(d) to a claimant who is participating in a work placement approved by the Secretary of State (or a person providing services to the Secretary of State) before the placement starts.

(6AA) In paragraph (6A)(d) 'work placement' means practical work experience which is not undertaken in expectation of payment."

From the same date, reg.5(9)(b) of the same amending regulations substituted the words "starting rate" for the words "lower rate", in each place in which they occur, in reg.42(8)(a).

pp.384–385, *annotation to the Income Support (General) Regulations 1987, reg.42(2)(g) and (2ZA) to (2CA)*

3.048 The amendments made to these paragraphs on July 16, 2007 reflect the fact that as a result of the changes made by Pt 4 of the Finance Act 2004 retirement annuity contracts are now subsumed under the general classification of "personal pension scheme" (see the amended definition of "personal pension scheme" in reg.2(1) above which reflects this change). As a consequence there is no longer any need to distinguish between retirement annuity contracts and personal pension schemes in the Income Support Regulations and so references to retirement annuity contracts have been removed from reg.42 and the other regulations in which they appear.

pp.389–390, *annotation to the Income Support (General) Regulations 1987, reg.42(6A)*

3.049 The effect of the amendment to reg.42(6A) is to introduce a further exclusion from the notional earnings rule in reg.42(6). A claimant will not be treated as having notional earnings if he is undertaking an unpaid work placement (defined in the new para.(6AA)); the work placement must have been approved by the Secretary of State before it started.

p.391, *annotation to the Income Support (General) Regulations, reg.42(8)*

3.050 The outdated references to "personal relief", "the Income and Corporation Taxes Act 1970" and "lower rate" have been updated. "Lower rate" was replaced by "starting rate" in relation to the rates at which income tax is charged by the Income Tax Act 2007 with effect from April 6, 2007 (see the new definition of "starting rate" inserted into reg.2(1) above).

pp.393–399, *annotation to the Income Support (General) Regulations 1987, reg.46*

See *CIS/647/2007* in the note to reg.23 above.   3.051

pp.394–397, *annotation to the Income Support (General) Regulations 1987, reg.46 (Claimant holding as trustee)*

In *CIS/213/2004 and CIS/214/2004* a property in France had been purchased in the claimant's name. However, the purchase price and the sums spent on renovating the property had been provided by Ms V (who lived in the same house in England as the claimant, although they were not living together as partners).   3.052

The claimant and Ms V had a son, S, and Ms V had four other children from another relationship. If the property had been purchased in Ms V's name, under French law all five of her children would have been entitled to an interest in the property on her death, whatever the terms of her will. However, Ms V wished to provide only for S and the property was therefore purchased in the claimant's name, so that only S would inherit on the claimant's death.

On the same day that the property was purchased the claimant executed a holograph will bequeathing a "usufruct" (the French equivalent of a life interest) in the property to Ms V.

The combined effect of the property being in the claimant's name and his will was that on his death S would inherit half the property with Ms V having a usufruct of the remainder.

The matter reached the Court of Appeal (under the name of *Martin v Secretary of State for Social Security*) which by consent remitted it back to a Commissioner to deal with three issues:

(i) *What, applying the provisions of the Hague Convention 1986 and the Recognition of Trusts Act 1987, was the applicable law governing the arrangement entered into between the claimant and Ms V for the purchase of the property?*

The 1987 Act implements the Hague Convention of 1986 on the law applicable to trusts and their recognition. Article 7 of the Convention provides that where no applicable law has been chosen the trust will be governed by the law "with which it is most closely connected". To ascertain this, reference is to be made in particular to

(a) the place of administration of the trust designated by the settlor;
(b) the situs of the assets of the trust;
(c) the place of residence or business of the trustee; and
(d) the objects of the trust and the places where they are to be fulfilled.

Looking at these four factors, the Commissioner states that (a) was inapplicable because Ms V did not designate a place of administration of the trust. As to (b), the property was in France. As to (c), the trustee's residence was in England. In relation to (d), the Commissioner concludes that the greater part of the objects of the trust were to be fulfilled in France, given that the beneficial interest in question was in land situated in France and the inheritance laws in question were French.

Furthermore, it seemed from the parties' actions that they assumed that any dispute would be litigated in accordance with French law.

The Commissioner therefore holds that, looking at the matter as a whole, the putative trust was more closely connected with France than with England. Thus French law was the applicable law. Since French law does not recognise the concept of a trust, it followed that there was no resulting or constructive trust in favour of Ms V.

(ii) If English law was the applicable law, did the facts gave rise to a presumed resulting trust or common intention constructive trust?

On the Commissioner's view as to the applicable law, this issue did not arise. However, in his opinion the purchase of the property in the claimant's name with money provided by Ms V and in accordance with the mutual understanding that Ms V would make the decisions in relation to the property and be entitled to the proceeds of sale if it was sold would give rise under English law to a resulting or constructive trust in favour of Ms V.

(iii) If French law was the applicable law, could the value of the French property nonetheless not be treated as capital for the purposes of income support?

The Commissioner felt unable to reach a conclusion on this without seeking a further opinion as to what remedies would have been available under French law to Ms V in the event of the claimant seeking to sell the property and treat the proceeds of sale as his own. He therefore directed the Secretary of State to obtain this further advice, with a view to him deciding whether those remedies (if any) would lead to the conclusion that the property was not the claimant's capital for income support purposes.

p.404, *amendment to the Income Support (General) Regulations 1987, reg.49 (Calculation of capital in the United Kingdom)*

3.053   With effect from October 1, 2007, reg.5(10) of the Social Security (Miscellaneous Amendments) (No.5) Regulations 2007 (SI 2007/2618) substituted the following regulation for reg.49:

"Calculation of capital in the United Kingdom
49. Capital which a claimant possesses in the United Kingdom shall be calculated at its current market or surrender value less—

(a) where there would be expenses attributable to sale, 10 per cent; and
(b) the amount of any incumbrance secured on it."

p.404, *annotation to the Income Support (General) Regulations 1987, reg.49*

3.054   The previous form of reg.49 reflected an old procedure under which valuations of National Savings and Investments were uprated annually on July 1. This no longer happens. Under the new form of reg.49

Income Support, Jobseekers' Allowance, etc.

National Savings Certificates will be valued in the same way as other capital.

p.407, *amendment to the Income Support (General) Regulations 1987, reg.51 (Notional capital)*

With effect from July 16, 2007, the words "or retirement annuity contract" in para.(2)(d) of reg.51 were omitted by reg.2(7) of the Social Security (Miscellaneous Amendments) (No.3) Regulations 2007 (SI 2007/1749).

3.055

pp.413–414, *annotation to the Income Support (General) Regulations 1987, reg.51(1) (Deprivation)*

In *R. (on the application of Hook) v Social Security Commissioner and Secretary of State for Work and Pensions* [2007] EWHC 1705 (Admin) the High Court dismissed the claimant's application for judicial review of the Commissioner's refusal of leave to appeal in *CIS/1757/2006*. Note that the main volume is wrong when it refers to an application for leave to appeal to the Court of Appeal being made against the decision in *CIS/1757/2006*. The decision in *CIS/1757/2006* was in fact a refusal of leave to appeal by the Commissioner and the application referred to in the main volume was the claimant's application for judicial review of the Commissioner's refusal of leave to appeal.

3.056

p.416, *annotation to the Income Support (General) Regulations 1987, reg.51(1) (Purpose)*

See *CIS/647/2007* in the note to reg.23 above.

3.057

pp.414–419, *annotation to the Income Support (General) Regulations 1987, reg.51(1) (Purpose)*

CIS/1775/2007 concerned the application of the deprivation rule in a case where the claimant had spent her inheritance from her mother on a wide range of items over a period of more than two years. The Commissioner states:

3.058

"Where an inheritance is spent over more than two years in many different ways, it is not possible, as the tribunal has done, to deal with all payments as being made with the same motivation, without looking at the different types of expenditure and the alleged reasons for them and coming to a conclusion in relation to each as to the significant operative purposes for which such expenditure was made. It is more than likely that at least some of the expenditure in question would have been incurred regardless of its effect on entitlement to income support. What the tribunal needs to look for is expenditure that, on the particular facts of this case, and taking into account the emotional state and budgeting capabilities of the claimant, would probably not have been made by her unless a significant motivation for it was to deprive herself of capital for the purpose of claiming income support or increasing the amount of that benefit."

The Commissioner also pointed out that if the tribunal concluded that all or part of the claimant's expenditure was with a significant operative purpose of securing or increasing entitlement to income support, it had to determine the amount by which the notional capital was to be treated as diminishing over future weeks/years. In assessing this it had to apply the diminishing notional capital rule in reg.51A and not some arbitrary figure that it considered represented the claimant's living expenses.

p.420, *annotation to the Income Support (General) Regulations 1987, reg.51(2)*

3.059　See the note to reg.42(2)(g) and (2ZA) to (2CA) above.

p.465, *amendment to the Income Support (General) Regulations 1987, reg.62(2A) (Calculation of grant income)*

3.060　With effect from September 1, 2007 (or if the student's period of study begins between August 1 and August 31, 2007, the first day of the period), reg.2(2)(a) of the Social Security (Students and Income-related Benefits) Amendment Regulations 2007 (SI 2007/1632) substituted the words "£290 per academic year" for "£285" in reg.62(2A)(a).

From the same date, reg.2(2)(b) of the same amending regulations substituted the words "£370 per academic year" for "£361" in reg.62(2A)(b).

p.473, *amendment to the Income Support (General) Regulations 1987, reg.66A(5) (Treatment of student loans)*

3.061　With effect from September 1, 2007 (or if the student's period of study begins between August 1 and August 31, 2007, the first day of the period), reg.2(3)(a) of the Social Security (Students and Income-related Benefits) Amendment Regulations 2007 (SI 2007/1632) substituted the words "£290 per academic year" for "£285" in reg.66A(5)(a).

From the same date, reg.2(3)(b) of the same amending regulations substituted the words "£370 per academic year" for "£361" in reg.66A(5)(b).

pp.482–485, *commentary to Income Support (General) Regulations 1987, reg.70 (Urgent cases)—Pre-April 3, 2000 asylum seekers—"on arrival"*

3.062　In *Kola and another v Secretary of State for Work and Pensions* [2007] UKHL 54 (to be reported as *R(IS) 1/08*), the House of Lords has allowed the claimant's appeal against the decision of the Court of Appeal. Their Lordships held that "on arrival" meant "as soon as reasonably practicable after arrival". Lord Brown of Eaton-under-Heywood (with whom the other members of the judicial committee agreed) stated (at para.38):

"If the asylum seeker could not reasonably have been expected to claim asylum any earlier than he did, having regard both to his practical opportunity for doing so and to his state of mind at the time, including the effect on him of anything said by his facilitating agent, then I see no good reason why his claim should not properly be accepted as one made 'on his arrival'."

Applying that test, Mrs Kola who had arrived in the UK hidden in the back of a lorry and did not go through immigration control, and Mr Mirzajani, who was smuggled into the UK through the Channel Tunnel in the back of a car, satisfied the "on arrival" test because neither could reasonably have been expected to claim asylum any earlier than they did.

The effect of the decision is to overrule all the case law at Commissioner on this point (with the possible exception of *R(IS) 14/99*) and also the decision of the Court of Appeal in *Shire v Secretary of State for Work and Pensions*.

Seven years ago—five years ago, even—*Kola* would have been a decision of the highest importance for asylum seekers. However, with the lapse of time, it has become of historical interest only: it is probable that it no longer affects anyone other than the parties to the case.

p.501, *Income Support (General) Regulations 1987, Sch.1B, para.18A (Refugees)*

With effect from June 14, 2007, s.12(2)(a)(ii) of the Asylum and Immigration (Treatment of Claimants, etc.) Act 2004 (c.19), revoked para.18A.

By Art.2(3) of the Asylum and Immigration (Treatment of Claimants, etc.) Act 2004 (Commencement No.7 and Transitional Provisions) Order 2007 (SI 2007/1602), the revocation of para.18A "shall not apply to a person who is recorded as a refugee on or before June 14, 2007". For those purposes a person is recorded as a refugee on the day on which the Home Secretary notifies him that he has been recognised as a refugee and granted asylum in the UK (see Art.2(4)).

3.063

p.516, *Income Support (General) Regulations 1987, Sch.2 para.8A (Bereavement premium)*

With effect from October 1, 2007, reg.2 of, and the Schedule to, the Social Security (Miscellaneous Amendments) (No.5) Regulations 2007 (SI 2007/2618), revoked para.8A.

3.064

p.521, *Income Support (General) Regulations 1987, Sch.2 para.15(1A) (Bereavement premium)*

With effect from October 1, 2007, reg.2 of, and the Schedule to, the Social Security (Miscellaneous Amendments) (No.5) Regulations 2007 (SI 2007/2618), revoked both columns of para.15(1A).

3.065

Income Support, Jobseekers' Allowance, etc.

p.527, commentary to Income Support (General) Regulations 1987, Sch.2 para.8A

3.066 By reg.6 of the Social Security Amendment (Bereavement Benefits) Regulations 2000 (SI 2000/2239), para.8A ceased to have effect from April 10, 2006. See also the updating entry for p.516 (above).

p.567, annotation to the Income Support (General) Regulations 1987, Sch.3, para.4

3.067 In *CIS/3382/2006* the tribunal found that the claimant's new house was not in fact more suitable for his needs as a disabled person than the one he was already occupying, and that the real purpose of the move had been to acquire accommodation to suit the broader needs of the household rather than his disability specifically. The Commissioner agreed that these crucial findings were altogether proper and reasonable on the facts. The evidence showed that far from being *more* suited to the claimant's needs as a disabled person than where he was living before, the new house was in fact impossible for him to live in at all until extensive work had been carried out to put it in a fit condition. The consequence was that the claimant's allowable housing costs were restricted to the amount of his original house purchase loan.

p.578, annotation to the Income Support (General) Regulations 1987, Sch.3, para.12

3.068 From August 12, 2007 the standard rate for interest on eligible loans has been 7.33 per cent.

p.603, amendment to the Income Support (General) Regulations 1987, Sch.8 (Sums to be disregarded in the calculation of earnings), para.1

3.069 With effect from October 1, 2007, reg.5(11)(a) of the Social Security (Miscellaneous Amendments) (No.5) Regulations 2007 (SI 2007/2618) substituted the following paragraph for para.1 of Sch.8:

"**1.**—(1) In the case of a claimant who has been engaged in remunerative work as an employed earner or, had the employment been in Great Britain, would have been so engaged—

(a) any earnings, other than items to which sub-paragraph (2) applies, paid or due to be paid from that employment which terminated before the first day of entitlement to income support;

(b) any earnings, other than a payment of the nature described in regulation 35(1)(e), paid or due to be paid from that employment which has not been terminated where the claimant is not—

(i) engaged in remunerative work, or
(ii) suspended from his employment.

(2) This sub-paragraph applies to—

Income Support, Jobseekers' Allowance, etc.

   (a) any payment of the nature described in regulation 35(1)(e); and
   (b) any award, sum or payment of the nature described in—
       (i) regulation 35(1)(g) or (h), or
       (ii) section 34 or 70 of the Employment Rights Act 1996 (guarantee payments and suspension from work: complaints to employment tribunals),
including any payment made following the settlement of a complaint to an employment tribunal or of court proceedings."

p.604, *amendment to the Income Support (General) Regulations 1987, Sch.8 (Sums to be disregarded in the calculation of earnings), para.2*

With effect from October 1, 2007, reg.5(11)(b) of the Social Security (Miscellaneous Amendments) (No.5) Regulations 2007 (SI 2007/2618) substituted the following paragraph for para.2 of Sch.8:

3.070

"**2.**—(1) In the case of a claimant to whom this paragraph applies, any earnings (other than a payment of the nature described in regulation 35(1)(e)) which relate to employment which ceased before the first day of entitlement to income support whether or not that employment has terminated.

(2) This paragraph applies to a claimant who has been engaged in part-time employment as an employed earner or, had the employment been in Great Britain, would have been so engaged; but it does not apply to a claimant who has been suspended from his employment."

p.608, *annotation to the Income Support (General) Regulations 1987, Sch.8, para.1*

The effect of the new form of para.1 is to significantly extend the disregard that applies to payments made on the termination of full-time work (i.e. 16 hours or more per week in the case of the claimant, 24 hours or more per week for a partner). The new rules are:

3.071

- Where the full-time employment terminated before the first day of entitlement to income support, all payments (except those referred to below) made on its cessation, including final earnings, payments in lieu of wages, or in lieu of notice, holiday pay and compensation payments (as defined in reg.35(3)) are ignored (sub-para.(1)(a)). This means that entitlement to income support can begin immediately (subject of course to the other conditions of entitlement being met).
- However, any retainer, and the employment protection payments referred to in reg.35(1)(g), reg.35(1)(h), and s.34 and s.70 of the Employment Rights Act 1996 (including any payment made in settlement of an employment tribunal claim or court action), will be taken into account (see sub-para.(2)). Regulation 35(1)(g) applies to compensation awards for unfair dismissal and reg.35(1)(h) to arrears of pay under an order for reinstatement or re-engagement;

Income Support, Jobseekers' Allowance, etc.

any sum payable under an award for the continuation of a contract of employment; and remuneration under a protective award. Section 34 of the Employment Rights Act 1996 provides for a complaint to an employment tribunal if an employer fails to pay under s.28 of the Act (right to guarantee payments); and s.70 similarly so provides if an employer fails to pay under s.64 (right to remuneration while suspended on medical grounds) or s.68 (right to remuneration while suspended on maternity grounds) or under s.67 fails to offer alternative suitable work where this is available before suspending on maternity grounds.

- The disregard is even more extensive where the employment has not terminated but the claimant is working less than 16 hours a week (or none at all) (sub-para.(1)(b)). In this case only payment of any retainer is taken into account. See *R(IS) 9/95* which decided that a guarantee payment under s.12 of the Employment Protection (Consolidation) Act 1978 counted as a retainer (presumably the same applies to guarantee payments under s.28 of the Employment Rights Act 1996). However the disregard in sub-para.(1)(b) does not apply if the person has been suspended from his employment. Note also that payments of sick pay, maternity pay, paternity pay or adoption leave pay are taken into account. This is because they do not count as earnings (see reg.35(2)).

pp.608–609, *annotation to the Income Support (General) Regulations 1987, Sch.8, para.2*

3.071A The new form of para.2, which contains the disregard that applies where a person's part-time work stops before the first day of entitlement to income support, appears to be merely a recasting of the previous form. For the rules that apply in this case see the notes to para.2 in the main volume.

p.618, *amendment to the Income Support (General) Regulations 1987, Sch.9 (Sums to be disregarded in the calculation of income other than earnings), para.50*

3.072 With effect from August 22, 2007, para.13(2) of the Schedule to The Secretary of State for Justice Order 2007 (SI 2007/2128) substituted the word "Justice" for the words "the Home Department" in para.50.

p.618, *Income Support (General) Regulations 1987, Sch.9 (Sums to be disregarded in the calculation of income other than earnings), para.57*

3.073 With effect from June 14, 2007, s.12(2)(a)(i) of the Asylum and Immigration (Treatment of Claimants, etc.) Act 2004 (c.19), revoked para.57.

By Art.2(3) of the Asylum and Immigration (Treatment of Claimants, etc.) Act 2004 (Commencement No.7 and Transitional Provisions) Order 2007 (SI 2007/1602), the revocation of para.57 "shall not apply to a person who is recorded as a refugee on or before June 14, 2007". For

Income Support, Jobseekers' Allowance, etc.

those purposes a person is recorded as a refugee on the day on which the Home Secretary notifies him that he has been recognised as a refugee and granted asylum in the UK (see Art.2(4)).

p.637, *annotation to Income Support (General) Regulations 1987, Sch.9 (Sums to be disregarded in the calculation of income other than earnings), para.57*

Paragraph 57 was revoked with effect from June 14, 2007. See the up-dating entry for pp.318–320 of the Main Volume (above). 3.074

p.644, *amendment to the Income Support (General) Regulations 1987, Sch.10 (Capital to be disregarded), para.23A*

With effect from July 16, 2007, the words "or retirement annuity contract" in para.23A of Sch.10 were omitted by reg.2(8) of the Social Security (Miscellaneous Amendments) (No.3) Regulations 2007 (SI 2007/1749). 3.075

p.644, *Income Support (General) Regulations 1987, Sch.10 (Capital to be disregarded), para.29*

With effect from October 1, 2007, reg.2(3) of the Independent Living Fund (2006) Order 2007 (SI 2007/2538), amended para.29 to read as follows: 3.076

"29. Any payment in kind made by a charity or under the Macfarlane (Special Payments) Trust, the Macfarlane (Special Payments) (No.2) Trust, [the Fund, the Independent Living (1993) Fund or the Independent Living Fund (2006)]"

p.645, *amendment to the Income Support (General) Regulations 1987, Sch.10 (Capital to be disregarded), para.40*

With effect from August 22, 2007, para.13(3) of the Schedule to the Secretary of State for Justice Order 2007 (SI 2007/2128) substituted the word "Justice" for the words "the Home Department" in para.40. 3.077

p.659, *annotation to the Income Support (General) Regulations 1987, Sch.10, para.7*

CIS/3760/2006 follows *CIS/2448/2006* (see the main volume) in deciding that a refund of charges by a local authority to a claimant because the claimant had been wrongly charged for after-care services under s.117 of the Mental Health Act 1983 (see the House of Lords' decision in *R. v Manchester City Council ex p. Stennett* [2002] UKHL 34) was not "arrears of income support" under para.7. 3.078

p.662, *annotation to the Income Support (General) Regulations 1987, Sch.10, para.23A*

See the note to reg.42(2)(g) and (2ZA) to (2CA) above. 3.079

Income Support, Jobseekers' Allowance, etc.

pp.663–664, *annotation to the Income Support (General) Regulations 1987, Sch.10, para.26*

3.080   In *CIS/1915/2007* the claimant left the matrimonial home (which she jointly owned with her husband) and started divorce proceedings. However she came under intense family pressure to return to her husband. She therefore decided that she had to postpone the divorce until she could arrange other accommodation in which she and her children could hide away from her family while the divorce went through.

The decision-maker had initially considered that the value of the claimant's interest in the home could be disregarded under para.26 because she was taking reasonable steps to gain her share of the property by bringing divorce proceedings but decided that the disregard no longer applied when she stopped taking these steps.

The Commissioner agreed that bringing divorce proceedings could constitute taking reasonable steps for the purposes of para.26. However he went on to point out that a flexible approach had to be taken to the question of reasonableness. If there was a temporary suspension of the divorce proceedings and the resulting disposal of the property, because of family pressures, or threats of violence, or to see if a reconciliation could be achieved, all the facts had to be looked at to see whether the claimant was still taking reasonable steps. In the circumstances of this case, by temporarily suspending her divorce proceedings until she had put herself in a position where she could safely proceed, the claimant was continuing to take such steps.

pp.698–699, *Social Security (Immigration and Asylum) Regulations 2000, reg.12(1) and (2) (Transitional arrangements and savings)*

3.081   With effect from June 14, 2007, s.12(3) of the Asylum and Immigration (Treatment of Claimants, etc.) Act 2004 (c.19), revoked paras (1) and (2) of reg.12.

By Art.2(3) of the Asylum and Immigration (Treatment of Claimants, etc.) Act 2004 (Commencement No.7 and Transitional Provisions) Order 2007 (SI 2007/1602), the revocation "shall not apply to a person who is recorded as a refugee on or before June 14, 2007". For those purposes a person is recorded as a refugee on the day on which the Home Secretary notifies him that he has been recognised as a refugee and granted asylum in the UK (see Art.2(4)).

p.704, *Accession (Immigration and Worker Registration) Regulations 2004, reg.2 ("Accession State worker requiring registration")*

3.082   With effect from November 19, 2007, reg.3 of the Accession (Worker Authorisation and Worker Registration) (Amendment) Regulations 2007 (SI 2007/3012), inserted the following paragraph after para.(5) of reg.2:

"(5A) A national of a relevant accession State is not an accession State worker requiring registration during any period in which he is a member of a mission or other person mentioned in section 8(3) of the 1971 Act (member of a diplomatic mission, the family member of such a person, or a person otherwise entitled to diplomatic immunity), other than a person who, under section 8(3A) of that Act, does not count as a member of a mission for the purposes of section 8(3).",

substituted the following head for head (iii) of para.6(b) of reg.2:

"(iii) an accession State national subject to worker authorisation who only has a right to reside under regulation 13 of those Regulations or under regulation 14 of those Regulations by virtue of being treated as a worker for the purpose of the definition of "qualified person" in regulation 6(1) of those Regulations.",

inserted the following head after head (i) of para.7(a) of reg.2:

"(ia) he was exempt from the provisions of the 1971 Act by virtue of section 8(3) of that Act; or"

and amended para.7(c) of reg.2 to read as follows:

"(c) a person shall also be treated as legally working in the United Kingdom on or after 1 May 2004 during any period in which he falls within [paragraph (5), (5A) or (6)]".

pp.713–714, *Accession (Immigration and Worker Authorisation) Regulations 2006, reg.2 ("Accession State national subject to worker authorisation")*

With effect from November 19, 2007, reg.2 of the Accession (Worker Authorisation and Worker Registration) (Amendment) Regulations 2007 (SI 2007/3012), inserted a new para.(6A) in reg.2 as follows:

3.083

"(6A) A national of Bulgaria or Romania is not an accession State national subject to worker authorisation during any period in which he is a member of a mission or other person mentioned in section 8(3) of the 1971 Act (member of a diplomatic mission, the family member of such a person, or a person otherwise entitled to diplomatic immunity), other than a person who, under section 8(3A) of that Act, does not count as a member of a mission for the purposes of section 8(3).",

substituted the following paragraph for para.(8) or reg.2:

"(8) A national of Bulgaria or Romania is not an accession State national subject to worker authorisation during any period in which he is a family member of—
  (a) an EEA national who has a right to reside in the United Kingdom under the 2006 Regulations, other than—
     (i) an accession State national subject to worker authorisation; or
     (ii) a person who is not an accession State national subject to worker authorisation solely by virtue of being the family member of a person mentioned in sub-paragraph (b); or

Income Support, Jobseekers' Allowance, etc.

(b) an accession State national subject to worker authorisation who has a right to reside under regulation 14(1) of the 2006 Regulations by virtue of being a self-employed person, a self-sufficient person or a student falling within sub-paragraph (c), (d) or (e) of regulation 6(1) of those Regulations ('qualified person')."

and amended para.(12)(a) of reg.2 by the addition of a new head (ia) as follows:

"(ia) he was exempt from the provisions of the 1971 Act by virtue of section 8(3) of that Act; or"

p.714, *Accession (Immigration and Worker Authorisation) Regulations 2006, reg.3 (Authorised family member)*

3.084   With effect from November 19, 2007, reg.2 of the Accession (Worker Authorisation and Worker Registration) (Amendment) Regulations 2007 (SI 2007/3012), substituted the following paragraph for para.(1) of reg.3:

"(1) A person is an authorised family member for the purposes of these Regulations if he is the family member of an accession State national subject to worker authorisation who has a right to reside in the United Kingdom under regulation 14(1) of the 2006 Regulations as a worker, unless—

(a) that worker is only authorised to work under these Regulations by virtue of holding an accession worker card issued in accordance with regulation 11 pursuant to an application as an authorised family member; or
(b) that worker is working as an au pair, a seasonal agricultural worker or under the Sectors Based Scheme."

p.715, *Accession (Immigration and Worker Authorisation) Regulations 2006, reg.4 ("Highly skilled person")*

3.085   With effect from November 19, 2007, reg.2 of the Accession (Worker Authorisation and Worker Registration) (Amendment) Regulations 2007 (SI 2007/3012), substituted the following heads for heads (i) and (ii) of para.(1)(b) of reg.4:

"(i) a Higher National Diploma awarded by a relevant institution in Scotland; or
(ii) a degree, postgraduate certificate or postgraduate diploma awarded by a relevant institution in the United Kingdom."

p.715, *commentary to Accession (Immigration and Worker Authorisation) Regulations 2006, reg.3 (Authorised family member)*

3.086   The November 19, 2007 amendment to reg.3(1) is subject to the transitional provision in reg.4 of SI 2007/3012 for applications made before that date by those who were "authorised family members" under the previous definition.

Income Support, Jobseekers' Allowance, etc.

p.803, *Jobseeker's Allowance Regulations 1996, reg.1(3) (Definition of "the Independent Living Fund (2006)" and "the Independent Living Funds")*

With effect from October 1, 2007, reg.4 of the Independent Living Fund (2006) Order 2007 (SI 2007/2538), inserted a new definition of "the Independent Living Fund (2006)" as follows:

3.087

" 'the Independent Living Fund (2006)' means the Trust of that name established by a deed dated 10th April 2006 and made between the Secretary of State for Work and Pensions of the one part and Margaret Rosemary Cooper, Michael Beresford Boyall and Marie Theresa Martin of the other part;"

and amended the definition of "the Independent Living Funds" to read as follows:

" 'the Independent Living Funds' means the Independent Living Fund, [the Independent Living (Extension) Fund, the Independent Living (1993) Fund and the Independent Living Fund (2006)];"

p.803, *amendment to the Jobseeker's Allowance Regulations 1996, reg.1(3) (lower rate)*

The definition of "lower rate" was revoked with effect from October 1, 2007 by reg.2 and the Sch. to the Social Security (Miscellaneous Amendments) (No.5) Regulations 2007 (SI 2007/2618).

3.088

p.804, *amendment to the Jobseeker's Allowance Regulations 1996, reg.1(3) (maternity leave)*

With effect from October 1, 2007, reg.8(2) of the Social Security (Miscellaneous Amendments) (No.5) Regulations 2007 (SI 2007/2618) amended the definition of "maternity leave" to substitute "Part VIII of the Employment Rights Act 1996" for "Part III of the Employment Protection (Consolidation) Act 1978".

3.089

p.806, *insertion of new definition in the Jobseeker's Allowance Regulations 1996, reg.1(3) ("starting rate")*

With effect from October 1, 2007, reg.8(2) of the Social Security (Miscellaneous Amendments) (No.5) Regulations 2007 (SI 2007/2618) inserted between the definitions of "sports award" and "subsistence allowance" a new definition to read:
"starting rate", where it relates to the rate of tax, has the same meaning as in the Income Tax Act 2007 (see section 989 of that Act);".

3.090

p.807, *amendment to the Jobseeker's Allowance Regulations 1996, reg.1(3) ("war widower's pension")*

With effect from July 16, 2007, reg.3(2) of the Social Security (Miscellaneous Amendments) (No.3) Regulations 2007 (SI 2007/1749)

3.091

Income Support, Jobseekers' Allowance, etc.

amended the definition of "war widower's pension" by adding at the end of it "or a pension or allowance for a widower or surviving civil partner granted under any scheme mentioned in section 641(1)(e) or (f) of the Income Tax (Earnings and Pensions) Act 2003."

p.823, *amendment to the Jobseeker's Allowance Regulations 1996, reg.5(3)*

3.092   With effect from October 1, 2007, reg.8(3) of the Social Security (Miscellaneous Amendments) (No.5) Regulations 2007 (SI 2007/2618) amended reg.5(3) by substituting "section 86 of the Employment Rights Act 1996" for "section 49 of the Employment Protection (Consolidation) Act 1978".

p.846, *annotation to the Jobseeker's Allowance Regulations 1996, reg.15*

3.093   In *CJSA/2663/2006* the claimant was a lone parent and full-time student whose claim for contribution-based JSA was refused as she was not a member of a couple. The Commissioner holds that reg.15(a) had to be read as if the references to partner were deleted as they were incompatible with Art.14, read with Art.1, Prot.1, ECHR.

p.855, *annotation to Jobseeker's Allowance Regulations 1996, reg.18(1)*

3.094   In deciding whether the test in reg.18(1) is met, the focus should be on what the claimant did in the week in question rather than on whether each of the steps set out in the jobseeker's agreement were performed. See *CJSA/1814/2007* noted in the update to p.62, above.

p.896, *Jobseeker's Allowance Regulations 1996, reg.52 (Persons treated as engaged in remunerative work)*

3.095   With effect from October 1, 2007, reg.8(4) of the Social Security (Miscellaneous Amendments) (No.5) Regulations 2007 (SI 2007/2618), amended reg.52(3) to read as follows:

"(3) [Subject to paragraph (3A), a person] who was, or was treated as being, engaged in remunerative work and in respect of that work earnings to which regulation 98(1)(b) and (c) (earnings of employed earners) applies are paid, shall be treated as engaged in remunerative work for the period for which those earnings are taken into account in accordance with Part VII."

and inserted a new paragraph immediately after para.3 as follows:

"(3A) Paragraph (3) shall not apply to earnings disregarded under paragraph 1 of Schedule 6 to these regulations."

p.927, *amendments to the Jobseeker's Allowance Regulations 1996, reg.71*

3.096   With effect from October 1, 2007, reg.8(5) of the Social Security (Miscellaneous Amendments) (No.5) Regulations 2007 (SI 2007/2618) amended reg.71(1)(c) by substituting "section 148 of the Employment

Income Support, Jobseekers' Allowance, etc.

Rights Act 1996" for "subsection (1) of section 88 of the Employment Protection (Consolidation) Act 1978". From the same date it amended reg.71(2) by substituting "139(1) of the Employment Rights Act 1996" for "81(2) of the Employment Protection (Consolidation) Act 1978".

p.944, *amendment to the Jobseeker's allowance regulations 1996, reg.75(1)(a)(iv) (Intensive Activity Period)*

With effect from June 1, 2007, reg.2 of the Jobseeker's Allowance (Extension of the Intensive Activity Period) Amendment Regulations 2007 (SI 2007/1316) amended the definition of Intensive Activity Period by substituting "60 years" for "50 years". 3.097

p.960, *Jobseeker's Allowance Regulations 1996, reg.85 (Special Cases)*

With effect from October 1, 2007, reg.8(6) of the Social Security (Miscellaneous Amendments) (No.5) Regulations 2007 (SI 2007/2618), corrected a drafting error by revoking the words "Subject to paragraph (2A)" in reg.85(1). 3.098

p.975, *amendment to the Jobseeker's Allowance Regulations 1996, reg.94 (Calculation of earnings derived from employed earner's employment and income other than earnings)*

With effect from October 1, 2007, reg.8(7) of the Social Security (Miscellaneous Amendments) (No.5) Regulations 2007 (SI 2007/2618) substituted the words "section 227(1) of the Employment Rights Act 1996" for the words "paragraph 8(1)(c) of Schedule 14 to the Employment Protection (Consolidation) Act 1978" in reg.94(8)(c)(ii). 3.099

p.976, *annotation to the Jobseeker's Allowance Regulations 1996, reg.94(6)–(9)*

Note the amendment to reg.52 (see above) and the extended disregard of payments made on the termination of full-time employment under the new para.1 of Sch.6 (see below). 3.100

pp.979–981, *amendment to the Jobseeker's Allowance Regulations 1996, reg.98 (Earnings of employed earners)*

With effect from October 1, 2007, reg.8(8)(a)(i) of the Social Security (Miscellaneous Amendments) (No.5) Regulations 2007 (SI 2007/2618) substituted the words "112(4), 113, 117(3)(a), 128, 131 and 132 of the Employment Rights Act 1996 (the remedies: orders and compensation, the orders, enforcement of order and compensation, interim relief)" for the words "68(2), 69, 71(2)(a), 77 or 79 of the Employment Protection (Consolidation) Act 1978 (remedies for unfair dismissal and compensation)" in reg.98(1)(f). 3.101

From the same date, reg.8(8)(a)(ii) of the same amending regulations substituted the words "28, 34, 64, 68 or 70 of the Employment Rights

Income Support, Jobseekers' Allowance, etc.

Act 1996 (right to guarantee payments, remuneration on suspension on medical or maternity grounds, complaints to employment tribunals)" for the words "12, 19 or 47 of the Employment Protection (Consolidation) Act 1978 (guaranteed payments, remuneration whilst suspended from work on medical or maternity grounds)" in reg.98(1)(ff).

From the same date, "157" was omitted in reg.98(1)(g) by reg.8(8)(a)(iii) of the same amending regulations.

From the same date, reg.8(8)(b) of the same amending regulations substituted the words "section 135(1) of the Employment Rights Act 1996" for the words "section 81(1) of the Employment Protection (Consolidation) Act 1978" in reg.98(2)(f).

pp.981–982, *annotation to the Jobseekers Allowance Regulations 1996, reg.98*

3.101A These amendments primarily replace references to revoked provisions in the Employment Protection (Consolidation) Act 1978 with references to the relevant provisions in the Employment Rights Act 1996.

p.986, *amendment to the Jobseeker's Allowance Regulations 1996, reg.102 (Deduction of tax and contributions for self-employed earners)*

3.102 With effect from July 16, 2007, reg.3(3)(a) of the Social Security (Miscellaneous Amendments) (No.3) Regulations 2007 (SI 2007/1749) substituted the words "personal allowance" for the words "personal relief" or "personal reliefs", in each place in which they occur, in reg.102(1).

From the same date, reg.3(3)(b) of the same amending regulations substituted the words "section 257(1)" for the words "sections 257(1), 257A(1) and 259" in reg.102(1).

With effect from October 1, 2007, reg.8(9) of the Social Security (Miscellaneous Amendments) (No.5) Regulations 2007 (SI 2007/2618) substituted the words "starting rate" for the words "lower rate", in each place in which they occur, in reg.102(1).

p.987, *annotation to the Jobseeker's Allowance Regulations, reg.102*

3.103 The outdated references to "personal relief" or "personal reliefs", to provisions in the Income and Corporation Taxes Act 1988, and to "lower rate" have been updated. "Lower rate" was replaced by "starting rate" in relation to the rates at which income tax is charged by the Income Tax Act 2007 with effect from April 6, 2007 (see the new definition of "starting rate" inserted into reg.1(3) above).

p.990, *amendment to the Jobseeker's Allowance Regulations 1996, reg.102D (Deduction in respect of tax for participants in the self-employment route)*

3.104 With effect from July 16, 2007, reg.3(3)(a) of the Social Security (Miscellaneous Amendments) (No.3) Regulations 2007 (SI 2007/1749) substituted the words "personal allowance" for the words "personal relief" or "personal reliefs", in each place in which they occur, in reg.102D.

Income Support, Jobseekers' Allowance, etc.

From the same date, reg.3(3)(b) of the same amending regulations substituted the words "section 257(1)" for the words "sections 257(1), 257A(1) and 259" in reg.102D.

With effect from October 1, 2007, reg.8(10) of the Social Security (Miscellaneous Amendments) (No.5) Regulations 2007 (SI 2007/2618) substituted the words "starting rate" for the words "lower rate", in each place in which they occur, in reg.102D(1)(c) and (2).

p.990, *annotation to the Jobseeker's Allowance Regulations, reg.102D*

The outdated references to "personal relief" or "personal reliefs", to provisions in the Income and Corporation Taxes Act 1988, and to "lower rate" have been updated. "Lower rate" was replaced by "starting rate" in relation to the rates at which income tax is charged by the Income Tax Act 2007 with effect from April 6, 2007 (see the new definition of "starting rate" inserted into reg.1(3) above).

3.105

pp.994–998, *amendment to the Jobseeker's Allowance Regulations 1996, reg.105 (Notional income)*

With effect from July 16, 2007, reg.3(4)(a) of the Social Security (Miscellaneous Amendments) (No.3) Regulations 2007 (SI 2007/1749) substituted the following paragraphs for para.(3) of reg.105:

3.106

"(3A) This paragraph applies where a person aged not less than 60—

(a) is entitled to money purchase benefits under an occupational pension scheme or a personal pension scheme;
(b) fails to purchase an annuity with the funds available in that scheme; and
(c) either—
  (i) defers in whole or in part the payment of any income which would have been payable to him by his pension fund holder, or
  (ii) fails to take any necessary action to secure that the whole of any income which would be payable to him by his pension fund holder upon his applying for it, is so paid, or
  (iii) income withdrawal is not available to him under that scheme.

(3A) Where paragraph (3) applies, the amount of any income foregone shall be treated as possessed by that person, but only from the date on which it could be expected to be acquired were an application for it to be made."

From the same date, reg.3(4)(b) of the same amending regulations substituted the words "where paragraph (3)(c)(i) or (ii)" for the words "to which either head (i) or (ii) of paragraph (3)(a)" in para.(4) of reg.105.

From the same date, reg.3(4)(c) of the same amending regulations substituted the words "where paragraph (3)(c)(iii)" for the words "to which either head (iii) of paragraph (3)(a), or paragraph (3)(b)" in para.(5) of reg.105.

From the same date, reg.3(3)(a) of the same amending regulations substituted the words "personal allowance" for the words "personal relief" or "personal reliefs" in each place that they appear in para.(15) of reg.105.

From the same date, reg.3(3)(b) of the same amending regulations substituted the words "section 257(1)" for the words "sections 257(1), 257A(1) and 259" in para.(15) of reg.105.

From the same date, reg.3(4)(d) of the same amending regulations inserted the words "or an occupational pension scheme" after the words "personal pension scheme" in the definition of "pension fund holder" in para.(16) of reg.105.

With effect from October 1, 2007, reg.8(11)(a) of the Social Security (Miscellaneous Amendments) (No.5) Regulations 2007 (SI 2007/2618) added the following new sub-paragraph at the end of para.(13A)(b)(ii) of reg.105:

" ; or
(c) to a claimant who is participating in a work placement approved by the Secretary of State (or a person providing services to the Secretary of State) before the placement starts.".

From the same date, reg.8(11)(b) of the same amending regulations substituted the words "starting rate" for the words "lower rate", in each place in which they occur, in reg.105(15)(a).

From the same date, reg.8(11)(c) of the same amending regulations added the following definition at the end of reg.105(16):

" "work placement" means practical work experience which is not undertaken in expectation of payment."

p.1000, *annotation to the Jobseeker's Allowance Regulations 1996, reg.105*

3.107   The amendments made by reg.3(4) of the Social Security (Miscellaneous Amendments) (No.3) Regulations 2007 reflect the fact that as a result of the changes made by Pt 4 of the Finance Act 2004 retirement annuity contracts are now subsumed under the general classification of "personal pension scheme". As a consequence there is no longer any need to distinguish between retirement annuity contracts and personal pension schemes in reg.105.

The amendments made by reg.8(11)(a) and (c) of the Social Security (Miscellaneous Amendments) (No.5) Regulations 2007 introduce a further exclusion from the notional earnings rule in reg.105(13). A claimant will not be treated as having notional earnings if he is undertaking an unpaid work placement; the work placement must have been approved by the Secretary of State before it started.

The other amendments update outdated references to "personal relief" or "personal reliefs", to provisions in the Income and Corporation Taxes Act 1988, and to "lower rate". "Lower rate" was replaced by "starting rate" in relation to the rates at which income tax is charged by

Income Support, Jobseekers' Allowance, etc.

the Income Tax Act 2007 with effect from April 6, 2007 (see the new definition of "starting rate" inserted into reg.1(3) above).

p.1003, *amendment to the Jobseeker's Allowance Regulations 1996, reg.111 (Calculation of capital in the United Kingdom)*

With effect from October 1, 2007, reg.8(12) of the Social Security (Miscellaneous Amendments) (No.5) Regulations 2007 (SI 2007/2618) substituted the following regulation for reg.111:

3.108

"Calculation of capital in the United Kingdom

111. Capital which a claimant possesses in the United Kingdom shall be calculated at its current market or surrender value less—
(a) where there would be expenses attributable to sale, 10 per cent; and
(b) the amount of any incumbrance secured on it.".

p.1004, *annotation to the Jobseeker's Allowance Regulations, reg.111*

See the note to reg.49 of the Income Support Regulations above.

3.109

p.1025, *amendment to the Jobseeker's Allowance Regulations 1996, reg.131 (Calculation of grant income)*

With effect from September 1, 2007 (or if the student's period of study begins between August 1 and August 31, 2007, the first day of the period), reg.3(2)(a) of the Social Security (Students and Income-related Benefits) Amendment Regulations 2007 (SI 2007/1632) substituted the words "£290 per academic year" for "£285" in reg.131(3)(a).

3.110

From the same date, reg.3(2)(b) of the same amending regulations substituted the words "£370 per academic year" for "£361" in reg.131(3)(b).

p.1031, *amendment to the Jobseeker's Allowance Regulations 1996, reg.136 (Treatment of student loans)*

With effect from September 1, 2007 (or if the student's period of study begins between August 1 and August 31, 2007, the first day of the period), reg.3(3)(a) of the Social Security (Students and Income-related Benefits) Amendment Regulations 2007 (SI 2007/1632) substituted the words "£290 per academic year" for "£285" in reg.136(5)(a).

3.111

From the same date, reg.3(3)(b) of the same amending regulations substituted the words "£370 per academic year" for "£361" in reg.136(5)(b).

p.1071, *Jobseeker's Allowance Regulations 1996, Sch.1 para.9A (Bereavement premium)*

With effect from October 1, 2007, reg.2 of, and the Schedule to, the Social Security (Miscellaneous Amendments) (No.5) Regulations 2007 (SI 2007/2618), revoked para.9A.

3.112

Income Support, Jobseekers' Allowance, etc.

p.1076, *Jobseeker's Allowance Regulations 1996, Sch.1 para.20(1A) (Bereavement premium)*

3.113   With effect from October 1, 2007, reg.2 of, and the Schedule to, the Social Security (Miscellaneous Amendments) (No.5) Regulations 2007 (SI 2007/2618), revoked both columns of para.20(1A).

p.1084, *commentary to Jobseeker's Allowance Regulations 1996, Sch.1 para.9A*

3.114   By reg.6 of the Social Security Amendment (Bereavement Benefits) Regulations 2000 (SI 2000/2239), para.9A ceased to have effect from April 10, 2006. See also the updating entry for p.1071 (above).

p.1113, *amendment to the Jobseeker's Allowance Regulations 1996, Sch.6 (Sums to be disregarded in the calculation of earnings), paras 1 to 2*

3.115   With effect from October 1, 2007, reg.8(14)(a) of the Social Security (Miscellaneous Amendments) (No.5) Regulations 2007 (SI 2007/2618) substituted the following paragraphs for paras 1 and 2 of Sch.6:

"**1.**—(1) In the case of a claimant who has been engaged in remunerative work as an employed earner or, had the employment been in Great Britain, would have been so engaged—

(a) any earnings, other than items to which sub-paragraph (2) applies, paid or due to be paid from that employment which terminated before the first day of entitlement to a jobseeker's allowance;

(b) any earnings, other than a payment of the nature described in regulation 98(1)(d), paid or due to be paid from that employment which has not been terminated where the claimant is not-
   (i) engaged in remunerative work, or
   (ii) suspended from his employment.

(2) This sub-paragraph applies to—

(a) any payment of the nature described in regulation 98(1)(d); and

(b) any award, sum or payment of the nature described in—
   (i) regulation 98(1)(f) or (g), or
   (ii) section 34 or 70 of the Employment Rights Act 1996 (guarantee payments and suspension from work: complaints to employment tribunals), including any payment made following the settlement of a complaint to an employment tribunal or of court proceedings.

1A. If the claimant's partner has been engaged in remunerative work as an employed earner or, had the employment been in Great Britain, would have been so engaged, any earnings paid or due to be paid on termination of that employment by way of retirement but only if—

Income Support, Jobseekers' Allowance, etc.

(a) on retirement the partner is entitled to a retirement pension under the Benefits Act, or
(b) the only reason the partner is not entitled to a retirement pension under the Benefits Act is because the contribution conditions are not satisfied.

2.—(1) In the case of a claimant to whom this paragraph applies, any earnings (other than items to which paragraph 1(2) applies) which relate to employment which ceased before the first day of entitlement to a jobseeker's allowance whether or not that employment has terminated.

(2) This paragraph applies to a claimant who has been engaged in part-time employment as an employed earner or, had the employment been in Great Britain, would have been so engaged; but it does not apply to a claimant who has been suspended from his employment.".

p.1113, *amendment to the Jobseeker's Allowance Regulations 1996, Sch.6 (Sums to be disregarded in the calculation of earnings), para.3*

With effect from October 1, 2007, reg.8(14)(b) of the Social Security (Miscellaneous Amendments) (No.5) Regulations 2007 (SI 2007/2618) substituted the words "118(1)(b) of the Employment Rights Act 1996" for the words "72(1)(b) of the Employment Protection (Consolidation) Act 1978" in para.3(b) of Sch.6.

3.116

pp.1117–1118, *annotation to the Jobseeker's Allowance Regulations 1996, Sch.6, paras 1 to 2*

See the notes to the new paras 1 and 2 of Sch.8 to the Income Support Regulations above. However, note that in the case of JSA the disregard is not more extensive where part-time work has ceased before the first day of entitlement to benefit (see para.2(1)). The same disregard applies as in the case of termination of full-time employment, although in the case of part-time work it is not necessary for the employment to have ended. Thus any employment protection payments referred to in reg.98(1)(g) or (h) or s.34 or s.70 of the Employment Rights Act 1966 (including any payment made in settlement of an employment tribunal claim or court action) are taken into account, as well as payment of any retainer. It is not entirely clear why this different rule for JSA is being maintained, since the stated intention behind the October 2007 changes is to align the treatment of final earnings on all new claims to benefit.

The new para.1A applies to a claimant's partner's earnings paid on termination of employment due to retirement. Such earnings will be disregarded in full, provided that the partner is retiring at pensionable age. For the equivalent income support provision see para.1A of Sch.8 to the Income Support Regulations in the main volume. Under that provision the disregard applies if the partner has reached the qualifying age for state pension credit. The difference between the two provisions reflects the fact that it is possible for a person to claim JSA up to pensionable age

3.117

Income Support, Jobseekers' Allowance, etc.

(i.e. 65 in the case of a man), whereas a person who has reached the qualifying age for state pension credit (currently 60) is not entitled to income support.

p.1128, *amendment to the Jobseeker's Allowance Regulations 1996, Sch.7 (Sums to be disregarded in the calculation of income other than earnings), para.49*

3.118   With effect from August 22, 2007, para.16(2) of the Schedule to The Secretary of State for Justice Order 2007 (SI 2007/2128) substituted the word "Justice" for the words "the Home Department" in para.49.

p.1138, *amendment to the Jobseeker's Allowance Regulations 1996, Sch.8 (Capital to be disregarded), para.38*

3.119   With effect from August 22, 2007, para.16(3) of the Schedule to The Secretary of State for Justice Order 2007 (SI 2007/2128) substituted the word "Justice" for the words "the Home Department" in para.38.

p.1150, *amendment to the State Pension Credit Regulations 2002, reg.1 (Citation, commencement and interpretation)*

3.120   With effect from October 1, 2007, Art.6(2) of the Independent Living Fund (2006) Order 2007 (SI 2007/2538) amended reg.1 by inserting the following definition before the definition of "the Independent Living Funds":

" 'the Independent Living Fund (2006)' means the Trust of that name established by a deed dated 10th April 2006 and made between the Secretary of State for Work and Pensions of the one part and Margaret Rosemary Cooper, Michael Beresford Boyall and Marie Theresa Martin of the other part;"

With effect from the same date, Art.6(3) the same Order substituted "the Independent Living (Extension) Fund, the Independent Living (1993) Fund and the Independent Living Fund (2006)" for the words "the Independent Living (Extension) Fund and the Independent Living (1993) Fund" in the definition of "the Independent Living Funds".

p.1151, *amendment to the State Pension Credit Regulations 2002, reg.1 (Citation, commencement and interpretation)*

3.121   With effect from October 1, 2007, reg.10(2) of the Social Security (Miscellaneous Amendments) (No.5) Regulations 2007 (SI 2007/2618) amended the definition of "pension fund holder" in reg.1 by inserting the words "an occupational pension scheme," after the words "with respect to".

p.1155, *annotations to the State Pension Credit Regulations 2002, reg.2(4) (Persons not in Great Britain)*

3.122   Note that the decision of the Tribunal of Commissioners on this point in *CPC/2920/2005* has been reversed in any event by the decision of the

Income Support, Jobseekers' Allowance, etc.

Court of Appeal in *Ullaslow v Secretary of State for Work and Pensions* [2007] EWCA Civ 657, noted in the main 2007 volume at para. 2.162.

p.1180, *amendment to the State Pension Credit Regulations 2002, reg.18 (Notional income)*

With effect from October 1, 2007, reg.10(3) of the Social Security (Miscellaneous Amendments) (No.5) Regulations 2007 (SI 2007/2618) amended reg.18 by substituting ", (1CA) and (1CB)" for "and (1C)" in para.(1A) and substituting for para.(1C) the following new sub-paragraphs:

3.123

"(1C) Paragraphs (1CA) and (1CB) apply for the purposes of paragraph (1) (or, where applicable, paragraph (1) read with paragraph (1B)).

(1CA) Where a benefit or allowance in payment in respect of the claimant would be adjusted under the Social Security (Overlapping Benefits) Regulations 1979 if the retirement pension income had been claimed, he shall be treated as possessing that income minus the benefit or allowance in payment.

(1CB) Where a benefit or allowance in payment in respect of the claimant would require an adjustment to be made under the Social Security (Overlapping Benefits) Regulations 1979 to the amount of retirement pension income payable had it been claimed, he shall be treated as possessing that retirement pension income minus the adjustment which would be made to it."

p.1182, *amendment to the State Pension Credit Regulations 2002, reg.19 (Calculation of capital in the United Kingdom)*

With effect from October 1, 2007, reg.10(4) of the Social Security (Miscellaneous Amendments) (No.5) Regulations 2007 (SI 2007/2618) substituted a new reg.19 as follows:

3.124

"Calculation of capital in the United Kingdom

19. Capital which a claimant possesses in the United Kingdom shall be calculated at its current market or surrender value less—

(a) where there would be expenses attributable to sale, 10 per cent; and'(b) the amount of any encumbrance secured on it."

p.1200, *amendment to the State Pension Credit Regulations 2002, Sch.II, para.8 (General provisions applying to housing costs)*

With effect from October 1, 2007, reg.10(5) of the Social Security (Miscellaneous Amendments) (No.5) Regulations 2007 (SI 2007/2618) substituted a new formula in para.8(8) as follows:

3.125

$$R \times \frac{S}{T}$$

Income Support, Jobseekers' Allowance, etc.

p.1236, *Social Fund Cold Weather Payments (General) Regulations 1988, Sch.1 (Identification of stations and postcode districts)*

3.126   With effect from November 1, 2007, reg.3 and Sch.1 of the Social Fund Cold Weather Payments (General) Amendment Regulations 2007 (SI 2007/2912), substituted a new Sch.1 as follows:

Column (1)	*Column (2)*
Meteorological Office Station	*Postcode Districts*
1. Aberporth	SA35–48, SA64–65.
2. Albemarle	DH1–7, DH9. DL4–5, DL14–17. NE1–13, NE15–18, NE20–21, NE23, NE25–43, NE44–46. SR1–7. TS21, TS28–29.
3. Andrewsfield	AL1–10. CB1–5, CB10–11, CB21–25. CM1–9, CM11–24, CM77. CO9. RM14–20. SG1–2, SG8–14.
4. Aultbea	IV21–22, IV26, IV40, IV52–54.
5. Aviemore	AB37. PH19–26.
6. Bedford	LU1–7. MK1–19, MK40–46. NN1–16, NN29. PE19. SG3–7, SG15–19.
7. Bingley	BB1–12, BB18. BD1–24. DE4, DE45. DL8, DL11. HD1–9. HX1–7. LS21, LS27, LS29. OL1–5, OL11–16. S32–33, S35–36. SK13, SK17, SK22–23. ST13. WF15–17.
8. Bishopton	G1–5, G11–15, G20–23, G31–34, G40–46, G51–53, G60–62, G64–69, G71–78, G81–84. KA–18, KA20–25, KA28–30. ML1–5. PA1–27, PA30, PA32.
9. Boscombe Down	BA12. RG28. SO20–23. SP1–5, SP7, SP9–11.
10. Boulmer	NE22, NE24, NE61–70. TD15.
11. Braemar	AB33–36. PH10–11, PH18.
12. Brize Norton	CV36. GL54–56. OX1–8, OX10–18, OX20, OX25–29, OX33, OX39, OX44, OX49. SN7.
13. Cardinham (Bodmin)	PL13–17, PL22–35. TR9.
14. Carlisle	CA1–8, CA13–15. DG12, DG16.
15. Cassley	IV27–28. KW11, KW13.

Income Support, Jobseekers' Allowance, etc.

Column (1) Meteorological Office Station	*Column (2)* Postcode districts
16. Charlwood	BN5–6, BN44. GU5–6. ME14–20. RH1–20. TN1–20, TN22, TN27.
17. Charterhall	NE71. TD3–6, TD8, TD10–12.
18. Chivenor	EX22–23, EX31–34, EX39.
19. Coleshill	B1–21, B23–38, B40, B42–50, B60–80, B90–98. CV1–12, CV21–23, CV31–35, CV37, CV47. DY1–14. LE10. WS1–15. WV1–16.
20. Crosby	CH1–8, CH41–49, CH60–66. FY1–8. L1–40. LL11–14. PR1–9, PR25–26. SY14. WA1–2, WA4–12. WN1–6, WN8.
21. Culdrose	TR1–8, TR10–20, TR26–27.
22. Dundrennan	DG1–2, DG5–7.
23. Dunkeswell Aerodrome	DT6–8. EX1–15, EX24. TA21. TQ1–6, TQ9–14.
24. Dyce	AB10–16, AB21–25, AB30–32, AB39, AB41–43, AB51–54. DD8–11.
25. Edinburgh Gogarbank	EH1–42, EH47–49, EH51–55. FK1–17. G63. KY3, KY11–13. PH3–5. TD13–14.
26. Eskdalemuir	DG3–4, DG10–11, DG13–14. ML12. TD1–2, TD7, TD9.
27. Filton	BS1–11, BS13–16, BS20–24, BS29–32, BS34–37, BS39–41, BS48–49. GL11–13. NP16, NP26.
28. Fylingdales	YO11–18, YO21–22, YO25.
29. Great Malvern	GL1–6, GL10, GL14–20, GL50–53. HR1–9. NP15, NP25. SY8. WR1–15.
30. Heathrow	BR1–8. CR0, CR2–9. DA1–2, DA4–8, DA14–18. E1–18. E1W. EC1–4. EN1–11. HA0–9. IG1–11. KT1–24. N1–22. NW1–11. RM1–13. SE1–28. SL0, SL3. SM1–7. SW1–20. TW1–20. UB1–10. W1–14. WC1–2. WD1–7, WD17–19, WD23–25.
31. Herstmonceux, West End	BN7–8, BN20–24, BN26–27. TN21, TN31–40.
32. High Wycombe	HP1–23, HP27. OX9. RG9. SL7–9.
33. Hurn (Bournemouth Airport)	BH1–25, BH31. DT1–2, DT11. SP6.

111

Income Support, Jobseekers' Allowance, etc.

Column (1)	Column (2)
Meteorological Office Station	Postcode districts
34. Isle of Portland	DT3–5.
35. Kinloss	AB38, AB44–45, AB55–56. IV1–3, IV5, IV7–20, IV30–32, IV36.
36. Kirkwall	KW15–17.
37. Lake Vyrnwy	LL20–21, LL23–25, LL41. SY10, SY15–17, SY19, SY21–22.
38. Lerwick	ZE1–3.
39. Leuchars	DD1–7. KY1–2, KY4–10, KY14–16. PH1–2, PH7, PH12–14.
40. Linton on Ouse	DL1–3, DL6–7, DL9–10. HG1–5. LS1–20, LS22–26, LS28. S62–64, S70–75. TS9, TS15–16. WF1–14. YO1, YO7–8, YO10, YO19, YO23–24, YO26, YO30–32, YO41–43, YO51, YO60–62.
41. Liscombe	EX16–21, EX35–38. TA22, TA24.
42. Loch Glascarnoch	IV4, IV6, IV23–24, IV63.
43. Loftus	SR8. TS1–8, TS10–14, TS17–20, TS22–27.
44. Lusa	IV41–49, IV51, IV55–56.
45. Lyneham	BA1–3, BA11, BA13–15. GL7–9. RG17. SN1–6, SN8–16, SN25–26.
46. Machrihanish	KA27. PA28–29, PA31, PA34, PA37, PA41–49, PA60–76. PH36, PH38–41.
47. Manston	CM0. CT1–21. DA3, DA9–13. ME1–13. SS0–17. TN23–26, TN28–30.
48. Marham	CB6–7. IP24–28. PE12–14, PE30–38.
49. Norwich Airport	NR1–35.
50. Nottingham	CV13. DE1–3, DE5–7, DE11–15, DE21–24, DE55–56, DE65, DE72–75. LE1–9, LE11–14, LE16–19, LE65, LE67. NG1–22, NG25, NG31–34. S1–14, S17–18, S20–21, S25–26, S40–45, S60–61, S65–66, S80–81. ST10, ST14.
51. Pembrey Sands	SA1–8, SA10–18, SA31–34, SA61–63, SA66–73.

Income Support, Jobseekers' Allowance, etc.

Column (1)	Column (2)
Meteorological Office Station	*Postcode districts*
52. Plymouth	PL1–12, PL18–21. TQ7–8.
53. Redesdale	CA9. DH8. DL12–13. NE19, NE47–49.
54. Rhyl	LL15–19, LL22, LL26–32.
55. St. Athan	CF3, CF5, CF10–11, CF14–15, CF23–24, CF31–36, CF61–64, CF71–72. NP10, NP18–20.
56. St. Catherine's Point	PO30, PO38–41.
57. Salsburgh	EH43–46. ML6–11.
58. Scilly, St. Mary's	TR21–25.
59. Sennybridge	CF37–48, CF81–83. LD1–8. NP4, NP7–8, NP11–13, NP22–24, NP44. SA9, SA19–20. SY7, SY9, SY18.
60. Shap	CA10–12, CA16–17. LA8–10, LA22–23.
61. Shawbury	ST1–9, ST11–12, ST15–21. SY1–6, SY11–13. TF1–13.
62. South Farnborough	GU1–4, GU7–35, GU46–47, GU51–52. RG1–2, RG4–8, RG10, RG12, RG14, RG18–27, RG29–31, RG40–42, RG45. SL1–2, SL4–6. SO24.
63. Stornoway Airport	HS1–9.
64. Thorney Island	BN1–3, BN9–18, BN25, BN41–43, BN45. PO1–22, PO31–37. SO14–19, SO30–32, SO40–43, SO45, SO50–53.
65. Tiree	PA77–78. PH42–44.
66. Trawsgoed	LL35–40. SY20, SY23–25.
67. Tulloch Bridge	FK 18–21, PA33, PA35–36, PA38, PA40. PH6, PH8–9, PH15–17, PH30–35, PH37, PH49–50.
68. Valley	LL33–40, LL42–49, LL51–78.
69. Waddington	DN1–22, DN31–41. HU1–20. LN1–13. NG23–24. PE10–11, PE20–25.
70. Walney Island	CA18–28. LA1–7, LA11–21.

Income Support, Jobseekers' Allowance, etc.

Column (1)	Column (2)
Meteorological Office Station	*Postcode districts*
71. Wattisham	CB8–9. CO1–8, CO10–16. IP1–23, IP29–33.
72. West Freugh	DG8–9. KA19, KA26.
73. Wick Airport	IV25. KW1–3, KW5–10, KW12, KW14.
74. Wittering	LE15. NN17–18. PE1–9, PE15–17, PE26–29.
75. Woodford	BL0–9. CW1–12. M1–9, M11–35, M38, M40–41, M43–46, M50, M90. OL6–10. SK1–12, SK14–16. WA3, WA13–16. WN7.
76. Yeovilton	BA4–10, BA16, BA20–22. BS25–28. DT9–10. SP8. TA1–20, TA23.

"

p.1239, *Social Fund Cold Weather Payments (General) Regulations 1988, Sch.2 (Specified alternative stations)*

3.127   With effect from November 1, 2007, reg.4 and Sch.2 of the Social Fund Cold Weather Payments (General) Amendment Regulations 2007 (SI 2007/2912), substituted a new Sch.2 as follows:

Column (1)	Column (2)
Meteorological Office Station	*Specified Alternative Station*
Charlwood	Kenley Airfield
Coleshill	Coventry
Fylingdales	Linton on Ouse
Kinloss	Lossiemouth
Linton on Ouse	Church Fenton
St. Athan	Mumbles
Shap	Keswick.

"

PART IV

UPDATING MATERIAL
VOLUME III

ADMINISTRATION, ADJUDICATION AND THE EUROPEAN DIMENSION

Administration, Adjudication and the European Dimension

p.27, *amendment to Administration Act 1992, s.2AA*

With effect from July 3, 2007, the Welfare Reform Act 2007, Sch.7(3) amends s.2AA(2) by substituting for para.(e) "(e) carer's allowance".　　4.001

p.37, *amendment to Social Security Administration Act 1992, s.7A and new s.7B*

With effect from October 1, 2007, the Welfare Reform Act 2007, s.41 amends s.7A to read as follows:　　4.002

[¹ **Sharing of functions as regards certain claims and information**

7A.—(1) Regulations may, for the purpose of supplementing the persons or bodies to whom claims for relevant benefits may be made, make provision—
  (a) as regards housing benefit or council tax benefit, for claims for that benefit to be made to—
    (i) a Minister of the Crown, or
    (ii) a person providing services to a Minister of the Crown;
  (b) as regards any other relevant benefit for claims for that benefit to be made to—
    (i) a local authority,
    (ii) a person providing services to a local authority, or
    (iii) a person authorised to exercise any function of a local authority relating to housing benefit or council tax benefit.
  [⁴ (c) as regards any relevant benefit, for claims for that benefit to be made to—
    (i) a county council in England,
    (ii) a person providing services to a county council in England, or
    (iii) a person authorised to exercise any function a county council in England has under this section.]
(2) Regulations may make provision for or in connection with—
  (a) the forwarding by a relevant authority of—
    (i) claims received by virtue of any provision authorised by subs.(1) above, and
    (ii) information or evidence supplied in connection with making such claims (whether supplied by persons making the claims or by other persons);
  (b) the receiving and forwarding by a relevant authority of information or evidence relating to social security [3 or work] matters supplied by, or the obtaining by a relevant authority of such information or evidence from—
    (i) persons making, or who have made, claims for a relevant benefit, or
    (ii) other persons in connection with such claims,

Administration, Adjudication and the European Dimension

including information or evidence not relating to the claim or benefit in question;
(c) the recording by a relevant authority of information or evidence relating to social security matters supplied to, or obtained by, the authority and the holding by the authority of such information or evidence (whether as supplied or obtained or recorded);
(d) the giving of information or advice with respect to social security matters by a relevant authority to persons making, or who have made, claims for a relevant benefit.
[4 (e) the verification by a relevant authority of information or evidence supplied to or obtained by the authority in connection with a claim for or an award of a relevant benefit.]
(3) In paragraphs (b) and [4 (d) and (e)] of subs.(2) above—
(a) references to claims for as relevant benefit are to such claims whether made as mentioned in subs.[4 (1)(a) (b) or (c)] above or not; and
(b) references to persons who have made such claims include persons to who awards of benefit have been made on the claims.
(4) Regulations under this section may make different provision for different areas.
(5) Regulations under any other enactment may make such different provision for different areas as appears to the Secretary of State expedient on connection with any exercise by regulations under this section of the power conferred by subs.(4) above.
(6) In this section—
(a) "benefit" includes child support or a war pension (any reference to a claim being read, in relation to child support, as a reference to an application [2 (or an application treated as having been made)] under the Child Support Act 1991 for a maintenance assessment [2 maintenance assessment]);
(b) "local authority" means an authority administering housing benefit or council tax benefit;
[4 (c) "relevant authority" means—
   (i) a Minister of the Crown;
   (ii) a local authority;
   (iii) a county council in England;
   (iv) a person providing services to a person mentioned in sub-paras (i) to (iii);
   (v) a person authorised to exercise any function of a local authority relating to housing benefit or council tax benefit;
   (vi) a person authorised to exercise any function a county council in England has under this section;]
(d) "relevant benefit" means housing benefit, council tax benefit or any other benefit prescribed for the purposes of this section;
[3 (e) "social security or work matters" means matters relating to—

Administration, Adjudication and the European Dimension

(i) social security, child support or war pensions, or

(ii) employment or training;]

and in this subsection "war pension" means a war pension within the meaning of s.25 of the Social Security Act 1989 (establishment and functions of war pensions committees).]

AMENDMENTS

1. Welfare Reform and Pensions Act 1999, s.71 (November 11, 1999).
2. Child Support, Pensions and Social Security Act 2000, s.26 and Sch.3, para.12 (March 3, 2003 for certain purposes only: see SI 2003/192).
3. Employment Act 2002, s.53 and Sch.7 (November 24, 2002).
4. Welfare Reform Act 2007, s.41 (July 3, 2007).

4.003

The same provision inserts a new s.7B with effect from October 1, 2007:

[¹ **7B Use of social security information**

(1) A relevant authority may use for a relevant purpose any social security information which it holds.

(2) Regulations may make provision as to the procedure to be followed by a relevant authority for the purposes of any function it has relating to the administration of a specified benefit if the authority holds social security information which—

(a) is relevant for the purposes of anything which may or must be done by the authority in connection with a claim for or an award of the benefit, and

(b) was used by another relevant authority in connection with a claim for or an award of a different specified benefit or was verified by that other authority in accordance with regulations under s.7A(2)(e) above.

(3) A relevant purpose is anything which is done in relation to a claim which is made or which could be made for a specified benefit if it is done for the purpose of—

(a) identifying persons who may be entitled to such a benefit;

(b) encouraging or assisting a person to make such a claim;

(c) advising a person in relation to such a claim.

(4) Social security information means—

(a) information relating to social security, child support or war pensions;

(b) evidence obtained in connection with a claim for or an award of a specified benefit.

(5) A specified benefit is a benefit which is specified in regulations for the purposes of this section.

(6) Expressions used in this section and in s.7A have the same meaning in this section as in that section.

Administration, Adjudication and the European Dimension

(7) This section does not affect any power which exists apart from this section to use for one purpose social security information obtained in connection with another purpose.]

Amendment

4.004   1. Welfare Reform Act 2007, s.41 (October 1, 2007).

p.50, *annotations to Administration Act 1992, s.71(1)*

4.005   In the discussion of the application of reg.14 of the Payments on Account etc Regulations at para.1.100, note that state pension credit needs to be added to the list of benefits to which reference is made.

p.50, *amendment of, and annotations to, Administration Act 1992, s.71*

4.006   With effect from July 3, 2007, the Welfare Reform Act 2007, s.44, amends s.71 so that subs.(5) ceases to have effect.

With effect from July 3, 2007, the Welfare Reform Act 2007, s.44, amends s.71(5A) to read as follows:

[⁴(5A) Except where regulations otherwise provide, an amount shall not be recoverable [under subs.(1) or under regulations under subs.(4)] above unless the determination in pursuance of which it was paid has been reversed or varied on an appeal or [² has been revised under s.9 or superseded under s.10 of the Social Security Act 1998]].

In *CIS/1960/2007,* the Commissioner ruled that income support and state pension credit are not inter-connected benefits, so that an appellant was not assisted by a disclosure of a relevant fact in connection with his claim for state pension credit whose non-disclosure in relation to his claim for income support resulted in an overpayment of income support.

The Secretary of State's appeal in the *Balding* case has been dismissed by the Court of Appeal: *Secretary of State for Work and Pensions v Balding,* [2007] EWCA Civ 1327.

p.88, *amendment to Administration Act 1992, s.71ZA(2)*

4.007   With effect from July 3, 2007, the Welfare Reform Act 2007, Sch.8 repeals the following words in s.71ZA(2): (a) in para.(a) the words "paragraph (a) of subsection (5) and"; and the whole of para.(b).

p.129, *amendment to Administration Act 1992, s.168*

4.008   With effect from July 3, 2007 the welfare Reform Act 2007, Sch.8 repeals the words in s.168(3)(d) from "to the same officer" to the end.

With effect from July 3, 2007, the Welfare Reform Act 2007, Sch.7(3) amends s.168 for the words "the amounts allocated to them" substitute the words "any amount allocated to them" and in subs.(6) for the words "payments from the social fund such as are mentioned in section 138(1)(b) of the Contributions and Benefits Act" substitute "section 138(1)(b) payments".

Administration, Adjudication and the European Dimension

p.161, *annotation to Social Security (Recovery of Benefits) Act 1997, s.1*

CCR/2658/2006 has been reported as *R(CR) 1/07*.   4.009

p.173, *annotation to Social Security (Recovery of Benefits) Act 1997, s.11(1)*

CCR/2658/2006 has been reported as *R(CR) 1/07*.   4.010

p.176, *annotation to Social Security (Recovery of Benefits) Act 1997, s.12(3)*

CCR/2658/2006 has been reported as *R(CR) 1/07*.   4.011

p.199, *annotation to Social Security Act 1998, s.6(3)*

CDLA/2379/2006 has been reported as *R(DLA) 3/07*.   4.012

pp.216–225, *annotation to Social Security Act 1998, s.12(2)*

    Questions of foreign law are treated as question of fact as to which   4.013
expert witnesses may give evidence. In the light of *Kerr v Department for Social Development* [2004] UKHL 23; [2004] 1 W.L.R. 1372 (also reported as an appendix to *R1/04(SF)*) (mentioned in the main work), it was held in *CIS/213/2004* that, where a question of French law arose when considering a claimant's possible interest in a property in France, it was reasonable to require the Secretary of State to obtain the necessary evidence of French law.

    Where a claimant suggests that a tribunal obtain evidence from a particular doctor and the tribunal does not do so, the claimant is entitled to be told that the tribunal will not obtain the evidence so that he can consider doing so (*CAF/1569/2007*, applying *R(M) 2/80*), although it may be sufficient that the Tribunals Service inform claimants in general terms that it is their responsibility to provide evidence themselves (see *CIB/5030/1998*, mentioned on p.260 of the main work).

    Approved disability analysts are doctors or other health care professionals who have received special training to make an assessment of the disabling effects of an impairment and relate this to the relevant legislation in order to provide advice or reports for those making decisions on behalf of the Secretary of State. Even where they have not examined a claimant, their opinions may be taken into account as evidence, provided the tribunal can identify the factual basis on which the opinion was given. It will usually also be necessary for the tribunal to know the professional qualification and areas of expertise of the analyst (*CDLA/2466/2007*).

    It is not a contempt of court to disclose to a tribunal information about proceedings before a court sitting in private unless the case comes within one of the categories specified in s.12(1)(a) to (d) of the Administration of Justice Act 1960 or the court has expressly prohibited publication of the information under s.12(1)(e) of that Act (*AF Noonan Ltd v*

Bournemouth and Boscombe AFC [2007] EWCA Civ 848; [2007] 1 W.L.R. 2614). Rule 10.21A(2) of the Family Proceedings Rules 1991 (SI 1991/1247), inserted by rr.21 of the Family Proceedings (Amendment) (No.2) Rules 2007 (SI 2007/2187), expressly permits information relating to ancillary relief proceedings held in private to be communicated to the Secretary of State, a McKenzie Friend or lay adviser or an appeal tribunal, but only for the purposes of child support appeals.

pp.239–246, annotation to Social Security Act 1998, s.14(1)

4.014   *Secretary of State for Work and Pensions v Morina* [2007] EWCA Civ 749 has now been reported at [2007] 1 W.L.R. 3033 and as *R(IS) 6/07*.

A tribunal may legitimately give assistance to the parties during a hearing by telling them what it thinks of the evidence it has heard so far, but it may not form, or give the impression of having formed, a firm view in favour of one side's credibility when the other side has not yet called its evidence on the relevant point. Where there is such a manifestation of bias, attention should be drawn to it straightaway, because a Commissioner may not look favourably on an allegation of bias if the dissatisfied party has taken his or her chance on the outcome of the case and found it unwelcome (*Amjad v Steadman-Byrne* [2007] EWCA Civ 625; [2007] 1 W.L.R. 2484).

Where a Commissioner has made a decision in the light of detailed medical evidence, tribunals are entitled to apply the Commissioner's approach to similar cases where such detailed evidence is not before them. Thus, Commissioners' decisions may have some precedential value on matters of fact. In *CDLA/2288/2007*, it has been held that such decisions are binding, unless they can be distinguished or have been overtaken by later medical research which at least casts significant doubt on its accuracy. In that case, a tribunal had found that arrested development or incomplete development of the brain had not occurred in a claimant with autism, contrary to the finding made in *CDLA/1678/1997*.

A senior immigration judge in the asylum and immigration tribunal is of the same seniority as a Social Security Commissioner and that tribunal has a system of reconsiderations in place of appeals. Accordingly, a Commissioner will give the same weight to a decision on a point of law given on reconsideration by an asylum and immigration tribunal presided over by a senior immigration judge as he or she would give to a decision of a Commissioner (*CIS/1794/2007*).

In *Howard de Walden Estates Ltd v Aggio* [2007] EWCA Civ 499; [2007] 3 W.L.R. 542, the Court of Appeal has held that the relationship between the Chancery Division of the High Court and a county court is the relationship of superior court to inferior court and that a county court is always bound to follow a decision of the High Court, even when the High Court is exercising the same first instance jurisdiction. This may cast some doubt on the approach taken in *R(IS) 15/99, R(SB) 52/83* and *R(AF) 1/07* (mentioned in the main work), but *Chief Supplementary*

Administration, Adjudication and the European Dimension

Benefit Officer v Leary [1985] 1 W.L.R. 84 (also reported as an appendix to *R(SB) 6/85*), another decision of the Court of Appeal, was not cited to the Court in *Howard de Walden Estates Ltd v Aggio*. It may be that a distinction must be drawn between cases where a jurisdiction of the High Court has subsequently been conferred on Commissioners and other cases and that *R(IS) 15/99* was wrongly decided on this point but *R(SB) 52/83* and *R(AF) 1/07* were not.

pp.254–255, *annotation to Social Security Act 1998, s.16(1)–(3)*

CIS/1363/2005 was reversed by the Court of Appeal in *Secretary of State for Work and Pensions v Morina* [2007] EWCA Civ 749; [2007] 1 W.L.R. 3033 (also reported as *R(IS) 6/07*). The Court agreed with the Commissioner that a decision of a legally qualified panel member must be treated as a decision of a tribunal but held that there was nonetheless no right of appeal.

4.015

p.258, *Social Security Act 1998, s.19*

In both subs.(1) and subs.(2)(b), "medical practitioner" is replaced by "health care professional approved by the Secretary of State" with effect from July 3, 2007 (s.62(1) and (2) of the Welfare Reform Act 2007). References in the annotation to medical practitioners must be read accordingly. Even where health care professionals have not examined a claimant, their opinions may be taken into account as evidence, provided the tribunal can identify the factual basis on which the opinion was given. It will usually also be necessary for the tribunal to know the professional qualification and areas of expertise of the person providing the opinion (*CDLA/2466/2007*). The term "health care professional" is defined in s.39 (see below).

4.016

pp.259–260, *Social Security Act 1998, s.20*

By s.62(1) and (3) of the Welfare Reform Act 2007, the term "medical practitioner" in subs.(2) is replaced by "health care professional approved by the Secretary of State". By s.62(1) and (4) of the 2007 Act, a new subs.(2A) is added—

4.017

"(2A) The power under subsection (2) to refer a person to a healthcare professional approved by the Secretary of State includes power to specify the description of health care professional to whom the person is to be referred."

These amendments came into force on July 3, 2007. The term "health care professional" is defined in s.39 (see below).

p.278, *Social Security Act 1998, s.39(1)*

By s.62(1) and (5) of the Welfare Reform Act 2007, there is inserted after the definition of Commissioner, with effect from July 3, 2007—

4.018

" 'health care professional' means—

Administration, Adjudication and the European Dimension

    (a) a registered medical practitioner,
    (b) a registered nurse,
    (c) an occupational therapist or physiotherapist registered with a regulatory body established by an Order in Council under section 60 of the Health Care Act 1999, or
    (d) a member of such other profession regulated by a body mentioned in section 25(3) of the National Health Service Reform and Health Care Professions Act 2002 as the Secretary of State may prescribe;".

p.290, *annotation to Social Security Act 1998, Sch.3, paras 10–19*

4.019   Further criticism of the handling of credits cases has been voiced in CIB/1620/2006. In particular, the Commissioner criticised instructions to staff causing them to make undisclosed assumptions about contributions and credits issues instead of issuing decisions in respect of such issues informing claimants of their rights of appeal.

p.362, *amendment to Claims and Payments Regulations 1987, reg.2*

4.020   With effect from July 3, 2007, The Social Security (Miscellaneous Amendments) (No.2) Regulations 2007 (SI 2007/1626) amends reg.2 by inserting the following new definition after the definition of "claim for benefit":

" 'health care professional' means—

    (a) a registered medical practitioner,
    (b) a registered nurse,
    (c) an occupational therapist or physiotherapist registered with a regulatory body established by an Order in Council under section 60 of the Health Care Act 1999, or
    (d) a member of such other profession, regulated by a body mentioned in section 25(3) of the National Health Service Reform and Health Care Professions Act 2002 prescribed by the Secretary of State in accordance with powers under section 39(1) of the Social Security Act 1998."

p.366, *amendment to Claims and Payments Regs 1987, reg.3*

4.021   With effect from September 24, 2007 The Social Security (Miscellaneous Amendments) (No.4) Regulations 2007 (SI 2007/2470) amends reg.3 as follows:
After sub-para.(c) insert—
"(ca) in the case of a Category A retirement pension where the beneficiary—
    (i) is entitled to any category of retirement pension other than a Category A retirement pension; and(ii) becomes divorced or the beneficiary's civil partnership is dissolved;
(cb) in the case of a Category B retirement pension where the beneficiary—

(i) is entitled to either a Category A retirement pension or to a graduated retirement benefit or to both; and(ii) marries or enters into a civil partnership;";

After sub-para.(d) insert—

"(da) in the case of a bereavement payment where the beneficiary is over pensionable age and satisfies the conditions of entitlement under section 36(1) of the Contributions and Benefits Act;".

p.367, *amendments to Claims and Payments Regs 1987, reg.4*

With effect from October 31, 2007 The Social Security (Claims and Information) Regulations 2007 (SI 2007/2911) amend reg.4 as follows:

4.022

In para.(6A)—
(i) for "Paragraphs (6B) and (6C) apply in relation to a person" substitute "This paragraph applies to a person";(ii) for sub-paragraphs (c) and (d) substitute—
"(c) who makes a claim for income support; or
(d) who has not attained the qualifying age and who makes a claim for a carer's allowance, disability living allowance or incapacity benefit."; and

In para.(6B), for sub-para.(b) substitute—

"(b) the offices of—
(i) a local authority administering housing benefit or council tax benefit,
(ii) a county council in England,
(iii) a person providing services to a person mentioned in head (i) or (ii),
(iv) a person authorised to exercise any function of a local authority relating to housing benefit or council tax benefit, or
(v) a person authorised to exercise any function a county council in England has under section 7A of the Social Security Administration Act 1992,
if the Secretary of State has arranged with the local authority, county council or other person for them to receive claims in accordance with this sub-paragraph,"; and

In para.(6C), after sub-para.(c) insert—

"(cc) may verify any non-medical information or evidence supplied or obtained in accordance with sub-paragraph (b) or (c) and shall forward it to the Secretary of State as soon as reasonably practicable;".

p.381, *amendment to Claims and Payments Regs 1987, reg.4D*

With effect from October 31, 2007 The Social Security (Claims and Information) Regulations 2007 (SI 2007/2911) amend reg.4D as follows:

4.023

Administration, Adjudication and the European Dimension

For para.(4) substitute—

"(4) A claim made in writing may also be made at the offices of—
  (a) a local authority administering housing benefit or council tax benefit;
  (b) a county council in England;
  (c) a person providing services to a person mentioned in sub-paragraph (a) or (b);
  (d) a person authorised to exercise any functions of a local authority relating to housing benefit or council tax benefit; or
  (e) a person authorised to exercise any function a county council in England has under section 7A of the Social Security Administration Act 1992,
if the Secretary of State has arranged with the local authority, county council or other person for them to receive claims in accordance with this paragraph."

In para.(5), after sub-para.(c) insert—

"(cc) may verify any non-medical information or evidence supplied or obtained in accordance with sub-paragraph (b) or (c) and shall forward it to the Secretary of State as soon as reasonably practicable;".

p.386, *amendments and annotations to Claims and Payments Regs 1987, reg.6*

4.024   With effect from September 24, 2007 The Social Security (Miscellaneous Amendments) (No.4) Regulations 2007 (SI 2007/2470) amends reg.6 as follows:

After reg.6(15) insert—

"(15A) Paragraphs (16) to (34) shall not apply in any case where it would be advantageous to the claimant to apply the provisions of regulation 19 (time for claiming benefit.".

In reg.6(19) (date of claim) for the words from "original award") to "the circumstances", substitute "original award") has been terminated or reduced or payment under that award ceases in the circumstances and in sub-paragraph (b) for "re-awarded," substitute "re-awarded or becomes payable again".

In reg.6(20)—
(a) after sub-para.(a) omit "or";
(b) at the end of sub-para.(b) add "or"; and
(c) after sub-para.(b) add—
    "(c) that the qualifying benefit has ceased to be payable in accordance with—
        (i) regulation 6(1) of the Social Security (Attendance Allowance) Regulations 1991 or regulation 8(1) of the Social Security (Disability Living Allowance) Regulations 1991 because the claimant is undergoing treatment as an in-patient in a hospital or similar institution, or

Administration, Adjudication and the European Dimension

(ii) regulation 7 of the Social Security (Attendance Allowance) Regulations 1991 or regulation 9 of the Social Security (Disability Living Allowance) Regulations 1991 because the claimant is resident in certain accommodation other than a hospital.".

In reg.6(21)—

(a) for "The additional" substitute "Subject to paragraph (21A), the additional" and in sub-para.(a), for "and" substitute "or"; and
(b) for sub-para.(b) substitute—

"(b) the qualifying benefit is re-awarded following revision, supersession or appeal; or
(c) the qualifying benefit is re-awarded on a renewal claim when an award for a fixed period expires; or
(d) the cessation of payment ends when the claimant leaves the hospital or similar institution or accommodation referred to in paragraph (20)(c); and
the further claim referred to in paragraph (19), is made within three months of the date on which the additional circumstances apply.".

After reg.6(21), insert—

"(21A) Paragraph (21) applies whether the benefit is re-awarded when the further claim is decided or following a revision of, or an appeal against, such a decision.".

In reg.6(30)(b) omit "not later than 10 working days after the termination,".
In reg.6(33), for "Where" substitute "Subject to paragraph (34), where".
After reg.6(33) add—

"(34) Paragraph (33) shall not apply where the decision awarding a qualifying benefit is made in respect of a renewal claim where a fixed period award of that benefit has expired, or is due to expire.".

With effect from October 31, 2007 The Social Security (Claims and Information) Regulations 2007 (SI 2007/2911) amend reg.6(1E) by omitting "who has attained the qualifying age".
In *CG/4060/2005* the Commissioner decides that reg.6(4AB) applies only to claim for a jobseeker's allowance, and so was of no assistance to persons claiming carer's allowance.

p.400, *annotations to Claims and Payments Regs 1987, reg.7*

CIS/51/2007 involved what had been a difficult case for the tribunal, 4.025
since they had been obliged for want of proper documentation from the Secretary of State to reconstruct the history of a claim and its refusal. It appears that the claimant's claim for income support had been refused

for his failure to provide satisfactory evidence of his identity and his address. The Commissioner observed:

> "7. . . . it seems to me that [the appellant's representative] was entirely right in defining the scope and subject matter of the appeal as he did at the start of his written submissions to the tribunal . . . ":
>
> "This appeal is about whether or not the appellant satisfied the evidence requirements."

What was thus challenged in the appeal was the correctness of the two decisions whose effect was that he got no award of benefit because those requirements were not considered to be satisfied on either claim.

8. As a matter of language it seems to me indifferent whether one expresses that by saying he had not shown he had a "valid claim" to each benefit being sought, or that his claims failed to show he qualified for entitlement and so they were disallowed. For all practical purposes it comes to the same thing. This is however an area where it is well to be careful of the language one uses, because it is easy enough to muddle up: (a) the requirements for making a *claim* under the regulations (which are purely a matter of form and procedure); and (b) the obvious and universal necessity for any person making such a claim to substantiate it by showing he meets the qualifying conditions for entitlement (which is a matter of fact and evidence). To complete the prescribed form giving a name, address and national insurance number complies with (a); to show that the name, address and number given are genuinely those of the person submitting the claim form is within (b). Rather than speaking of a "valid claim" I therefore prefer the formulation adopted by the tribunal chairman in the opening paragraph of her statement of reasons, when she recorded that the claimant appealed against two decisions made by the Secretary of State on March 29 and 31, 2006 "that he was not entitled" to income support and incapacity benefit from January 6 2006. That was in my judgment a correct assessment of the substance and effect of the decisions given, even if not of their actual terms.

9. . . .

10. [The evidence requirements] are to be found in reg.7 of the Social Security (Claims and Payments) Regulations 1987 SI No.1968, under the heading "Evidence and Information":

> . . .

At the risk of stating the blindingly obvious, this is a provision that applies in relation to *claims* once they have been made in a procedurally effective manner so that they have got to be processed: it enables the Secretary of State to require any additional or confirmatory information or evidence to ensure that they are processed properly, so that claimants are awarded the benefit to which they are shown to be entitled, and not awarded benefits to which they are not.

11. The provisions of reg.7(1) thus apply only to persons who have made something that can be identified as a procedurally effective *claim*. They are separate and distinct from the provisions earlier in the same regulations that define what amounts to such a claim, and set out the procedural requirements for making claims if they are to be recognised as such and require the claims adjudication process to be put in motion

Administration, Adjudication and the European Dimension

at all. Particularly in relation to income support and jobseeker's allowance those earlier provisions, now in regs 4 to 6A, have been greatly encumbered and complicated with a plethora of additional provisions attempting to circumscribe and define more closely what is and is not to be accepted as amounting to a "claim" for benefit for this purpose, and the date on which such a claim is treated as effectively made. It is important to bear in mind that those earlier provisions are not concerned with the confirmation or correctness of the information entered by a claimant on his claim form or otherwise supplied by him as part of his claim: only with the question of whether the claim is procedurally an effective one at all, so as to require that information to be looked at and the substance of the claim to entitlement evaluated. For these reasons it seems to me better nowadays to avoid expressions such as "valid" or "invalid" in relation to claims unless one also makes very clear whether this refers to procedural effectiveness, in the sense of something requiring the adjudication process to be started, or substantive validity in the sense of a claim on which the qualifying conditions for an actual award of benefit are shown to be met."

p.408, *amendment to Claims and Payments Regs 1987, reg.13*

With effect from May 23, 2007, reg.13 is amended by The Social Security, Housing Benefit and Council Tax benefit (Miscellaneous Amendments) Regulations 2007 (SI 2007/1331) as follows: 4.026

Advance claims and awards

13.—(1) Where, although a person does not satisfy the requirements for entitlement to a benefit on the date on which the claim is made, the [6 Secretary of State] is of the opinion that unless there is a change of circumstances he will satisfy those requirements for a period beginning on a day ("the relevant day") not more than three months after the date on which the claim is made, then [6 Secretary of State] may—   4.027
  (a) treat the claim as if made for a period beginning with the relevant day; and
  (b) award benefit accordingly, subject to the condition that the person satisfies the requirements for entitlement when benefit becomes payable under the award.
  (2) [6 A decision pursuant to para.(1)(b) to award benefit may be revised under s.9 of the Social Security Act 1998] if the requirements for entitlement are found not to have been satisfied on the relevant day.
  (3) [5 [10 . . .] paras (1) and (2) do not] apply to any claim for maternity allowance, attendance allowance [10 . . .], [8 state pension credit] retirement pension or increase, [9 a shared additional pension] [10 . . .] [2 disability living allowance], or any claim within reg.11(1)(a) or (b).
  [10 . . .]
  [10; Paragraphs (1) and (2) do not apply to—

Administration, Adjudication and the European Dimension

(a) a claim for income support made by a person from abroad as defined in reg.21AA of the Income Support (General) Regulations 1987 (special cases: supplemental—persons from abroad) or;
(b) a claim for a jobseeker's allowance made by a person from abroad as defined in regs 85A of the Jobseeker's Allowance Regulations (special cases: supplemental—persons from abroad).]

AMENDMENTS

4.028
1. The Social Security (Miscellaneous Provisions) Amendment Regulations 1991 (SI 1991/2284), reg.7 (November 1, 1991).
2. The Social Security (Claims and Payments) Amendment Regulations 1991 (SI 1991/2741) (SI 1991/2741), reg.6(a) (February 3, 1992).
3. The Social Security (Miscellaneous Provisions) Amendment Regulations 1992 (SI 1992/247), reg.13 (March 9, 1992).
4. The Social Security (Claims and Payments) Amendment Regulations 1991 (SI 1991/2741), reg.6(b) (March 10, 1992).
5. The Social Security (Claims and Payments) Amendment Regulations 1994 (SI 1994/2319), reg.3 (October 3, 1994).
6. The Social Security Act 1998 (Commencement No.9, and Savings and Consequential and Transitional Provisions) Order 1999 (SI 1999/2422), Sch.7 (September 6, 1999).
7. The Tax Credits (Claims and Payments) (Amendment) Regulations 1999 (SI 1999/2572), reg.7 (October 5, 1999).
8. State Pension Credit (Consequential, Transitional and Miscellaneous) Regulations 2002 (SI 2002/3019), reg.6 (April 7, 2003).
9. The Social Security (Shared Additional Pension) (Miscellaneous Amendments) Regulations 2005 (SI 2005/1551) (July 6, 2005).
10. The Social Security, Housing Benefit and Council Tax benefit (Miscellaneous Amendments) Regulations 2007 (SI 2007/1331) (May 23, 2007)

GENERAL NOTE

4.029
These amendments reverse the effect of the Court of Appeal's decision in *Bhakta* which ruled that the Secretary of State could not automatically exclude a claim from being treated as made in advance where the claimant might at some future date meet the habitual residence test.

p.413, *amendment to Claims and Payments Regs 1987, reg.13D*

4.030
With effect from May 23, 2007 The Social Security, Housing Benefit and Council Tax benefit (Miscellaneous Amendments) Regulations 2007 (SI 2007/1331) amend reg.13D by inserting a new para.(4) after para.(3) as follows:

"(4) This regulation does not apply to a claim made by a person not in Great Britain as defined in regulation 2 of the State Pension Credit Regulations (persons not in Great Britain)."

Administration, Adjudication and the European Dimension

p.420, *amendment to Claims and Payments Regs 1987, reg.19*

With effect from September 24, 2007 The Social Security (Miscellaneous Amendments) (No.4) Regulations 2007 (SI 2007/2470) amends reg.19 as follows:
After para.(3B) insert—

"(3C) In any case where the application of paragraphs (16) to (34) of regulation 6 would be advantageous to the claimant, this regulation shall apply subject to those provisions.".

4.031

p.440, *amendment to Claims and Payments Regs 1987, reg.26*

With effect from July 3, 2007, The Social Security (Miscellaneous Amendments) (No.2) Regulations 2007 (SI 2007/1626) amends reg.26(1)(a) by substituting for the words "medical practitioner" the words "health care professional approved by the Secretary of State".

4.032

p.443, *amendments to Claims and Payments Regs 1987, reg.30*

With effect from September 24, 2007 The Social Security (Miscellaneous Amendments) (No.4) Regulations 2007 (SI 2007/2470) amends reg.30 as follows:
In reg.30(4) (payments on death), for "Paragraphs" substitute "Subject to paragraph (4B), paragraphs".
After reg.30(4A) insert—

4.033

"(4B) A written application is not required where—
(a) an executor or administrator has not been appointed;
(b) the deceased was in receipt of a retirement pension of any category or state pension credit including where any other benefit was combined for payment purposes with either of those benefits at the time of death;
(c) the sum payable by way of benefit to the deceased is payable to a person who was the spouse or civil partner of the deceased at the time of death; and
(d) either—
   (i) the spouse or civil partner and the deceased were living together at the time of death; or
   (ii) they would have been living together at the time of death but for the fact that either or both of them were in a residential care or a nursing home or in a hospital.".

p.453, *amendment to Claims and Payments Regs 1987, reg.32B*

With effect from October 31, 2007 The Social Security (Claims and Information) Regulations 2007 (SI 2007/2911) add a new reg.32B after reg.32B as follows:

4.034

"Information relating to awards of benefit

32B.—(1) Where an authority or person to whom paragraph (2) applies has arranged with the Secretary of State for the authority or

person to receive claims for a specified benefit or obtain information or evidence relating to claims for a specified benefit in accordance with regulation 4 or 4D, the authority or person may—
(a) receive information or evidence which relates to an award of that benefit and which is supplied by—
  (i) the person to whom the award has been made; or
  (ii) other persons in connection with the award,
  and shall forward it to the Secretary of State as soon as reasonably practicable;
(b) verify any information or evidence supplied; and
(c) record the information or evidence supplied and hold it (whether as supplied or recorded) for the purpose of forwarding it to the Secretary of State.
(2) This paragraph applies to—
(a) a local authority administering housing benefit or council tax benefit;
(b) a county council in England;
(c) a person providing services to a person mentioned in sub-paragraph (a) or (b);
(d) a person authorised to exercise any function of a local authority relating to housing benefit or council tax benefit;
(e) a person authorised to exercise any function a county council in England has under section 7A of the Social Security Administration Act 1992.
(3) In paragraph (1), 'specified benefit' means one or more of the following benefits—
(a) attendance allowance;
(b) bereavement allowance;
(c) bereavement payment;
(d) carer's allowance;
(e) disability living allowance;
(f) incapacity benefit;
(g) income support;
(h) jobseeker's allowance;
(i) retirement pension;
(j) state pension credit;
(k) widowed parent's allowance;
(l) winter fuel payment."

p.454, *amendment to Claims and Payments Regs 1987, reg.33*

4.035 With effect from September 24, 2007 The Social Security (Miscellaneous Amendments) (No.4) Regulations 2007 (SI 2007/2470) amends reg.33 as follows:

"In regulation 33(1)(c) (persons unable to act) for 'receiver' substitute 'deputy' and after 'Court of Protection' insert 'under Part 1 of the Mental Capacity Act 2005 or receiver appointed under Part 7 of the Mental Health Act 1983 but treated as a deputy by virtue of the Mental Capacity Act 2005' ".

Administration, Adjudication and the European Dimension

p.480, *amendment to Claims and Payments Regs 1987, Sch.9*

With effect from July 31, 2007 The Social Security (Claims and Payments) Amendment (No.2) Regulations 2007 (SI 2007/1866) make a number of amendments to Sch.9 as follows:
In para.1(1) (interpretation) after the definition of "the Income Support Regulations" insert—

4.036

" 'integration loan which is recoverable by deductions' means an integration loan which is made under the Integration Loans for Refugees and Others Regulations 2007 and which is recoverable from the recipient by deductions from a specified benefit under regulation 9 of those Regulations".

After para.7C insert—

"Integration loans

7D. Subject to paragraphs 2(2), 8 and 9, where a person has an integration loan which is recoverable by deductions, any weekly amount payable shall be equal to 5 per cent. of the personal allowance of a single claimant aged not less than 25 years, including where the loan is a joint loan.".

In para.8 (maximum amount of payments to third parties)—
  (i) in sub-para.(1) after "Fines Regulations" insert ", and in respect of an integration loan which is recoverable by deductions"; and
  (ii) in sub-para.(2) for "and 7" substitute ",7 and 7D";
In para.9 (priority as between certain debts)—
  (i) in sub-para.(1A)(b), for "and regulation 5 of the Council Tax Regulations" substitute ", regulation 5 of the Council Tax Regulations and regulation 9 of the Integration Loans for Refugees and Others Regulations 2007"; and
  (ii) after sub-para.(1B)(g) insert—
    "(ga) any liability to repay an integration loan which is recoverable by deductions.".

p.492, *amendment to Claims and Payments Regs 1987, Sch.9A*

With effect from December 17, 2007, The Social Security (Housing Costs and Miscellaneous Amendments) Regulations 2007 (SI 2007/3183) amend Sch.9A as follows:
In para.2A(4) (specified circumstances for the purposes of reg.34B) of Sch.9A (deductions of mortgage interest from benefit and payment to qualifying lenders), for "19" substitute "20".

4.037

p.547, *annotation to Decisions and Appeals Regulations, reg.1(3)*

CAF/857/2006 has been reported as *R(AF) 5/07. Secretary of State for Work and Pensions v Morina* [2007] EWCA Civ 749 has now been reported at [2007] 1 W.L.R. 3033 and as *R(IS) 6/07*.

4.038

Administration, Adjudication and the European Dimension

pp.550–560, *Decisions and Appeals Regulations, reg.3*

4.039   Regulation 3(5) is amended and new paras (5ZA) to (5ZC) are added immediately afterwards. These provisions now read as follows—

"(5) A decision of the Secretary of State under section 8 or 10—
(a) [² except where paragraph (5ZA) applies] which arose from an official error; or
(b) [¹ except in a case to which sub-paragraph (c) or (d) applies,] where the decision was made in ignorance of, or was based upon a mistake as to, some material fact and as a result of that ignorance of or mistake as to that fact, the decision was more advantageous to the claimant than it would otherwise have been but for that ignorance or mistake,
(c) [¹ subject to subparagraph (d),] where the decision is a disability benefit decision, or is an incapacity benefit decision where there has been an incapacity determination (whether before or after the decision), which was made in ignorance of, or was based upon a mistake as to, some material fact in relation to a disability determination embodies in or necessary to the disability benefit decision, or the incapacity determination, and—
  (i) as a result of that ignorance or mistake as to that fact the decision was more advantageous to the claimant than it would otherwise have been but for that ignorance or mistake and,
  (ii) the Secretary of State is satisfied that at the time the decision was made the claimant or payee knew or could reasonably have been expected to know of the fact in question and that it was relevant to the decision,
[¹(d) where the decision is a disability benefit decision, or is an incapacity benefit decision, which was made in ignorance of, or was based upon a mistake as to, some material fact not in relation to the incapacity or disability determination embodied in or necessary to the incapacity benefit decision or disability benefit decision, and as a result of that ignorance of, or mistake as to that fact, the decision was more advantageous to the claimant than it would otherwise have been but for the ignorance or mistake,]
may be revised at any time by the Secretary of State.
[² (5ZA) This paragraph applies where—
(a) the decision which would otherwise fall to be revised is a decision to award a benefit specified in paragraph (5ZB), whether or not the award has already been put in payment;
(b) that award was based on the satisfaction by a person of the contribution conditions, in whole or in part, by virtue of credits of earnings for incapacity for work or approved training in the tax years from 1993–94 to 2007–08;
(c) the official error derives from the failure to transpose correctly information relating to those credits from the Department for Work and Pensions' Pension Strategy Computer System to Her

Majesty's Revenue and Customs' computer system (NIRS2) or from related clerical procedures; and

(d) that error has resulted in an award to the claimant which is more advantageous to him than if the error had not been made.

(5ZB) The specified benefits are—
(a) bereavement allowance;
(b) contribution-based jobseeker's allowance;
(c) incapacity benefit;
(d) retirement pension;
(e) widowed mother's allowance;
(f) widowed parent's allowance; and
(g) widow's pension.

(5ZC) In paragraph (5ZA)(b), "tax year" has the meaning ascribed to it by section 122(1) of the Contributions and Benefits Act.]".

AMENDMENTS

1. Social Security (Miscellaneous Amendments) (No.4) Regulations 2007 (SI 2007/2470), reg.3(2) to (4) (September 24, 2007).
2. Social Security (National Insurance Credits) Amendment Regulations 2007 (SI 2007/2582), reg.3 (October 1, 2007).

4.040

The amendment to para.(5)(a) and the insertion of paras (5ZA) to (5ZC) make it unnecessary to revise decisions awarding the benefits listed in para.(5ZB) made as a result of errors in claimants' favour in transposing information on the Department for Work and Pensions' computer system to Her Majesty's Revenue and Customs computer system. The claimants will continue to receive the benefits.

The explanation for the insertion of the new para.(5)(d) is more complicated. As observed in the annotation in the main work, the legislation would be a lot simpler if ignorance and mistake of material facts were in all cases grounds for supersession under reg.6, rather than revision, and the circumstances in which supersession on those grounds were effective from the same date as the superseded decision were set out in reg.7. Indeed, where the decision being replaced is a decision of a tribunal or Commissioner, that is the position (see regs 6(2)(c)(i) and 7(5)). However, where the decision being replaced is a decision of the Secretary of State, ignorance and mistake of material facts are grounds for supersession under reg.6(2)(b) except where they are grounds for revision (see reg.6(3)). The general rule is that revision (and therefore backdating) applies where the need to make a new decision is due to official error or where the original decision was advantageous to a claimant (see sub-paras (a) and (b)). The point of making revision (and therefore backdating by virtue of s.9(3) of the Social Security Act 1998) necessary in the latter case is so that there is an overpayment that may be recovered under s.71 of the Social Security Administration Act 1992 if it was due to misrepresentation or a failure to disclose a material fact. However, in order to avoid the necessity of considering whether an overpayment should be recovered in most incapacity benefit and disability benefit cases, ignorance and mistake are not made grounds for

Administration, Adjudication and the European Dimension

revision in cases where the ignorance or mistake relates to the extent of the claimant's incapacity or disability, save where the "claimant or payee knew or could reasonably have been expected to know of the fact in question and that it was relevant to the decision" (sub-paras (c) and (d)). That is similar to the test in s.71 of the 1992 Act (*R(A) 2/06*), but the Secretary of State has to deal with the issue when making the entitlement decision and cannot only return to it later. It is the new sub-para.(d) that makes it plain that, where the ignorance or mistake relates to an issue other than the extent of the claimant's incapacity or disability, the general rule applies.

A new para.(5B) is inserted by reg.3(5) of the Social Security (Miscellaneous Amendments) (No.4) Regulations 2007 (SI 2007/2470) with effect from September 24, 2007. It provides—

> "(5B) A decision by the Secretary of State under section 8 or 10 awarding incapacity benefit may be revised at any time if—
> (a) it incorporates a determination that the condition in regulation 28(2)(b) of the Social Security (Incapacity for Work) (General) Regulations 1995 (conditions for treating a person as incapable of work until the personal capability assessment is carried out) is satisfied;
> (b) the condition referred to in sub-paragraph (a) was not satisfied at the time when the further claim was first determined; and
> (c) there is a period before the award which falls to be decided."

Regulation 28 of the 1995 Regulations provides that a person is to be deemed to satisfy the personal capability assessment before the assessment is carried out if a medical certificate is provided and he or she has not failed a personal capability assessment in the last six months (subject to certain exceptions). In *R(IB) 1/01*, it was held that, where those conditions are not satisfied, the claimant is still entitled to benefit in respect of the claim if he or she subsequently passes the personal capability assessment and, in *R(IB) 8/04*, it was held that a new claim is not necessary once the six months have elapsed. The new para.(5B) enables the Secretary of State to revise a decision awarding benefit from a date later than the date of claim (presumably because the claimant had failed a personal capability assessment less than six months before the date of claim but six months before the date from which the award was made) if the claimant subsequently satisfies the personal capability assessment.

p.568, *annotation to Decisions and Appeals Regulations, reg.6(1)*

4.041   *C8/06–07(IB)* has been reported as *R1/07(IB)*.

p.576, *Decisions and Appeals Regulations, reg.7(2)*

4.042   With effect from September 24, 2007, the words "subject to sub-para.(bd)," are inserted at the beginning of reg.7(2)(bc) and a new sub-para.(bd) is added (reg.3(6) and (7) of the Social Security (Miscellaneous Amendments) (No.4) Regulations 2007 (SI 2007/2470)). Sub-paragraph (bd) provides—

"(bd) sub-paragraph (bc) shall only apply to the disabled person whose benefit is affected by the cessation of payment of carer's allowance;".

p.588, *Decisions and Appeals Regulations, reg.7A(1)*

With effect from September 24, 2007, there are added at the end of the definition of "incapacity benefit decision" the words "or an award of long term incapacity benefit under regulation 17(1) (transitional awards of long-term incapacity benefit) of the Social Security (Incapacity Benefit) (Transitional) Regulations 1995" (reg.3(8) of the Social Security (Miscellaneous Amendments) (No.4) Regulations 2007 (SI 2007/2470)). This fills the lacuna revealed in *Hooper v Secretary of State for Work and Pensions* [2007] EWCA Civ 495 (reported as *R(IB) 4/07*).

4.043

p.594, *Decisions and Appeals Regulations, reg.12*

Amendments are made to reg.12 by reg.4(2) of the Social Security (Miscellaneous Amendments) (No.2) Regulations 2007 (SI 2007/1626) with effect from July 3, 2007. In para.(2), "health care professional approved by the Secretary of State" is substituted for "medical practitioner" and, in para.(3)(b), for the first occurrence of "medical practitioner" there is substituted "health care professional" and for the second occurrence of "medical practitioner" there is substituted "health care professional approved by the Secretary of State". Approved health care professionals receive special training to make an assessment of the disabling effects of an impairment and relate this to the relevant legislation in order to provide advice or reports for those making decisions on behalf of the Secretary of State. Even where a health care professional has not examined a claimant, his or her opinion may be taken into account as evidence, provided the tribunal can identify the factual basis on which the opinion was given. It will usually also be necessary for the tribunal to know his or her professional qualification and area of expertise (*CDLA/2466/2007*). The term "health care professional" is defined in s.39 of the Social Security Act 1998 (see above).

4.044

p.602, *annotation to Decisions and Appeals Regulations, reg.18*

A decision that entitlement has ceased under reg.19(3) will usually be a supersession decision against which an appeal lies (*R(H) 4/08*). A refusal to allow a home visit is not, in itself, a refusal to provide information and there can usually be no termination if the claimant has not been given a deadline by which the information must be provided (*CH/2995/2006*).

4.045

p.602, *Decisions and Appeals Regulations, reg.19(1)*

With effect from July 3, 2007, "health care professional approved by the Secretary of State" is substituted for "medical practitioner" (reg.4(3)

4.046

Administration, Adjudication and the European Dimension

of the Social Security (Miscellaneous Amendments) (No.2) Regulations 2007 (SI 2007/1626)). The term "health care professional" is defined in s.39 of the Social Security Act 1998 (see above).

p.603, *annotation to Decisions and Appeals Regulations, reg.19*

4.047 A decision that entitlement has ceased under reg.19(3) will usually be a supersession decision against which an appeal lies (*R(H) 4/08* and see also para.22 of *CH/2995/2006*).

p.616, *annotation to Decisions and Appeals Regulations, reg.32(1)*

4.048 *Secretary of State for Work and Pensions v Morina* [2007] EWCA Civ 749 has now been reported at [2007] 1 W.L.R. 3033 and as *R(IS) 6/07*.

pp.628–629, *annotation to Decisions and Appeals Regulations, reg.39*

4.049 Where a claimant asks for a paper hearing and asks for it not to take place until a certain date because further evidence will be provided, the tribunal must either wait until that date or inform the claimant that it will not do so (*CDLA/792/2006*). It will seldom be appropriate not to wait for evidence unless the time requested is unreasonably long or there has been previous delay on the part of the claimant.

p.635, *annotation to Decisions and Appeals Regulations, reg.46*

4.050 *Secretary of State for Work and Pensions v Morina* [2007] EWCA Civ 749 has now been reported at [2007] 1 W.L.R. 3033 and as *R(IS) 6/07*.

p.644, *annotation to Decisions and Appeals Regulations, reg.51*

4.051 The appeal against *CIS/1216/2005* (mentioned in the main work) has been dismissed (*Mote v Secretary of State for Work and Pensions* [2007] EWCA Civ 1324).

p.645, *annotation to Decisions and Appeals Regulations, reg.52*

4.052 Where a tribunal has the power to examine a claimant it need not do so if it considers that an examination is unnecessary. It is not always necessary to carry out a physical clinical examination in order to assess functional loss. It may be better in some cases simply to question the claimant about the practical effects of an injury. However, if it is not minded to conduct a physical examination, it is good practice for the tribunal to state as much during the course of the hearing so that the claimant has an opportunity to make representations on the point (*R(I) 10/62, CI/3384/2006*). Whether a failure to do so renders a decision liable to be set aside on appeal is likely to depend on the circumstances and, in particular, whether the claimant can show that an examination might have led to a different outcome.

pp.661–662, *annotation to Decisions and Appeals Regulations, reg.57(1)*

Where there has been a breach of natural justice that does not fall within the narrow scope of reg.57 and an application under para.(1) has been rejected for that reason, the legally qualified panel member should consider setting the decision aside under s.13 of the Social Security Act 1998 if an application for leave to appeal is submitted (*CDLA/ 792/2006*).

4.053

p.677, *Decisions and Appeals Regulations, Sch.3B, para.6*

With effect from September 24, 2007, "Social Security (Hospital In-Patients) Regulations 2005" is substituted for "Social Security (Hospital In-Patients) Regulations 1975" (reg.3(9) of the Social Security (Miscellaneous Amendments) (No.4) Regulations 2007 (SI 2007/2470)).

4.054

p.681, *annotations to General Benefit Regs 1982, reg.2*

A Commissioner has ruled in *CSS/239/2007* that, without a certificate of the type referred to in reg.2(4) of the General Benefit Regulations, an appellant could not obtain the advantage of the regulation. Paragraphs 8 to 10 of the decision address questions arising in relation to devolved government in Scotland.

4.055

p.755, *Payments on Account etc Regs 1988, correction to text of Case 1*

There is a typographical error in the text of Case 1, which should read as follows:

[⁶ *Case 1: Payment pursuant to a decision which is revised or superseded, or overturned on appeal*

Where a person has been paid a sum by way of benefit [or by way of a shared additional pension under s.55A of the Social Security Contributions and Benefits Act 1992] pursuant to a decision which is subsequently revised under s.9 of the Social Security Act 1998, superseded under s.10 of that Act or overturned on appeal.]

4.056

p.765, *Payments on Account etc Regs, reg.14*

Some errors were contained in the text of reg.14, which should read as follows:

4.057

Quarterly diminution of capital

14.—(1) For the purposes of s.53(1) of the Act [SSAA, s.71(1)], where income support, [⁴ or state pension credit] [², or income-based jobseeker's allowance] [¹, working families' tax credit or disabled person's tax credit] has been overpaid in consequence of a misrepresentation as to the capital a claimant possesses or a failure to disclose its existence, the adjudicating authority shall treat that capital as having been reduced at the end of each quarter from the start of the

Administration, Adjudication and the European Dimension

overpayment period by the amount overpaid by way of income support, [⁴ or state pension credit] [², or income based jobseeker's allowance] [¹ working families' tax credit or disabled person's tax credit] within that quarter.

(2) Capital shall not be treated as reduced over any period other than a quarter or in any circumstances other than those for which para.(1) provides.

(3) In this regulation—

"a quarter" means a period of 13 weeks starting with the first day on which the overpayment period began and ending on the 90th consecutive day thereafter;

"overpayment period" is a period during which income support [³ or an income based jobseeker's allowance,] [¹ working families' tax credit or disabled person's tax credit] is overpaid in consequence of a misrepresentation as to capital or a failure to disclose its existence.

p.904, *annotations to Art.18 EC*

4.058   The *Abdirahman and Ulluslow* decisions in the Court of Appeal are now reported as *R(IS) 8/07*.

In *CIS/2358/2006* (A case concerning a Polish student who had undertaken some work in the United Kingdom but had ceased work following the birth of a daughter) the Commissioner provides a helpful explanation of the proper approach to using Art.18 EC following the decision in the *Baumbast Case* to give a right to reside:

"15. One can derive from the judgment in *Baumbast*, therefore, the principle that, where a right of residence is not expressly conferred by subordinate Community legislation, Article 18(1) confers a right of residence where it would be disproportionate to imply from the subordinate legislation that there is no right of residence. However, it seems to me that to rely on Article 18(1) where the Council of the European Communities has apparently deliberately excluded a class of persons from the scope of a directive would be to attack the directive and, if such an attack had any substance, it would be necessary to consider referring the case to the European Court of Justice because only that Court has the power to hold a directive to be incompatible with the Treaty. On the other hand, one can derive from the Advocate General's opinion in *Baumbast* the idea that there may be a lacuna in a directive, in which case there is no implication that exclusion from the scope of a right of residence was deliberate because the situation of the claimant in question simply was not considered by the Council. In other words, Article 18(1) may be relied upon to supplement a directive but, in proceedings before a national court or tribunal, it cannot be relied upon to remove limitations necessarily implicit in a directive."

In *CIS/408/2006*, the same Commissioner said that he regarded Directive 2004/38/EC "sets a standard by reference to which proportionality must be judged for the purpose of Article 18(1) in a case arising before the directive came into force." (para.33). This case is an important authority on when a burden on the public purse will be regarded as reasonable, though the decision may turn on its rather special facts (which involved the rights of a Cameroon national married to a French national. The Commissioner summarises the position as follows:

"54. In my judgment, having regard to all these considerations, the claimant's wife's right of free movement for the purpose of working, guaranteed to her by Article 39 of the Treaty, would be infringed if she and the claimant were not recognised as having the right to reside in the United Kingdom in the circumstances of this case. There was a lacuna in the directives in force at the time of the claimant's claim for income support and there is now a lacuna in Directive 2004/38/EC but I am satisfied that the claimant and his wife retained rights of residence by virtue of Article 18(1) of the Treaty. Where a worker exercising rights under Article 39 of the Treaty in the United Kingdom is obliged to cease work and cannot be available for alternative work due to a need to care for his or her spouse who is a not a citizen of the Union but who is temporarily seriously disabled, they both retain rights of residence in the United Kingdom in the circumstances that arise in this case. Among those circumstances are the facts that—

(a) the disabled person had been exercising his Community law right to work in the United Kingdom and had become temporarily incapable of work;
(b) the disability had first manifested itself some considerable time after the disabled person had arrived in the United Kingdom, after he had married and after he had started work;
(c) the disabled person had qualified for free National Health Service treatment by virtue of his period of residence in the United Kingdom, which was at least in part by virtue of his right of residence under Community law, and was continuing to undergo such treatment while being cared for by his wife;
(d) the recognition of the claimant's right of residence under Community law when he married had led to him losing the opportunity of establishing a right of residence in his own right as a refugee.

Whether any of those circumstances is determinative can be decided when the need arises. (If point (a) is not determinative, it may follow that a person retains a right of residence while temporarily unable to be available for work due to the need to care for a dependant child, although, I would suggest, only where the child's need for care is temporary and is wholly due to the seriousness of the disability rather than the child's age.)"

In *CIS/4010/2006*, which concerned a French woman who has lived in the United Kingdom for just over a year and had become pregnant, the Commissioner noted:

"9. The claimant argues that it is enough that she had been living in the United Kingdom for just over a year. She refers to CIS/3182/2005 and relies on Articles 12 and 18 of the EC Treaty. I do not agree that a years' residence is long enough. When considering Article 18, regard must be had to the standard set by Directive 2004/38/EC under which a right of permanent residence giving access to social assistance to people who are not economically active is not generally acquired until after five years' residence, although there are specified exceptions, and, in the light of *Abdirahman v Secretary of State for Work and Pensions* [2007] EWCA Civ 657, it is clear that Article 12 cannot be relied upon independently."

However, the Commissioner makes no reference to Art.24(2) of Directive 2004/38/EC which provides that "the host Member State shall not be obliged to confer entitlement to social assistance during the first three months of residence"; it remains to be seen what this provision means in the light of the other provisions of the Directive. That same provision also makes reference to entitlement to grant maintenance aid for studies only after a period of residence of five years.

See *CIS/419/2007* which considered the position of a Polish student whose studies were in suspense, and who was found not to have a right of residence.

For an example of a decision of a Commissioner exploring some of the issues raised in the line of cases referred to in the annotations, including issues of student status and entitlement to reside as the parent of a child born in the United Kingdom, see *CIS/1545/2007*.

p.910, *annotations to Art.39 EC*

4.059   Note that the relevant regulations relating to worker authorisation and worker registration are The Accession (Immigration and Worker Authorisation) Regulations 2006 (SI 2006/3317) as amended by SI 2007/475 and SI 2007/3012.

In *CJSA/1475/2006* the Commissioner addressed some important questions on a person's position as a worker and as a work seeker, and made the following statements in his decision:

"13. The Secretary of State also concedes that a claimant who satisfies the conditions of entitlement to jobseeker's allowance set out in section 1(1) of the Jobseekers Act 1995, which include being available for employment, entering into a jobseeker's agreement and actively seeking employment, will satisfy the *Antonissen* test of seeking employment and having genuine chances of being engaged in employment. Moreover, in this particular case, Mr Kolinsky conceded that the *Antonissen* test was satisfied in respect of the period from 9 September 2005 and he supported the claimant's appeal in respect of that period.

14. I accept the Secretary of State's concessions. The "right to reside" test imposed by regulation 85(4B) does not, in practice, provide an additional hurdle for citizens of the European Union claiming jobseeker's allowance, save where there is a derogation from the usual rules. . . . "

p.925, *annotations to Art. 7 of reg. 1612/68*

Tow judgments of the Grand Chamber of the Court of Justice of the European Communities handed down on July 18, 2007 reveal both the power and the limitations of Art.7(2). 4.060

In Case C-212/05 *Hartmann v Freistaat Bayern*, the Court ruled:

"1. A national of a Member State who, while maintaining his employment in that State, has transferred his residence to another Member State and has since then carried on his occupation as a frontier worker can claim the status of migrant worker for the purposes of Regulation (EEC) No 1612/68 of the Council of 15 October 1968 on freedom of movement for workers within the Community.

2. In circumstances such as those at issue in the main proceedings, Article 7(2) of Regulation No 1612/68 precludes the spouse of a migrant worker carrying on an occupation in one Member State, who does not work and is resident in another Member State, from being refused a social advantage with the characteristics of German child-raising allowance on the ground that he did not have his permanent or ordinary residence in the former State."

But in Case C-213/05 *Geven v Land Nordrhein-Westfalen*, the Court ruled:

"Article 7(2) of Regulation (EEC) No 1612/68 of the Council of 15 October 1968 on freedom of movement for workers within the Community does not preclude the exclusion, by the national legislation of a Member State, of a national of another Member State who resides in that State and is in minor employment (between 3 and 14 hours a week) in the former State from receiving a social advantage with the characteristics of German child-raising allowance on the ground that he does not have his permanent or ordinary residence in the former State."

p.972, *annotations to Art. 10a, reg. 1408/71*

The Court of Justice of the European Communities has now handed down its judgment in Case C-299/05 *Commission v European Parliament and Council*, Judgment of October 18, 2007. The Court has ruled that attendance allowance, care allowance, and the care component of a disability living allowance constitute sickness benefits and not special non-contributory benefits. The problem of the care component being part of a single benefit, namely, disability living allowance, is acknowledged, with the possibility of severing the two components of the allowance. To give the United Kingdom an opportunity to reconstitute the two components of the disability living allowance as separate benefits, the Court attached a temporally limitation to its judgment in the following terms: 4.061

"74 It is necessary, however, for the Court to state that the straightforward annulment of the inclusion of the DLA in the list in Annex IIa as amended would lead to the United Kingdom being forced to grant the 'mobility' element of that benefit to an unspecified number of recipients throughout the European Union, although the fact that that part of the DLA is in the nature of a non-contributory benefit cannot be disputed and it could lawfully be included in that list as a non-exportable benefit.

75 That fact warrants the Court exercising the power expressly conferred on it by the second paragraph of Article 231 EC in the event of annulment of a regulation, provisionally to maintain the effects of inclusion of the DLA as regards solely the 'mobility' part so that, within a reasonable period, appropriate measures can be taken to include it in Annex IIa as amended."

In Case C-287/05 *Hendrix v Raad van Vestuur van het Uitvoeringsinstituut Werknemersversekeringen,* Judgment of September 11, 2007, the Grand Chamber ruled:

"1. A benefit such as that provided under the Law on provision of incapacity benefit to disabled young people (Wet arbeidsongeschiktheidsvoorziening jonggehandicapten) of 24 April 1997 must be regarded as a special non-contributory benefit within the meaning of Article 4(2a) of Council Regulation (EEC) No 1408/71 of 14 June 1971 on the application of social security schemes to employed persons, to self employed persons and to members of their families moving within the Community, as amended and updated by Council Regulation (EC) No 118/97 of 2 December 1996, as amended by Council Regulation (EC) No 1223/98 of 4 June 1998, with the result that only the coordinating provision in Article 10a of that regulation must be applied to persons who are in the situation of the applicant in the main proceedings and that payment of that benefit may validly be reserved to persons who reside on the territory of the Member State which provides the benefit. The fact that the person concerned previously received a benefit for disabled young people which was exportable is of no relevance to the application of those provisions.

2. Article 39 EC and Article 7 of Regulation (EEC) No 1612/68 of the Council of 15 October 1968 on freedom of movement for workers within the Community must be interpreted as not precluding national legislation which applies Article 4(2a) and Article 10a of Regulation No 1408/71, as amended and updated by Regulation No 118/97, as amended by Regulation No 1223/98, and provides that a special non-contributory benefit listed in Annex IIa to Regulation No 1408/71 may be granted only to persons who are resident in the national territory. However, implementation of that legislation must not entail an infringement of the rights of a person in a situation such as that of the applicant in the main proceedings which goes beyond what is required to achieve the legitimate objective pursued by the national legislation. It is for the national court, which must, so far as possible, interpret the national legislation in conformity with Community law, to take account, in particular, of the fact that the worker in question has maintained all of his economic and social links to the Member State of origin."

p.1183, *annotations to Art. 4, Dir. 79/7/EEC*

CIB/2248/2006 concerned a claim to incapacity benefit by a female to male transsexual. The claimant, who was born on August 18, 1942, and his gender at birth was registered as female. He began to live as a man from the age of 19, and underwent gender re-assignment surgery early in 2003. His assigned gender from that date was male, but his registered gender remained as female. The claimant reached the age of 60 in August 2002 (when his registered gender remained female). He had not option but to claim a retirement pension on the cessation of his entitlement to incapacity benefit on attaining the age of 60. On November 30, 2005 the claimant obtained a gender recognition certificate as a man. He was then 63. His entitlement to retirement pension ceased. He reclaimed incapacity benefit on December 2, 2005, but his claim was refused. The Commissioner first considered any issue arising under the European Convention on Human Rights, but could not conclude that it was possible to interpret s.30A of the Contributions and Benefits Act in such a way as to avoid the discrimination on grounds of sex which arose when Art.8 was read together with Art.14 of the European Convention.

The Commissioner then turned to the application of Directive 79/7/EEC to the circumstances presented by the appellant. The Commissioner concludes that there is a breach of the equal treatment requirement in Art.4:

> "37. Persons who are incapable of work and whose legal gender changes from female to male between the ages of 60 and 65 are entitled to incapacity benefit until the age of 60, then to a retirement pension until the change in their legal gender. Thereafter, depending on the time that has elapsed, they may be entitled to neither. That makes them unique in that the link between the loss of incapacity benefit and entitlement to a retirement pension is broken. And it is broken solely because of the change in legal gender between those ages. The claimant has not been treated equally with persons in the other categories because his legal gender changed as a result of having acquired an assigned gender. Unlike the persons in every other category, he is deprived of the opportunity of ensuring a continuity between entitlement to incapacity benefit and a retirement pension. . . .
>
> 38. That effect is a direct result of the change in the claimant's legal gender and prohibited by the wording of Article 4(1). Alternatively, it is attributable to the acquisition of the claimant's acquisition of an assigned gender and is prohibited on the authority of *Richards*."

But once again the Commissioner finds, for the same reasons as is relation to the European Convention, that interpretation is of no assistance. But a remedy can be provided by disapplying the national law to the extent necessary to remove the prohibited discriminatory treatment:

> "43. The 2004 Act fails to comply with Article 4, because it deprives the claimant of the link between entitlement to incapacity benefit and a retirement pension. I can remove that discrimination by disapplying

Administration, Adjudication and the European Dimension

the legislation to the extent necessary in order to allow that link to be maintained in the circumstances of his case. For practical purposes, that result can be achieved by deciding the claim for incapacity benefit as if it was made the day that his entitlement previously ceased. The claimant must, of course, be incapable of work, but for other purposes the gap in entitlement is to be disregarded."

p.1225, *annotations to Art.4 ECHR*

4.063 In joined decisions *CSJSA/495/2007 and CJSA/505/2007*, the Commissioner dismissed as unarguable a complaint by an appellant that the requirements of the New Deal programme with its requirement for an "intensive activity period employment programme constituted a modern form of slavery."

p.1226, *annotations to Art.6, ECHR*

4.064 Note in relation to the *Tsfayo* case referred to in para.4.58, the admissibility decision of the Strasbourg Court in *BH v United Kingdom* (App.59580/00), Decision of September 25, 2007).

CSIB/85/2007 concerned an appellant whose appeal had been heard in her absence. An application to set that decision aside was successful on the grounds that a family emergency had prevented the appellant's attendance. The renewed hearing was before a tribunal with the same chairman. That chairman drew this fact to the appellant's attention and she did not object. An appeal against the decision of the tribunal raised the question of whether there had been a fair hearing. Applying the fair-minded and informed observe test, the Commissioner, somewhat reluctantly and clearly viewing the case as "exceedingly borderline", set aside the tribunal's decision and remitted the case for a further rehearing before an entirely differently composed tribunal. The Commissioner, having observed that the claimant in this case *might* not have had sufficient time to consider all the pros and cons of agreeing to a hearing before a tribunal chaired by the same chairman who had dealt with the case at an earlier stage, notes:

> "22. . . . The very fact that an adjudicator offers a claimant an opportunity to object means that the adjudicator appreciates that justice must not only be done but be seen to be done . . . and judges that present appearances could seem to suggest the contrary even if this was not the actual position; if the adjudicator then gives inadequate scope to the claimant's freedom to object, if the latter so wishes, this is one factor which *could* support objective bias."

p.1251, *annotations to Art.14 ECHR*

4.065 It is understood that the applicant in *R. (on the application of RJM) v Secretary of State for Work and Pensions* has petitioned for leave to appeal to the House of Lords.

For an informative decision on time limits and claims for bereavement benefits (covering both European Union Law and Convention law), see *CG/2488/2006*.

PART V

UPDATING MATERIAL VOLUME IV

TAX CREDITS AND EMPLOYER PAID SOCIAL SECURITY

Tax Credits and Employer Paid Social Security

p.21, *amendment to Taxes Management Act 1970, s.118*

With effect from April 6, 2007, the reference to s.20C in the definition of "tax" in s.118(1) was repealed by Finance Act 2007, Sch.27, Pt 5. 5.001

p.77, *amendment to Social Security Administration Act 1992, s.122AA (Disclosure of contributions etc. information by Inland Revenue),*

With effect from April 18, 2005, s.50(4) of, and Sch.4, para.46 to, the Commissioners for Revenue and Customs Act 2005 substituted "Her Majesty's Revenue and Customs" in the heading for "Inland Revenue" and in subs.(1) substituted the expression "Revenue and Customs officials (within the meaning of section 18 of the Commissioners for Revenue and Customs Act 2005 (confidentiality)" for the words "persons employed in relation to the Inland Revenue". 5.002

With effect from April 6, 2005, s.319 of, and Sch.12, para.7 to, the Pensions Act 2004 substituted "Pensions Regulator" for "Occupational Pensions Regulatory Authority" in subs.(2)(d).

p.92, *amendment to Social Security Act 1998, s.39 (Interpretation of Ch.2)*

With effect from July 3, 2007, s.62(5) of the Welfare Reform Act 2007 inserted in subs.(1) after the definition of "Commissioner" the following definition: 5.003

" 'health care professional' means—
   (a) a registered medical practitioner,
   (b) a registered nurse,
   (c) an occupational therapist or physiotherapist registered with a regulatory body established by an Order in Council under section 60 of the Health Care Act 1999, or
   (d) a member of such other profession regulated by a body mentioned in section 25(3) of the National Health Service Reform and Health Care Professions Act 2002 as the Secretary of State may prescribe;"

p.102, *amendment to Social Security Contributions (Transfer of Functions) Act 1999, s.12(5) (Exercise of right of appeal)*

With effect from May 11, 2001, s.88(2) of, and Sch.29, para.39 to, the Finance Act 2001 amended subs.(5) by substituting "(2) to (7) of section 31D" for "(5A) to (5E) of section 31" and "subsection (1) of that section" for "subsection (4) of that section". 5.004

p.124, *amendment to Tax Credits Act 2002, s.6 (Notification of changes of circumstances)*

Subsections (3A) and (3B), inserted by the Tax Credits Notification of Changes of Circumstances (Civil Partnership) (Transitional Provisions) Order 2005 (SI 2005/828) have been inserted in the wrong place in the 5.005

text; they belong immediately after subs.(3). Note also that these provisions have effect only for the tax year 2005/06.

p.124, *annotation to Tax Credits Act 2002, s.6 (Notification of changes of circumstances)*

5.006   Both the Parliamentary Ombudsman and the Citizens Advice Bureaux published further reports about tax credits in October 2007. *Tax Credits: Getting it wrong?* was published as the 5th Report of the Parliamentary Ombudsman (HC 1010, Session 2006–07). The report contains detailed case studies about, in particular, overpayments and their recovery, and notes that complaints about tax credits continue to form a growing part of the workload of the Ombudsman. In the year starting on April 1, 2007 to the end of August, tax credits complaints formed 26 per cent of the Ombudsman's workload, and three quarters of those complaints were upheld either in whole or in part. It also comments on the complaints and appeals procedures. Nearly all current complaints are about overpayments.

The National Association of Citizens Advice Bureaux published a report at the same time entitled *Tax Credits: the current picture*. This summarises the comments of 1,500 respondents to a survey on their experiences of tax credits—drawn from 186,000 people helped by CABs in handling their tax credits in the last year. The report notes as worrying the number of respondents who stopped claiming tax credits because of the problems involved.

p.158, *annotation to Tax Credits Act 2002, s.31 (Incorrect statements, etc)*

5.007   The provisions of the TMA 1970 on which s.31 and related sections of TCA 2002 are based have been recast by Finance Act 2007, s.97, introducing a new code of penalties in Sch.24. The provisions were discussed in a consultation document published by HMRC in December 2006 entitled *Modernising Powers, Deterrents and Safeguards: a new approach to penalties for incorrect tax returns*. HMRC will be publishing detailed guidance about the new provisions, which will apply to all income tax, capital gains tax, corporation tax and VAT provisions, but not tax credits.

p.164, *annotation to Tax Credits Act 2002, s.36 (Powers in relation to documents)*

5.008   With effect from a date to be ordered by HM Treasury, s.36(2) and (3) are to be repealed by Finance Act 2007, s.84 and Sch.27, Pt 5. The repeal is because s.84 of that Act amends the provisions of the Police and Criminal Evidence Act 1994 to give HMRC officers new powers to obtain documents under that Act.

p.167, *annotation to Tax Credits Act 2002, s.38 (Appeals)*

5.009   The 2007 special report of the Parliamentary Ombudsman noted above in relation to p.124 of the main Vol.4 continues to recommend

Tax Credits and Employer Paid Social Security

that appeal rights should be given to an independent tribunal in connection with overpayments. It also sets out the government response to that recommendation, which is an enhanced complaints procedure. This procedure is now applied by both HMRC and the Ombudsman to all tax credits complaints, including appeals. In effect, a complaint only gets to the Ombudsman or an appeal to a tribunal as a fourth level of review.

p.225, *amendment to Income Tax (Earnings and Pensions) Act 2003, s.219 (Extra amounts to be added in connection with a car)*

With effect from April 6, 2007, s.62 of the Finance Act 2007 repealed subs.(5) and (6).   5.010

p.334, *amendment to Commissioners for Revenue and Customs Act 2005, s.13 (Exercise of Commissioners' functions by officers)*

With effect from a date to be ordered by HM Treasury, s.84 of, and Sch.27, Pt 5 to, the Finance Act 2007 repeal subs.(3)(b) and (c).   5.011

p.373, *insertion of the Working Tax Credit (Entitlement and Maximum Rate) Regulations 2002, reg.7D (Ceasing to undertake work or working for less than 16 hours per week)*

The following missing reference should be inserted immediately below the text of reg.7D: 5.012

AMENDMENT

1. Working Tax Credit (Entitlement and Maximum Rate) (Amendment) Regulations 2007 (SI 2007/968, reg.2(3) (April 6, 2007).   5.013

pp.383–384, *amendment of the Working Tax Credit (Entitlement and Maximum Rate) Regulations 2002, reg.14(2) (Definition of "child care" for the purposes of the child care element)*

With effect from October 1, 2007, reg.2 of the Working Tax Credit (Entitlement and Maximum Rate) (Amendment No.2) Regulations 2007 (SI 2007/2479) amended reg.14(2) by omitting para.(iv) in sub-para.(a) (but not the word "or" following it), by omitting "or" at the end of sub-para.(f)(i), by adding "or" at the end of sub-para.(f)(ii) and inserting after sub-para.(f)(ii) the following: 5.014

"(iii) by a child care provider approved by an accredited organisation within the meaning given by regulation 4 of the Tax Credit (New Category of Child Care Provider) Regulations 1999."

p.404, *amendment to the Tax Credits (Definition and Calculation of Income) Regulations 2002, reg.2(2) (Interpretation)*

5.015 With effect from October 1, 2007, Art.7 of the Independent Living Fund (2006) Order 2007 (SI 2007/2538) inserted before the definition of "the Independent Living Funds" the following definition:

" 'the Independent Living Fund (2006)' means the Trust of that name established by a deed dated 10th April 2006 and made between the Secretary of State for Work and Pensions of the one part and Margaret Rosemary Cooper, Michael Beresford Boyall and Marie Theresa Martin of the other part;"

The same amending provision substituted "the Independent Living (Extension) Fund, the Independent Living (1993) Fund and the Independent Living Fund (2006)" in the definition of "the Independent Living Funds" for the expression "the Independent Living (Extension) Fund and the Independent Living (1993) Fund".

p.405, *amendment to the Tax Credits (Definition and Calculation of Income) Regulations 2002, reg.2(2) (Interpretation)*

5.016 With effect from May 16, 2007, reg.3 of the Tax Credits (Definition and Calculation of Income) (Amendment) Regulations 2007 (SI 2007/1305) inserted after the definition of "the Independent Living (1993) Fund" the following new definition:

" 'ITA' means the Income Tax Act 2007;"

p.408, *amendment to the Tax Credits (Definition and Calculation of Income) Regulations 2002, reg.3 (Calculation of income of claimant)*

5.017 With effect from May 16, 2007, reg.4 of the Tax Credits (Definition and Calculation of Income) (Amendment) Regulations 2007 (SI 2007/1305) substituted "Chapter 2 of Part 8 of ITA (gift aid)" for "section 25 of the Finance Act 1990 (donations to charity by individuals)" in para.(7)(b) and "section 120 of ITA (deduction of property losses from general income)" for "section 379A(2) and (3) of the Taxes Act" in para.(8)(b).

p.428, *amendment to the Tax Credits (Definition and Calculation of Income) Regulations 2002, reg.8 (Student income)*

5.018 With effect from May 16, 2007, reg.5 of the Tax Credits (Definition and Calculation of Income) (Amendment) Regulations 2007 (SI 2007/1305) substituted for sub-paras (d)(i) and (ii) the following:

"(i) under regulation 22 of the Assembly Learning Grants and Loans (Higher Education) (Wales) Regulations 2006 in relation to an academic year which begins on or after 1st September 2006 but before 1st September 2007; or

(ii) under regulation 26 of the Assembly Learning Grants and Loans (Higher Education) (Wales) Regulations 2007 in relation to an academic year which begins on or after 1st September 2007."

p.435, *amendment to the Tax Credits (Definition and Calculation of Income) Regulations 2002, reg.11 (Property income)*

With effect from May 16, 2007, reg.6 of the Tax Credits (Definition and Calculation of Income) (Amendment) Regulations 2007 (SI 2007/1305) substituted "contained in sections 118 (carry forward against subsequent property business profits) and 119 (how relief works) of ITA" for the expression for "of section 379A of the Taxes Act" in para.(3) and "those sections" for the words "subsection (1) of that section".

5.019

p.437, *amendment to the Tax Credits (Definition and Calculation of Income) Regulations 2002, reg.12 (Foreign income)*

With effect from May 16, 2007, reg.7 of the Tax Credits (Definition and Calculation of Income) (Amendment) Regulations 2007 (SI 2007/1305) substituted "contained in sections 118 (carry forward against subsequent property business profits) and 119 (how relief works) of ITA apply" for "of section 379A of the Taxes Act apply by virtue of section 379B of that Act" in para.(4) and "those sections" for "section 379A(1)".

5.020

p.438, *amendment to the Tax Credits (Definition and Calculation of Income) Regulations 2002, reg.14 (Claimants treated for any purpose as having income by virtue of the Income Tax Acts)*

With effect from May 16, 2007, reg.8 of the Tax Credits (Definition and Calculation of Income) (Amendment) Regulations 2007 (SI 2007/1305) omitted from para.(2) the following sub-paras: (a)(xi) (s.730A); (a)(xii) (s.739); (a)(xiii) (s.740); and (a)(xv) (s.776). In addition, the following new sub-para. was inserted after sub-para.(2)(b):

5.021

"(ba) the following provisions of ITA—
(i) Chapter 5 of Part 11 (price differences under repos);
(ii) Chapter 2 of Part 13 (transfer of assets abroad); and
(iii) Chapter 3 of Part 13 (transactions in land)."

p.454, *amendment to the Child Tax Credit Regulations 2002, reg.3 (Circumstances in which a person is or is not responsible for a child or qualifying young person)*

With effect from August 16, 2007, reg.3 of the Child Tax Credit (Amendment) Regulations 2007 (SI 2007/2151) amended reg.3 so as to omit the sentence beginning "This Case shall not apply" in Case A of r.4 and to insert after r.4.1 the following new rule—

5.022

"4.2. Where a child or qualifying young person is in residential accommodation referred to in regulation 9 of the Child Benefit (General) Regulations 2006 and in the circumstances prescribed in paragraphs (a) or (b) of that regulation, he shall be treated as being the responsibility of any person who was treated as being responsible for him immediately before he entered that accommodation."

p.459, *amendment to the Child Tax Credit Regulations 2002, reg.5 (Maximum age and prescribed conditions for a qualifying young person*

5.023   With effect from August 16, 2007, reg.4 of the Child Tax Credit (Amendment) Regulations 2007 (SI 2007/2151) amended reg.5 by inserting ", is enrolled or has been accepted to undertake such training," in para.(3)(ab) after "training", by inserting ", or he enrolled or was accepted to undertake that course before he attained that age" at the end of para.(3A), and omitting ", and shall include" in para.(5) to the end of the paragraph.

pp.609–614, *revocation of the Tax Credits (Approval of Child Care Providers) Scheme 2005*

5.024   With effect from October 1, 2007, Art.4 of the Tax Credits (Child Care Providers) (Miscellaneous Revocation and Transitional Provisions) (England) Scheme 2007 revoked the Tax Credits (Approval of Child Care Providers) Scheme 2005 (SI 2005/93) in its entirety but with some transitional protection—see New Regulations and Orders above, at para.1.000.

p.712, *amendment to the Statutory Paternity Pay and Statutory Adoption Pay (Weekly Rates) Regulations 2002, reg.3 (Weekly rate of payment of statutory adoption pay)*

5.025   The correct citation for the Social Security Benefits Up-rating Order 2007 is SI 2007/688.

p.871, *HMRC Codes of Practice and Guidance*

5.026   Updated versions of leaflets WTC5 and WTC 6 were issued by HMRC in August 2007 but only online. Printed versions are no longer available. Updated versions of leaflets WTC1 and WTC2 were issued by HMRC in October 2007 but only online. Printed versions are no longer available. The intended revision of COP26 in 2007 was still under consideration at the time of writing this Supplement. While its content has been considered in draft by the Tax Credits Consultation Group, no details have so far been published. For minutes of the Group see *http://www.hmrc.gov.uk/taxcredits/meetings.htm*.

PART VI

FORTHCOMING CHANGES AND UP-RATING OF BENEFITS

FORTHCOMING CHANGES

6.001 This section aims to give users of Social Security Legislation 2007 some information on significant changes coming into force between December 6, 2007—the date to which this Supplement is up to date—and mid-April 2008, the date to which the 2008 edition will be up to date. The information here reflects our understanding of sources available to us as at December 6, 2007, and users should be aware that there will no doubt be further legislative amendment between then and mid-April 2008. This section of the Supplement will at least enable users to access the relevant legislation on the TSO website (*http://www.hmso.gov.uk/legis.htm*).

REGULATIONS

The Social Security (Housing Costs and Miscellaneous Amendments) Regulations 2007 (SI 2007/3183)

6.002 These Regulations make amendments to the Income Support (General) Regulations 1987, the Jobseeker's Allowance Regulations 1996, the State Pension Credit Regulations 2002 and the Social Security (Claims and Payments) Regulations 1987 with effect from December 17, 2007.

The main effect is to amend the income support mortgage run-on provisions so that claimants who were receiving help with "other housing costs", *e.g.* service charges, ground rent, etc., are also entitled to the run-on. Previously the run-on only applied where a claimant had been receiving mortgage interest or interest on a loan (or loans) for repairs or improvements as part of his income support or JSA.

In addition, the provisions which allow a claimant who moves from income-based JSA to income support (and vice versa) within a linked period to receive the same amount for housing costs on any eligible loan are extended so that they also apply

(i) to any "other housing costs", e.g. service charges, ground rent, etc., he was receiving;

(ii) if the claimant or his partner was getting state pension credit and one of them becomes entitled to income support or income-based JSA.

The amending regulations also clarify that if a person is treated as in receipt of benefit by virtue of the linking rules this does not mean that he is to be treated as entitled to income support for the purpose of the rule that housing costs are not met if the loan was incurred when the claimant was entitled to benefit or in a 26-week period between claims.

NEW BENEFIT RATES FROM APRIL 2008

(Benefits covered in Volume I)

	April 2007 £ pw	April 2008 £ pw
Disability benefits		
Attendance allowance		
higher rate	64.50	67.00
lower rate	43.15	44.85
Disability living allowance		
care component		
highest rate	64.50	67.00
middle rate	43.15	44.85
lowest rate	17.10	17.75
mobility component		
higher rate	45.00	46.75
lower rate	17.10	17.75
Carer's allowance	48.65	50.55
Severe disablement allowance		
basic rate	49.15	51.05
age related addition—higher rate	17.10	17.75
age related addition—middle rate	11.00	11.40
age related addition—lower rate	5.50	5.70
Maternity benefits		
Maternity allowance		
standard rate	112.75	117.18
Bereavement benefits and retirement pensions		
Widowed parent's allowance or widowed mother's allowance	87.30	90.70
Bereavement allowance or widow's pension		
standard rate	87.30	90.70
Retirement pension		
Category A	87.30	90.70
Category B (higher)	87.30	90.70
Category B (lower)	52.30	54.35
Category C (higher)	52.30	54.35
Category C (lower)	31.30	32.50
Category D	52.30	54.35

Up-Rating of Benefits

	April 2007 £ pw	April 2008 £ pw
Incapacity benefit		
Long-term incapacity benefit		
basic rate	81.35	84.50
increase for age—higher rate	17.10	17.75
increase for age—lower rate	8.55	8.90
invalidity allowance—higher rate	17.10	17.75
invalidity allowance—middle rate	11.00	11.40
invalidity allowance—lower rate	5.50	5.70
Short-term incapacity benefit		
under pension age—higher rate	72.55	75.40
under pension age—lower rate	61.35	63.75
over pension age—higher rate	81.35	84.50
over pension age—lower rate	78.05	81.10
Dependency increases		
Adult		
carer's allowance	29.05	30.20
severe disablement allowance	29.05	30.20
maternity allowance	37.90	39.40
retirement pension	52.30	54.35
long-term incapacity benefit	48.65	50.55
short-term incapacity benefit under pension age	37.90	39.40
short-term incapacity benefit over pension age	46.80	48.65
Child	11.35*	11.35*
Industrial injuries benefits		
Disablement benefit		
aged 18 and over or under 18 with dependants—100%	131.70	136.80
90%	118.53	123.12
80%	105.36	109.44
70%	92.19	95.76
60%	79.02	82.08
50%	65.85	68.40
40%	52.68	54.72
30%	39.51	41.04
20%	26.34	27.36
aged under 18 with no dependants—100%	80.70	83.85
90%	72.63	75.47
80%	64.56	67.08

Forthcoming Changes

		April 2007 £ pw	April 2008 £ pw
aged under 18 with no dependants— (cont.)	*70%*	56.49	58.70
	60%	48.42	50.31
	50%	40.35	41.93
	40%	32.28	33.54
	30%	24.21	25.16
	20%	16.14	16.77
unemployability supplement			
basic rate		81.35	84.50
increase for adult dependant		48.65	50.55
increase for child dependant		11.35*	11.35*
increase for early incapacity—higher rate		17.10	17.75
increase for early incapacity—middle rate		11.00	11.40
increase for early incapacity—lower rate		5.50	5.70
constant attendance allowance			
exceptional rate		105.40	109.60
intermediate rate		79.05	82.20
normal maximum rate		52.70	54.80
part-time rate		26.35	27.40
exceptionally severe disablement allowance		52.70	54.80
Reduced earnings allowance			
maximum rate		52.6	54.72
Death benefit			
widow's pension			
higher rate		87.30	90.70
lower rate		26.19	27.21
widower's pension		87.30	90.70
Benefits in respect of children			
Child benefit			
only, elder or eldest child (couple)		18.10	18.80
only, elder or eldest child (lone parent)		18.10	18.80
each subsequent child		12.10	12.55
Child's special allowance		11.35*	11.35*
Guardian's allowance		12.95	13.45

* These sums payable in respect of children are reduced if payable in respect of the only, elder or eldest child for whom child benefit is being paid (see reg.8 of the Social Security (Overlapping Benefits) Regulations 1979).

NEW BENEFIT RATES FROM APRIL 2008

(Benefits covered in Volume II)

	April 2007 £ pw	April 2008 £ pw
Contribution-based jobseeker's allowance		
personal rates—*aged under 18*	35.65	47.95
aged 18 to 24	46.85	47.95
aged 25 or over	59.15	60.50
Income support and income-based jobseeker's allowance		
personal allowances		
single person—*aged under 18 (usual rate)*	35.65	47.95
aged under 18 (higher rate)	46.85	47.95
aged 18 to 24	46.85	47.95
aged 25 or over	59.15	60.50
lone parent *aged under 18 (usual rate)*	35.65	47.95
aged under 18 (higher rate)	46.85	47.95
aged 18 or over	59.15	60.50
couple *both aged under 18*	35.65	47.95
both aged under 18, one disabled	46.85	47.95
both aged under 18, with a child	70.70	72.35
one aged under 18, one aged 18 to 24	46.85	47.95
one aged under 18, one aged 25 or over	59.15	60.50
both aged 18 or over	92.80	94.95
child	47.45	52.59
premiums		
family—*ordinary*	16.43	16.75
lone parent	16.43	16.75
bereavement		
pensioner—*single person (JSA only)*	59.90	63.55
couple	88.90	94.40
enhanced pensioner	88.90	94.40
higher pensioner—*single person (JSA only)*	59.90	63.55
couple	88.90	94.40
disability—*single person*	25.25	25.85
couple	36.00	26.85
enhanced disability—*single person*	12.30	12.60
couple	17.75	18.15
child	18.76	19.60

Forthcoming Changes

	April 2007 £ pw	April 2008 £ pw
severe disability—*single person*	48.45	50.35
couple (one qualifies)	48.45	50.35
couple (both qualify)	96.90	100.70
disabled child	46.69	48.72
carer	27.15	27.75

Pension credit

Standard minimum guarantee		
single person	119.05	124.05
couple	181.70	189.35
Additional amount for severe disability		
single person	48.45	50.35
couple (one qualifies)	48.45	50.35
couple (both qualify)	96.90	100.70
Additional amount for carers	27.15	27.75
Savings credit threshold		
single person	87.30	91.20
couple	139.60	145.80
Maximum savings credit		
single person	19.05	19.71
couple	25.26	26.13

NEW TAX CREDIT AND EMPLOYER-PAID BENEFIT RATES 2008–09

(Benefits covered in Volume IV)

	2007–08 £pa	2007–08 £pa
Working tax credit		
Basic element	1,730	1,800
Couple and lone parent element	1,700	1,770
30 hour element	705	735
Disabled worker element	2,310	2,405
Severe disability element	980	1,020
50+ Return to work payment (under 30 hours)	1,185	1,235
50+ Return to work payment (30 or more hours)	1,770	1,840
Child tax credit		
Family element	545	545
Family element, baby addition	545	545
Child element	1,845	2,085
Disabled child element	2,440	2,540
Severely disabled child element	980	1.020
Tax credit income thresholds		
Income disregard	25,000	25,000
First threshold	5,220	6,420
First threshold for those entitled to child tax credit only	14,495	15,575
First withdrawal rate - 37% in 2007–08, 39% in 2008–09		
Second threshold	50,000	50,000
Second withdrawal rate—6.67%		

	2007–08 £pw	2008–09 £pw
Employer paid benefits		
Standard rates		
Statutory sick pay	72.55	75.40
Statutory maternity pay	112.75	117.18
Statutory paternity pay	112.75	117.18
Statutory adoption pay	112.75	7.18
Income threshold	87.00	90.00